To the memory of
Vernon and Vella D. Williams
and to
Karen V. Williams
and
Beverly L. Mason-Williams

FROM A CASTE
TO A
MINORITY

Recent Titles in
Contributions in Afro-American and African Studies

Take Five: Collected Poems
Kenneth A. McClane

Pride Against Prejudice: The Biography of Larry Doby
Joseph Thomas Moore

Sacred Symphony: The Chanted Sermon of the Black Preacher
Jon Michael Spencer

He, Too, Spoke for Democracy: Judge Hastie, World War II, and the Black
Soldier
Phillip McGuire

The Trinidad Awakening: West Indian Literature of the Nineteen-Thirties
Reinhard W. Sander

The Crisis and Challenge of African Development
Harvey Glickman, editor

African Literature, African Critics: The Forming of Critical Standards,
1947–1966
Rand Bishop

Their Place on the Stage: Black Women Playwrights in America
Elizabeth Brown-Guillory

Ghanaian Literatures
Richard K. Priebe, editor

From Folklore to Fiction: A Study of Folk Heroes and Rituals in the Black
American Novel
H. Nigel Thomas

Visible Now: Blacks in Private Schools
Diana T. Slaughter and Deborah J. Johnson, editors

Feel the Spirit: Studies in Nineteenth-Century Afro-American Music
George R. Keck and Sherrill V. Martin, editors

FROM A CASTE
TO A
MINORITY

Changing Attitudes of American Sociologists Toward Afro-Americans, 1896–1945

VERNON J. WILLIAMS, JR.

Contributions in Afro-American and African Studies,
Number 121

Henry Louis Gates, Jr., Series Editor

GREENWOOD PRESS
New York · Westport, Connecticut · London

Library of Congress Cataloging-in-Publication Data

Williams, Vernon J.
    From a caste to a minority : changing attitudes of American
sociologists toward Afro-Americans, 1896–1945 / Vernon J. Williams,
Jr.
        p. cm. — (Contributions in Afro-American and African
studies, ISSN 0069-9624 ; no. 121)
    Bibliography: p.
    Includes index.
    ISBN 0-313-26420-1 (lib. bdg. : alk. paper)
    1. Afro-Americans—History—1877–1964.   2. Sociologists—United
States—Attitudes—History.   3. Sociology—United States—History.
I. Title.   II. Series.
E185.6.W734 1989
305.8′96073—dc19   88-24654

British Library Cataloguing in Publication Data is available.

Library of Congress Catalog Card Number: 88-24654
ISBN: 0-313-26420-1
ISSN: 0069-9624

First published in 1989

Greenwood Press, Inc.
88 Post Road West, Westport, Connecticut 06881

Printed in the United States of America

The paper used in this book complies with the
Permanent Paper Standard issued by the National
Information Standards Organization (Z39.48–1984).

10 9 8 7 6 5 4 3 2 1

Copyright Acknowledgment

Grateful acknowledgment is given to the University of Chicago Press as the
publisher of the *American Journal of Sociology* for permission to use excerpts
from W. Lloyd Warner's "American Caste and Class," *AJS* 42 (September
1936):234–237, including the diagram.

Contents

Acknowledgments   *ix*

Abbreviations   *xi*

Introduction   *1*

1. Slow and Protracted Change: Northern Sociologists and the "Negro Problem," 1896–1910   *5*

2. Southern Sociology Defends Jim Crow, 1900–1910   *33*

3. The Influence of Franz Boas, 1894–1910   *59*

4. The Dynamics of Change, 1911–1920   *81*

5. The Triumph of Liberal Environmentalism, 1920–1929   *113*

6. The Triumph of Assimilationist Theory, 1930–1945   *149*

Conclusion   *177*

Appendix: The Internalist-Externalist Controversy in the History of Racial Thought   *181*

Bibliography   *185*

Index   *195*

Acknowledgments

Several scholars read this work at various stages in its development and offered constructive criticisms. I offer my sincere thanks to William G. McLoughlin, Harold W. Pfautz, Rhett Jones, George M. Fredrickson, Nancy Grant, Nell I. Painter, Wilson Moses, Ridgeway Shinn, Jr., Richard Lobban, Carolyn Fluehr-Lobban, and Amritjit Singh.

Above all, I would like to thank my sister, Karen V. Williams, who provided me with financial and moral support during my eight-year stint of marginal employment.

Abbreviations

AA	*American Anthropologist*
AAA	*American Anthropological Association*
AAAS	*American Association for the Advancement of Science*
AHR	*American Historical Review*
AJS	*American Journal of Sociology*
Annals	*Annals of the American Academy of Political and Social Science*
APS	*American Philosophical Society*
AP	*Archives of Psychology*
ASR	*American Sociological Review*
AUL	*Atlanta University Leaflet*
AUP	*Atlanta University Publication*
JAFL	*Journal of American Folk-Lore*
JAS	*Journal of Applied Sociology*
JEP	*Journal of Educational Psychology*
JNE	*Journal of Negro Education*
Mem(s).	*Memoir(s)*
PASS	*Publications of the American Sociological Society*
PR	*Psychological Review*
Procs.	*Proceeding(s)*
PS	*Pedagogical Seminary*
PSQ	*Political Science Quarterly*
SF	*Social Forces*
SG	*Survey Graphic*

Introduction

This book, which is a history of the evolution of the idea of black progress in American sociology during the years 1896 to 1945, seeks to answer one fundamental question: How and why did sociology transform itself from a discipline that rationalized castelike arrangements in the United States to one that actively advocated and supported the full assimilation of Afro-Americans into the American mainstream? Like most questions involving the ethics of an established academic discipline on an issue on which it has traditionally attempted to provide insight and guidance, this one has elicited a variety of responses that have been both conflicting and controversial.[1]

It is my argument that the ascendancy of assimilationist theory in post–World War II sociology represented the triumph of the ideals of black progress and assimilation that had been significant arguments in American sociological theory since 1896. Thus, despite a capitulation before 1911 to the forces of racism and reaction, sociologists eventually achieved a unified voice against social Darwinist determinism. As a result, they transformed their discipline into one of the most forward-looking of all social science disciplines. The ideals of black progress and eventual assimilation that were stimulated perceptibly by the adoption after 1911 of naturalism as a worldview were influential in the undermining of racial determinism in the discipline, the adoption of the Boasian idea of cultural determinism, and the eventual integration of Afro-American scholars into the prestigious positions of authority on all issues pertinent to the study of Afro-Americans.

I have integrated three themes in my argument: the changing views of the leading sociologists; biographical/educational material on each sociologist (when relevant); and the demographic shift of blacks from the South to the urban-industrial areas in the North.

One of the most obvious results of my research has been to document the great reluctance of some sociologists to accept the findings of progressive colleagues and to fight instead for the validity of older theories years after competent research demonstrated their inadequacy. Thomas S. Kuhn has described the pattern of resistance to new paradigms as follows:

Usually the opponents of a new paradigm can legitimately claim that even in the area of crisis it is little superior to its traditional rival. Of course, it handles some problems better, has disclosed some new regularities. But the older paradigm can presumably be articulated to meet these challenges as it has met others before. . . . In addition, the defenders of traditional theory and procedure can always point to problems that its rival has not solved but that for their view are no problems at all.[2]

Kuhn's generalizations are certainly useful for my analysis of the various ways in which sociologists explained the purported inferiority of blacks and their prospects for assimilation. Despite the emergence of the Boasian position in the 1890s, the idea of the innate inferiority of blacks persisted well into the 1930s. That idea was usually buttressed by arguments based on anthropometry, psychological testing, the theory of African inferiority, and the theory of temperamental differences. Although the generalizations that were a product of anthropometry influenced sociological arguments on race from the 1890s to the 1920s, anthropometry was the special province of physical anthropologists and biologists; thus it was seldom used by competent sociologists. Arguments based on psychological testing, on the other hand, appeared in the 1900s, and, despite the criticism leveled at them, persisted well into the 1920s. The arguments based on the theory of racial temperamental differences appeared first in the 1890s and did not disappear until after 1930. The theory of African inferiority, a corollary of the innate biological difference argument, had been postulated in the 1900s; it was less potent than any of the aforementioned arguments and did not persist after 1920.

In addition to arguments of innate black inferiority, some sociologists during the period 1896 to 1945 utilized concepts of prejudice that rationalized the exclusion of blacks from full participation in the mainstream of American society. The concepts of "instinctive prejudice," "consciousness of kind," "ethnocentrism," and "the mores" suggested that race relations defied political and economic solutions, and that white prejudice would necessarily confine blacks to a low status.

This study relies wholly on the published writings of American sociologists in the years 1896 to 1945. Of particular importance are the articles published in the *American Journal of Sociology*, founded in 1895. This journal became the arena of scholarly debate at the turn of the century; through its articles one can trace the battle of polemics and ideas in the efforts of sociologists to free themselves from the racist assumptions of nineteenth-century social science. It is clear that sociologists made considerable progress away from early efforts to rationalize a castelike system on the assumed innate differences of both blacks and whites. Yet it is also true that even the most enlightened sociologists proposed no significant government action to hasten assimilation. As a result, sociologists sanctioned the laissez-faire or do-nothing approach which prevailed in these years.

I have used the term *racism*, despite its evisceration in recent years, because it denotes precisely the mind-set to which I am referring. Racism is used here to denote, as Pierre L. van den Berghe has defined clearly, "any set of beliefs that organic genetically transmitted differences (whether real or imagined) between human groups are intrinsically associated with the presence or absence of certain socially relevant abilities or characteristics, hence that such differences are a legitimate basis of invidious distinctions between groups socially defined as races."[3]

Finally, it should be noted that this work is neither an exercise in the history of science nor in the pure history of ideas. Rather, I have attempted, using some of the techniques of the sociology of knowledge, to demonstrate that before 1911 white sociologists, regardless of generational, regional, and amateur/professional factors, held conservative ideas supporting the status quo of black inequality. I have, however, avoided the Marxist assessment which stresses that "the ideas of the ruling class are in every epoch the ruling ideas," for I have pointed out that internal conceptual stresses on the issue of black capabilities existed between Afro-American and white Northern and white Southern sociologists writing before 1911. I have also clearly established that Afro-American and white Northern sociologists, unlike their white Southern counterparts, viewed assimilation and black progress as ideals. Although Southern racists who rationalized castelike arrangements dominated the discussion of the "Negro problem" before 1911, it was the ideals of Afro-Americans and white Northerners that triumphed in the next five decades.

By 1911, the "ruling ideas" were those of the forward-looking Afro-

American and white Northern sociologists who held the ethical beliefs of black progress and eventual assimilation. Unlike their pre-
decessors, who had concurred in Southern racist arguments, this
new generation of sociologists who had received their graduate
training in the late 1890s and in the 1900s was attracted to a naturalistic worldview. The rise of naturalism in post–1911 sociology
generated more internal conceptual stress on the issue of racial
capabilities and fostered an interest in the social structural changes
that were perceptibly transforming the demographic character of
the Northern urban and industrial areas in which most sociologists
lived and worked. There was, however, no monocausal relation
between the rise of naturalism and the decline of conservative thinking in sociology. Prior internal conceptual stresses, which were
exacerbated by Boasian anthropology and psychological testing in
the 1910s, and contemporaneous social structural changes were
necessary conditions for the development of progressive theories of
race and race relations. Nevertheless, it should be emphasized that
it was naturalism that provided the style of thought for the two
generations of sociologists who shaped the orientation of their discipline on white–black relations for more than fifty years.

Hopefully, this analysis of the hows and whys of the change from
an ideology of racial determinism to one of cultural determinism,
and from an ideology rationalizing castelike arrangements to one
advocating assimilation of Afro-Americans will provide some insight
into the emergence of a social science orientation that prepared the
way for *Brown v. Board of Education* and the subsequent success of
the Civil Rights movement in the 1960s.

NOTES

1. See Appendix, "The Internalist–Externalist Controversy in the History
of Racial Thought" in this volume.
2. Thomas S. Kuhn, *The Structure of Scientific Revolutions* (Chicago:
University of Chicago Press, 1970), 156–57.
3. Pierre L. van den Berghe, *Race and Racism* (New York: Wiley and Sons,
1967), 11.

Slow and Protracted Change: Northern Sociologists and the "Negro Problem," 1896–1910

When sociology emerged as an academic discipline in American universities in the 1890s, few contemporaries could have predicted that many of its distinguished future students would shape the ideas of present-day liberals on race and race relations. At that time, sociology was based primarily in Midwestern and Eastern universities, and the orientations of its "fathers"—Franklin H. Giddings, Edward A. Ross, Lester F. Ward, William G. Sumner, and Albion W. Small—reflected the peculiar concerns of Northern, middle-class Americans of British ancestry. The fathers of American sociology—most of whom were status-seeking, self-made, reform-minded men—were either clergymen or the descendants of clergymen who had transferred their moral concerns and careers from the "pulpit to the lectern." They were preoccupied with creating "grand theories" of society that would provide frameworks for analyzing and solving the "social problems" emanating from the rapid industrialization and urbanization that wracked the Gilded Age.[1] To these men, who had come of age during a period of inexorable social and economic change, problems stemming from the recent influx of numerous and diverse Southern and Eastern European immigrant groups, industrial and labor strife, political corruption, and the conflict between blacks and whites in the South seemed to be far more pressing concerns than the problems confronting Northern, urban blacks in their midst.

Nevertheless, it cannot be assumed that the pressing concerns of the fathers should have precluded them from constructing theories that would have directed empirical research on Northern, urban blacks. For although blacks constituted only 1 percent of the Northern population in 1900, their increasing migration from the South

into such major cities as New York, Chicago, and Philadelphia—
cities in which or near which the fathers taught —was beginning to
close much of the physical distance.[2] To the most perceptive young
sociologist of the period, W.E.B. DuBois, it was apparent as early as
the 1890s that the North, despite its relatively small black population, had an incipient race problem. In *The Philadelphia Negro*
(1899) and later in a series of five articles that were published in *The
New York Times* in 1901, the young Afro-American sociologist and
historian demonstrated that the rapid growth of the black population—especially in Southern New England and the Middle Atlan-
tic States—precipitated increasing prejudice and discrimination in
public accommodations, housing, and labor. Furthermore, he
pointed out that the obvious "social problems," such as alcoholism,
crime, and pauperism, which plagued many Northern blacks, were
the direct result of prejudice and discrimination. Emphasizing the
extent to which white determinants adversely affected the life
chances of the vast majority of blacks, DuBois wrote in 1901:

It is plain that with negative indifference, positive prejudice and some pecu-
niary interests against the Negro, and simply a general humanitarian feeling on the part of a few for him, it is easy to make his opportunities narrow
and his life burdensome. There can be no reasonable doubt that the Northern Negro receives less wages for his work and pays more for worse houses
than white workmen and that it is not altogether a matter of fitness that
confines his work chiefly to common labor and menial service.[3]

DuBois could have added that race relations in the North, like
those in the South, were extremely tense. During the 1900s race
riots broke out in New York City; Akron, Ohio; Greensburg, Indiana;
and Springfield, Illinois. As a portent of future developments in race
relations in the North, the muckraking journalist and amateur sociologist Ray Stannard Baker noted correctly in 1908 that "in every
important Northern city, a distinct race-problem already exists,
which must, in a few years, assume serious proportions."[4] John J.
Halsey, a professor at a college in suburban Chicago, was far more
emphatic about the immediate consequences of the steady migration of blacks from the South to Northern urban areas. Halsey noted
that: "He [the Negro] is pouring into the northern states, and where
there is an appreciable negro infusion, we have a negro problem just
as truly in the North as in the South."[5] The founding fathers of
American sociology nevertheless ignored the problems raised by the
presence of blacks in the North—despite the fact that "social problems" composed a province their discipline claimed as its own. Their

theories of slow and protracted social change and the ideology of the nation's leading black spokesmen were mutually reinforcing.

THE GREAT ACCOMMODATION: THE FOUNDING FATHERS ON RACE RELATIONS

In recent years August Meier and Louis R. Harlan have argued, on the basis of evidence gathered from Booker T. Washington's once private papers, that the Tuskegeean was involved in a surreptitious struggle against the forces of reaction in the South.[6] The new interpretation of Washington's role in the struggle for equality certainly provides needed insights into the complexity of his eclectic strategy. Few scholars will deny, however, that Washington's "Atlanta Exposition Address," through its skillful manipulation of sectional, nativist, and racial symbolism, rationalized perfectly the South's unfair and often brutal treatment of its citizens of discernible African descent.

During the 1890s, whites in the South were attempting to consolidate their higher caste position over blacks. The region, which was undergoing a period of relatively rapid industrialization, could not accommodate its surplus labor force. As a consequence, the intense search for work had resulted in substantial contact between lower-class blacks and whites in areas—especially in the cities of the lower South—where it had not occurred before. During this period of "competitive race relations," opportunistic politicians used blacks as scapegoats for the region's ills.[7] Disfranchisement by amended state constitutions had taken place in Mississippi in 1890 and was taking place in South Carolina at the time of Washington's address in 1895. Furthermore, lynching, the gradual proliferation of Jim Crow laws, and the removal of blacks from positions in skilled labor were all aided and abetted by the unethical political climate in the South, and by the North's ignorance of Southern racial affairs and ethical schizophrenia concerning its own black population.

Washington's address, delivered to a mixed audience at the opening of the Atlanta Cotton States and International Exposition on September 18, 1895, began by scolding black emigrationists "who depend on bettering their condition in a foreign land," and those militant blacks "who underestimate the importance of cultivating friendly relations with the Southern white man, who is his next-door neighbor." The ex-slave's interpretation of black history stressed the idea that blacks had been loyal servants "nursing your children, watching by the sick bed of your mothers and fathers, and often following them with tear-dimmed eyes to their graves." Revealing his nativist thought, he argued that whites "who look to the incoming of those of foreign birth and strange tongue and habits for the prosperity of the South" had a limited knowledge of the black contribution to Southern history. For blacks, "without strikes and labour wars, tilled your fields, cleared your forests, built your railroads and cities, and brought forth treasures from the bowels of the earth, and helped make possible this magnificent representation of the progress of the South."[8]

Despite Washington's emphasis on the monumental role blacks had played in whatever achievements the South made during the antebellum period, he argued that blacks were not prepared for the coming of industrialization. During Reconstruction, Washington asserted, "ignorant and inexperienced" blacks "began at the top instead of at the bottom." For those blacks "a seat in Congress or the state legislature was more sought than real estate or industrial skill . . . the political convention of stump speaking had more attractions than starting a dairy farm or truck garden." In effect, he exonerated white Southerners of any responsibility for the so-called Negro problem, and placed it squarely on the shoulders of blacks. Learning the virtues of common labor, he argued, would yield far more gains for blacks than politics. In regard to the role of blacks in the South's economy, he suggested that some would find a place in the professions. For the overwhelming number of blacks, however, Washington asserted: "It is at the bottom of life we must begin, and not at the top." Sociologically speaking, he envisioned a South where there would be great social distance between blacks and whites, yet considerable intergroup collaborations in those affairs "essential to mutual progress." Projecting the social Darwinist mind-set, with its emphasis on "the survival of the fittest," and a buoyant spirit of optimism, the Tuskegee Wizard argued that blacks would eventually achieve equality—not by agitation for social equality, but by a "severe and constant" struggle in the marketplace.[9]

Historical interpretations implying that Washington's Atlanta Exposition address either soothed the consciences of the justices of the Supreme Court that legitimized Jim Crow laws in the *Plessy v. Ferguson* case in 1896, or was an expedient strategy, have generated heated scholarly debates.[10] Those debates, however, seem unresolvable—especially when the adversaries take into account the virulent racism that pervaded the nation and the scheming of the Tuskegee political and patronage machines. Regardless of what positions the adversaries assume, Washington's speech clearly justified the status quo and thereby contributed to a permissive intellectual climate in which the distinguished sociologist, Franklin H. Giddings, could assert in 1896 without fear of censure: "The negro is plastic. He yields easily to environing influences. Deprived of the support of stronger races, he still relapses into savagery, but kept in contact with whites, he readily takes the external impress of civilization, and there is a reason to hope that he will acquire a measure of its reason."[11]

Professor Giddings's assessment of the character and capabilities of blacks and his cautious optimism concerning their future contain assumptions that adversely affected for twenty years a rational discussion of blacks in the American social science community. By using the term *the negro,* he revealed the assumption that blacks were a homogeneous group—an assumption held by most blacks and whites of the period. W.E.B. DuBois attacked this assumption as early as 1899, when he identified diverse social, religious, and economic groups within a major community of blacks in his classic study, *The Philadelphia Negro.* By asserting that blacks were "plastic," Giddings revealed an imagination with no bases in either past or present reality. Giddings's statements were not documented by either historical or anthropological evidence, and his insistence that blacks were adaptive was a sophisticated rationalization of Jim Crow laws, economic exploitation, social oppression, and disfranchisement. Like Washington's argument that blacks should acquiesce to the status quo in order to prepare for first-class citizenship, Giddings's statements imply that blacks were easily persevering despite enormous hardships, and would continue to do so in the foreseeable future.

The armchair sociologist's argument that "contact with whites" prevented blacks from lapsing into savagery was not only cultural snobbery, it was also impressionistic and nonsociological. Should one assume that servants, field hands, and bootblacks somehow received beneficial tutelage from the various classes they served? Did such contact prevent blacks from lapsing into savagery during their free time—when they were not under the scrutiny of whites, but were subject to the values and codes of other blacks? Giddings's commonsense generalizations about blacks, in essence, reflected the smug and often callous attitudes of most American intellectuals toward blacks. On a more specific level, his statements reflected an unwillingness to consider the reasonableness of arguments published as early as 1894 by an anthropologist of German-Jewish ancestry, Franz Boas.

Giddings's background, education, and career were both similar and dissimilar to the other fathers of sociology. Like most of them, he was born before the Civil War, and raised in a small town. Giddings's birthplace was Sherman, Connecticut, in 1855, and he grew up in Great Barrington, Massachusetts. Yet, unlike most of the oth-

er fathers, he was solidly middle-class, the son of a Congregationalist minister. A graduate of Union College, Giddings had pursued
careers in teaching and journalism before he entered academia in
1888, replacing Woodrow Wilson as lecturer in political economy at
Bryn Mawr. By 1892, the New Englander had succeeded in gaining a
position as a lecturer in sociology at Columbia University. Finally, in
1894, Giddings became the first full professor of sociology in the
United States.

Giddings was an assimilationist whose basic philosophy combined Comtean positivism and Spencerian evolutionism. He believed that the "equilibrium of energy" among individuals and
groups resulted in differentiation, integration, segregation, and assimilation, successively. The social order was, in essence, always in
a state of moving equilibrium. In the lower stages of society "ethnical
subordination" was a feature of the social order. In contradistinc-
tion, the "advanced stages of the development of highly organized
communities" were marked "by the differentiation [of the social constitution from the social composition] . . . so nearly complete that all
ethnical elements make their way into any part of the purposive
association." As Professor George M. Fredrickson has argued, Giddings, like many sociologists of the Progressive Era, "suggested the
evolution of society in the direction of assimilation and equality of
its ethnic components."[12] Giddings, however, believed that the racial inferiority of blacks was an obstacle to their assimilation in the
foreseeable future.

Perhaps none among the fathers was as confident as Lester F.
Ward that assimilation would occur and that racial differences
would not exist. Ward, who had experienced a slow and protracted
rise in his socioeconomic status, was born in Joliet, Illinois, in
1841, to an itinerant mechanic and a clergyman's daughter. He
suffered poverty and extreme hardship during his youth, yet
through sheer pluck and hard work, he learned biology and physiology and several foreign languages while working at menial jobs.
Eventually he qualified to teach high school. After serving in the
Civil War, in which he was wounded three times, Ward entered eve-
ning classes at Columbian (now George Washington) University and
earned degrees in art, law, and botany successively. At the same
time, he entered government service, working first as a clerk in the
Treasury Department, then as chief of the Division of Navigation
and Immigration, and later as a librarian at the Bureau of Statistics.
Then, after a tenure as a geologist in charge of paleobotany in the
federal government, Ward was promoted to the position of chief pal-
eontologist in the United States Geological Survey in 1892. The
"American Aristotle" made several contributions to the literature in

botany and geology, and established himself as one of the pre-academic pioneers of sociology with the publication of his so-ciobiological tome, *Dynamic Sociology* (1883). After lecturing in summer sessions at several universities, he resigned his government post in 1906 and accepted an appointment as professor of sociology at Brown University, a post he held until his death in 1913.

In his discussion of assimilation, "Evolution of Social Structures," published in the *American Journal of Sociology* in 1905, the political liberal drew on the racial conflict theories of Ludwig Gumplowicz and Gustav Ratzenhofer. Ward pointed out that racial conflicts were the means by which social assimilations were initiated. A society's initial social assimilation occurred in prehistorical times, when one race, through fortuitous circumstances, obtained a military advantage over another race and subjugated it. From the interaction of the two races, the following social structures emerged in succession: (1) the system of caste; (2) the institution of slavery; (3) labor in the economic sense; (4) the industrial system; (5) landed property; (6) priesthood; (7) a leisure class; (8) government by law; (9) the state; (10) political liberty; (11) property; (12) a business class; (13) a people; (14) a nation.[13]

Ward's ideas on the manner in which social assimilation takes place are developed in his statements on the creation of a people from two disparate races. At that stage in the evolution of the social structures, members of the dominant race outside the ruling classes and members of the subordinate race who are not enslaved realize, in their struggle for subsistence, that they have common interests. Race prejudice between the groups dissipates and they merge into an industrial class to which the ruling classes must relinquish some of their power. Greater interaction then takes place between classes and eventually both races intermarry, creating a new people "as homogeneous in its constitution as was either of its original components." In modern nations, the process has been repeated several times, each time moving the society to a higher plane of civilization.[14]

The present state of society in England, Ward believed, was illustrative of the effects of repeated social assimilation:

No less than four typical assimilations have taken place on English soil since the earliest recorded annals of the country began. Think of the animosities and hostilities, the bitter race hatred, the desperate struggles, the prolonged wars that characterize the history of England. What became of all these warring elements? There is no country in all the world where patriotism is higher than in England, and it is shared alike by Saxon and Celt, by

Scot and Briton. Who now are the Normans that constituted the last con-
quering race? And do the Saxons, when they can be distinguished any
longer feel the chains that once manacled them? The equilibration is complete, all class distinctions, at least those arising out of the race question,
have totally disappeared. On the other hand, consider the achievements of
England. Contemplate the wonderful social efficiency of that many times
amalgamated people. The sociologist cannot shut his eyes to the fact that
the social efficiency is mainly due to the repeated amalgamations and to the
intensity of the resultant social struggles, developing, molding, and
strengthening social structures.[15]

Throughout the rest of the world, social assimilations similar to
those that had taken place in England were occurring. This led Ward
to predict that "if we could peer far enough into the great future, we
should see this planet of ours ultimately peopled with a single homogeneous and completely assimilated race of men—the human race—
in the composition of which could be detected all the great com-
manding qualities of every one of its racial components."[16] Despite
Ward's optimism concerning the eventual assimilation of the world's
different races, he failed to predict when the process would be completed.

The climb from poverty to academia did not always mean that a
sociologist would embrace liberal views and believe that society was
evolving in the direction of the assimilation and equality of its ethnic components. William G. Sumner, who was born into a working-
class household in Paterson, New Jersey, in 1840, was a purveyor of
a conservative brand of social Darwinism. His meteoric rise from the
working class to Yale and then to advanced studies in theology at
Geneva, Gottingen, and Oxford seems to have enabled him to rationalize his own rapid upward socioeconomic mobility in one of the
most cutthroat and corrupt periods in recent American history. His
Darwinian educational struggle, which was facilitated by the money
of a few rich friends such as William C. Whitney, enabled him to
obtain a tutorship at Yale in 1868 and finally a post as professor of
political and social science at Yale in 1872. At Yale, this former
editor of a religious newspaper and rector of an Episcopal Church in
Morristown, New Jersey, indoctrinated his wide following with the
Spencerian ideology of the "survival of the fittest."

Nevertheless, Sumner was an excellent scholar. His magnum
opus, *Folkways* (1906), was a consummate piece of scholarship.
Emphasizing the theoretical significance of that volume, Howard W.
Odum wrote in 1951: "His study [*Folkways*] was based upon the
assumption that the first function of life is to live, and that in the
struggle for existence the ability to adapt to change is vital. Through

trial and error and experimentation, through pain and struggle, through the constant meeting of new needs, society itself not only has survived, but has developed its cultures." Along with A. G. Keller, Sumner was the first American scholar "to emphasize the importance of comparative societies, which was much later to be featured in *group* concepts," Odum concluded.[17] Hagiography aside, Sumner was a primitive when he discussed race relations. While Ward had based his theories of race relations on English and Continental developments, Sumner based his conservative theory on the behavior of primitive peoples and his analysis of race relations in the South. When Sumner accounted for the hostility of most whites toward those few whites who associated with blacks, he attributed that phenomenon to "the differences in the mores" of the whites and blacks. "The mores," as he defined them in 1906, "are the folkways, including the philosophical and ethical generalizations as to societal welfare, which are suggested by them and inherent in them, as they grow."[18]

Clearly, Sumner's usage of the concept of "the mores" approximated the concept of culture that was emerging in the writings of Franz Boas. Like the concept of culture, the concept of "the mores" had both liberal and conservative implications. When applied to the question of innate racial differences between blacks and whites, it suggested that those supposed differences were the product of the total social environment rather than race. When applied to the problems of race relations in the South, the concept of "the mores" suggested that little could be done to solve these problems, since they were the product of traditional differences between blacks and whites. Since the concept of the mores was an environmental concept, it did not come under attack from the Boasians and their followers in sociology; thus it persisted as an important part of the argument for those who viewed segregation as inevitable until Gunnar Myrdal exposed its "laissez-faire, do-nothing" bias in 1944.

As could be expected, Sumner clung to a conservative position in regard to the relations between whites and blacks. The problem between those races, he argued, stemmed from the fact that in freedom blacks were "living by their own mores." Interpreting the era of slavery as one of mild race relations, Sumner wrote that "whites and blacks had formed habits of action and feelings toward each other. They lived in peace and concord, and each one grew up in the way which was traditional and customary." Since the Civil War, the relationship of whites and blacks had changed. With no legal basis for asserting white superiority, the two races were attempting "to learn how to live together under other relations than before." Whites had resisted the change and had "never been converted from the old mores." There were indications, nevertheless, that new mores were forming which signaled a greater separation between the races. Emphasizing his laissez-faire attitude toward race relations, Sumner argued that the attempts on the part of humanitarians to monitor the natural relations between the races through legislation were destined to fail: "Some are anxious to interfere and try to control. They take their stand on ethical views of what is going on. It is evidently impossible for anyone to interfere. We are like spectators at a great natural convulsion. The results will be such as the facts and forces call for."[19]

Sumner betrayed several biases shared by Booker T. Washington and both Northern and Southern sociologists writing before 1911. The idea that slavery was a halcyon period where antagonisms between blacks and whites did not develop was a pivotal argument of Washington which was further developed by Southern sociologists such as Joseph A. Tillinghast and Jerome Dowd. By suggesting that race relations were mild during slavery, the pre—1911 sociologists wanted their readers to infer that the institution was an ideal solution to the racial problems in the South. Sumner's emphasis on the "traditional and customary" imbued those conservative ideas with a type of mythical significance. Surely, race relations in the ante-bellum period did not deserve such glorification.

Sumner's insistence on the omnipotence of natural laws clearly reveals his justification for the Jim Crow system. Like the other pre—1911 sociologists, Sumner believed that neither the intervention of the government nor the efforts of reformers could change the superordinate—subordinate relationship of whites and blacks. Such an approach did not admit that the local government had a role in the disfranchisement of blacks and the separation of the races. Why was it necessary to legalize Jim Crow laws if the natural laws dictated the relations between whites and blacks? Sumner, in essence, argued that natural laws ensured that blacks would occupy a permanently subordinate position in American society.

In his examination of Sumner's point of view, Gunnar Myrdal, a social economist at the University of Stockholm, argued in his monumental work, *An American Dilemma* (1944), that Sumner's political views and social scientific thought reinforced one another. On political issues, Sumner was a conservative. As a social scientist, he was mainly interested in explaining the role of the folkways and the mores in social life. Thus, the internationally renowned Myrdal pointed out: "His [Sumner's] observation that there were folkways and mores which gave societies a static stability buttressed his belief that social change was difficult to achieve. His desires to maintain the *status quo* led him to conclude that there should be no attempt to change the folkways and mores." Furthermore, Myrdal noted that the "static and fatalistic valuations" that permeated Sumner's concept of the mores implied "a whole social theory and an entire laissez-faire ('do-nothing') metaphysics, and is so utilized." Even if one ignored the political connotations of the concept of mores, Myrdal insisted, its "usefulness as a scientific tool" was limited to the study of primitive cultures and folk communities.[20] Sumner's concept of "mores" was not only deceptive, but also imprecise.

The flaws of deceptiveness and imprecision also weakened the theories of liberal assimilationists. Although liberals such as Giddings and Ward believed that society was evolving in the direction of the assimilation of different races, they did not come to grips with the problem of *how* blacks would achieve full social and political equality. An attempt to solve this perplexing problem was made by Edward A. Ross, the youngest father of American sociology. Ross was born into an itinerant Scotch–Irish family in rural Illinois in 1866. Orphaned at an early age, he was nevertheless able to gain the financial support of his foster parents. Ross attended Coe College, a Presbyterian-financed institution in Cedar Rapids, Iowa. After graduating from Coe in 1887, Ross traveled to Germany to study comparative literature—an experience that he found extremely disillusioning because of the pessimism that permeated German culture during those years. Upon returning to the United States, he received his doctorate in political economy at Johns Hopkins in 1891.

After teaching one year at Indiana University and one year at Cornell University, he was appointed to the faculty of Leland Stanford Junior University in 1893. An outspoken reformer, Ross soon came into conflict with the conservative views of Mrs. Leland Stanford, widow of the founder. Finally, in 1900, after Ross advocated that the government place immigration restrictions on Asians, the president of the university, David Starr Jordan, who had interceded on Ross's behalf on several occasions, obeyed Mrs. Stanford's wishes and fired him. Several of Ross's colleagues subsequently resigned or were dismissed. He continued his career at the University of Nebraska, and in 1906, his long and protracted struggle to obtain a permanent position ended when he secured an appointment at the University of Wisconsin, a position he held until his retirement in 1937.

Ross's most important contribution to sociological literature, *Social Control* (1901), was dedicated to his "Master" and father-in-law, Lester F. Ward. Like Ward, he believed that society was evolving towards the assimilation of disparate races. For Ross, the process of assimilation began with the acculturation of minority groups. "The all inclusive group," he argued, must necessarily find a means to "assimilate and reconcile its members and weaken the ties that bind men into minor groups." He believed that the social valuations of the dominant group would be employed as a means of controlling individuals and groups and bringing about the depreciation of "pleasures which are exclusive, collision-provoking, or liable to excess." Although Ross argued that blacks were an "idle, quarreling, sensual" race, he believed that they were capable of improvement. Like Booker T. Washington, he believed that the social valuations provided by the churches, schools, whites, and industry would compel blacks to acquire "a high estimate of cleanliness, family privacy, domestic privacy and literacy."[21] Unfortunately, Ross did not address himself to the problem of whether blacks would achieve full social and political equality as a consequence of their exposure to the dominant group's social valuations.

Most Northern, professional sociologists who were influenced by the fathers were progressive evolutionists who predicted the eventual coming of a color-blind society; none of them, however, indicted the white South for its castelike system. As a consequence, their theories were ambivalent when they attempted to analyze race relations in that region. Charles H. Cooley, one of the United States' most influential social psychologists, revealed his ambivalences in his treatise, *Social Organization* (1909). This Midwesterner, who was the son of a prominent Michigan jurist, had corresponded with Lester F. Ward regarding Sir Francis Galton's views on genius as early as 1890, and had taken a minor field in sociology for his doctorate under Franklin H. Giddings. Although Cooley did not write as a defender of the system in the South, he, like Giddings, could not envision that a system other than caste could exist. Believing that "an impulse toward caste is found in human nature itself," he nonetheless declared that it was an "inferior principle." As an evolutionist, Cooley thought caste tended to be "supplanted by something freer and more rational."[22]

Despite his contention that the caste system was inferior to the democratic system, Cooley conjured up a sociological law that purportedly accounted for the existence of the caste system. Revealing a belief in the existence of innate racial differences, he argued: "Two races of different temperament and capacity distinct to the eye living side by side in the same community tend strongly to become castes, no matter how equal the social system may otherwise be." Aware of the contradiction between democratic values and the values of the caste system, he rationalized the existence of that system by arguing its existence indicated the "impotence of democratic traditions to overcome the caste system when fostered by obvious physical and psychical differences."[23]

Cooley was in a quandary, for although he believed that innate racial differences between blacks and whites "fostered" the existence of the caste system, he felt that it was despicable. An advocate of the brotherhood of races, he could not countenance "that caste arrogance which does not recognize in the negro a spiritual brotherhood underlying all race differences and possible inferiority." The question of racial differences, Cooley suggested, could be separated "from that sharing in common spirit and service from which no human being can rightly or Christianly be excluded." Furthermore, he believed that "science, religion and the democratic spirit" supported the argument that the black was "fundamentally a man like the rest of us." Cooley hoped that the attitude of whites toward blacks was "transitory, since it is calculated, in a modern atmosphere, to generate continuing disquiet and hatred." Such an attitude, he concluded, belonged "with slavery and is incongruous in the newer world."[24]

Despite his hatred of the caste system and his advocacy of the brotherhood of different races, Cooley was fatalistic. Revealing his accommodationist stance, which was similar to that of Southerners like Howard W. Odum, Cooley wrote: "The practical question is not that of abolishing castes but of securing just and kindly relations between them, of reconciling the fact of caste with the ideals of freedom and right."[25] Such a reconciliation was impossible. Yet in the age of Booker T. Washington, the argument was acceptable to the vast majority of social scientists.

Unlike most Northern sociologists, Albion W. Small did not make any major theoretical contributions to the study of race relations. He did play an important role in the professionalization of sociology. Small was born in Waterville, Maine, in 1854, the son of a middle-class Baptist minister. He spent three years studying for the ministry at Colby University (now Colby College) and Newton Theological Institute. After leaving seminary, Small spent two years in Berlin and Leipzig, acquainting himself with "scientific procedures" of the German historical school.[26] Small returned to the United States in 1881 and taught history and political economy until 1888, when he entered Johns Hopkins. He received his doctorate in constitutional history at that institution in 1889 and was appointed president of Colby that same year.

When his fellow Baptist, William Rainey Harper, the founder and first president of the University of Chicago, began negotiations with Small in 1891, Small sketched out his grand scheme for the development of the department of sociology at that institution:

The academic work which I would do for the rest of my life, if perfectly free to select for myself, would be to organize such a department of Sociology as does not exist to my knowledge. It should include a collegiate foundation in history, and economics, more thorough and comprehensive than any required for entrance upon graduate study in the United States. . . . It should then, on the *historic* side, contain courses for three years, first in English and American institutional history, second in English and American economic history; on the *economic* side, upon a required basis of familiarity with the substance of all that may be called contemporary economic doctrine, original studies of the actual conditions of American economic problems with a view to comprehension of the status of these questions in their concrete relations, rather than to a doctrine about them in the abstract; on the *sociological* side, first courses filling one year in exposition of the philosophies of history. Second, courses filling the last year in Sociology proper—a synthesis of the facts of social physiology, as derived from the tributary biological, psychological, historical and economic sciences—being an inductive substitute for the antiquated metaphysical philosophies of history, and a clinical preparation for the practical diagnosis of specific social developments. . . . I would never grant the doctorate to men of the microscope alone, but would insist that they shall have acquired a sharp sense of the relation of what their microscope discovers to the laws of society as a whole.[27]

Small's twenty-year protracted transfer of his moral career from the pulpit to the lectern was completed in 1892, when he accepted the chairmanship of the Department of Social Science and Anthropology at the University of Chicago.

During the period between 1892 and 1912, Small appointed several reform-minded evangelical clergymen and descendants of clergymen to the department. They were: Charles R. Henderson, a Baptist minister and a leader in the reform of social services in Chicago; Charles Zueblin, a minister interested in municipal improvement, parks, and extension education; George Vincent, the son of a Methodist Episcopal bishop; and William I. Thomas, the son of a Methodist minister.[28] These urban progressives were providing the direction for reform movements. Like most of the fathers of sociology, they identified "social change as social evolution and interpreted it as *progress* toward a better society," as Roscoe C. Hinkle, Jr., and Gisela J. Hinkle put it.[29]

Furthermore, Small published the writings of a group of progressives in the *American Journal of Sociology* during the 1900s. Many of them were social reformers, social commentators, and teachers who had not received advanced academic training in sociology or were not actively engaged in the discipline. Although most of them believed in black inferiority, they did not attempt to justify slavery and the contemporaneous castelike system in the South. In fact, they thought blacks had made significant progress since slavery, and though they disagreed about the solution to the race problem, many of them believed that blacks had a progressive future. The argument of the amateur progressives became one of the most effective weapons in the liberal arsenal during the next two decades.

In 1902, Sarah E. Simons, a Washington, D.C., schoolteacher who had received an M.A. in history at Stanford University in 1900, marshalled a significant amount of statistical data indicating that blacks had made substantial progress since slavery. Data showing a significant decline in black illiteracy, the enrollment of blacks in schools and institutions of higher education, the development of a class of skilled tradesmen and professionals, and the founding of business and cultural organizations suggested to her that blacks had made obvious progress. Furthermore, Simons believed that the future for blacks was filled with excellent possibilities for success. She went so far as to hazard that: "Perhaps when [the black man] is as well-equipped for entrance into the field of society, business, or politics as the white man, the privilege will not be denied him, he may yet be able to achieve recognition."[30] Simons could state confidently that the intellectual capacity of blacks was alterable because she adhered to the Lamarckian doctrine of the inheritance of acquired characteristics. Simons believed that the American environment, despite the obstacles present, provided blacks with the opportunity to evolve to a higher stage of intellectual development. Thus, she remarked, "the social environment has already accomplished much, and will work more and more toward the assimilation of the negro."[31]

For Charlotte Perkins Gilman, one of the first women sociologists, a rigorous program was needed to "accelerate" the progress of blacks. Like Simons, Gilman admitted in an article published in the *American Journal of Sociology* (1908) that blacks had made remarkable progress in the United States. "The African race," she asserted, "with the advantage of contact with our more advanced stage of evolution, has made more progress in a few generations than any other race has ever done in the same time, except the Japanese." The progress of blacks, she thought, was due to the "direct transference of institutions and their result." She also acknowledged that there were a "number of cases" where the black has paralleled the business success of the white. That success indicated to her the "capacity of the race" to achieve in that endeavor.[32]

Despite her praise of the achievements of blacks, Gilman was not immune to making disparaging comments about their abilities. Revealing a belief in intrinsic differences between the black and the white, Gilman argued that the black was "widely dissimilar and in many respects inferior" to the white. Occupying, for the most part, a low position in the social order, the black was a "social injury" to the population as a whole. Like the Southern sociologists, she believed the disabilities of the black were due to their purported primitive African inheritance. Gilman argued that the black, even after slavery, was living "under social, economic, political, and religious conditions to which he was by heredity a stranger."[33]

Gilman is primarily remembered for her book *Women and Economics* (1898)—a work influenced significantly by Lester F. Ward's *Dynamic Sociology* (1883). In her work, the feminist Gilman argued that financial independence for women could be achieved through economic and social planning. Gilman's solution to the race problem required a type of long-range planning similar to that which she advocated for women. She proposed that the development of the black could be enhanced most effectively by the compulsory enlistment of the large "degenerate" element of the group in state-sponsored, forced-labor "armies." Children were to be guided from nursery to trade schools, and those who showed marked ability, to institutions of higher learning. Blacks of working age were to be employed on farms, producing goods that would not only feed, but also provide income for the army. In addition to their agricultural tasks, the members of the army would work on internal improvements that were badly needed in the South. Once an individual demonstrated the ability to work on his own, he would be given the funds that he had accumulated and allowed to leave the army. Those individuals who over a period of time did not achieve the standards necessary for their release were to be brought together to form shops and farms where they would remain until they graduated.[34]

Although this forced-labor program was intended to develop a self-sufficient black population, Gilman did not feel that she was promoting equality. Embracing an organic view of society, she wrote: "Society is an organic relation, it is not composed of constituents all alike and equally developed, but most diverse and unequal." Indeed, she thought it was "possible to have in a society members" who were racially inferior "to other members, but yet essential to the life of the whole."[35]

Perhaps the most influential amateur sociologist to publish an article in the *American Journal of Sociology* during the decade was Monroe N. Work, a transplanted black Southerner who would receive an M.A. in sociology at the University of Chicago in 1903. In his 1900 article, "Crime Among the Negroes of Chicago," the former African Methodist Episcopal minister took Frederick L. Hoffman to task for the argument that blacks had retrogressed since slavery. Like other sociologists of Afro-American ancestry, such as Kelly Miller and W.E.B. DuBois, Work attacked the degeneracy thesis of the reactionaries by arguing that blacks were evolving to a higher stage of evolution in which their true racial genius would reach fruition. Basing his long article on a large body of statistical data on crime in Chicago, Work argued cogently that the large number of crimes committed by blacks was due to "the fact that he [the black] is in this transitional state from a lower to a higher plane of development." He conceded to racists that some of the criminality was a result of "race characteristics peculiar to him [the black]," but went on to declare that "the economic phase of this transition . . . accounts for a large part of the excess of negro crime in the United States."[36]

Like W.E.B. DuBois, Monroe N. Work differed from many scholars of the period insofar as he emphasized the use of empirical data to support generalizations. His biennial *Negro Yearbook* and his other publications written during his tenure as director of the Department of Records and Research at Tuskegee provided a wealth of evidence that supported the argument that blacks were making considerable progress, despite their history of slavery, oppression, and economic exploitation. His publications influenced a whole generation of sociologists and laymen.

Despite the proclamations of moderates like Work, Simons, and Gilman concerning black progress, they severely undercut their own argument. By arguing that blacks were either presently inferior to whites or dominated by peculiar "race characteristics," they unwittingly excused the treatment of blacks. Furthermore, they failed to consider several important questions about the future status of blacks in the American social order. How long would it take blacks to raise themselves to the level of equality with whites? Would racial prejudice disappear? Would all of the purported "racial characteristics" vanish? The moderate amateurs did not attempt to answer those questions, for they were entangled in the labyrinth of the progressive evolutionist argument.

Thus, despite the oppressive conditions that confronted blacks in both North and South, the liberal fathers and their followers were optimistic about the eventual outcome of race relations. Their progressive evolutionism contrasted sharply with the reactionism of Frederick L. Hoffman, Walter F. Willcox, and Paul B. Barringer, amateur social scientists who thought blacks were degenerating and facing ultimate extinction.[37] Although the fathers were not pessimistic, they were unable to envision an egalitarian society in the foreseeable future, for their theories reflected uncertainties on the issue of the capabilities of nonwhites and a strong belief in the inevitability of racial prejudice.

THE PROBLEM OF THE CAPABILITIES OF NONWHITES

For the fathers of sociology, the question of whether blacks could participate fully in American society on an equal basis with whites was fraught with problems, primarily because turn-of-the-century social scientists believed that all generalizations about human behavior were qualified by race. Most of them thought that nonwhites were either different from or inferior to whites. Giddings, who voiced the opinion of most abstract social thinkers regarding the capabilities of what he labelled the "lower races," rejected the liberal environmentalist argument that it was impossible to determine the abilities of nonwhites because of their limited opportunities. Stating his case in his *Principles of Sociology*, Giddings wrote in 1896: "They [the lower races] have been in existence . . . much longer than the European races and have accomplished immeasurably less. We are, therefore, warranted in saying that they have not the same inherent abilities."[38]

Despite his dogmatic views, Giddings was not an extreme racist when judged by the standards of academics in his day. This New Englander, like most sociologists writing between 1896 and 1919, believed not only that social change was resulting in progress toward a better society, but also that the social behavior of races would affect their genetic makeup. In regard to the ability of blacks to adapt to new conditions, Giddings argued that they had greater evolutionary potential than the Tasmanians and the North American Indians. Although Giddings felt that blacks were intellectually inferior to Indians, he insisted that blacks exhibited "plasticity." Giddings's predictions concerning the potential of blacks to become equals with whites were cautious, however, because he believed that "a truly progressive type . . . must have not only plasticity, but also strength of character to make independent advances, and without outside help, to hold an advantage when it has been gained." Emphasizing the social Darwinist mind-set that stressed the superiority of Western civilization, Giddings concluded that both plasticity and character were held only by the peoples of Northern and Western Europe.[39] Like most Lamarckians, Giddings avoided the extreme racist view of the permanency of racial characteristics and at the same time avoided the ethical burdens of the liberal environmentalist creed.

It is incorrect nevertheless to relegate all of the fathers of sociology to the status of racists. While it is clear that the comments of Giddings were "sophisticated" rationalizations for attempts by Americans of Northern and Western European origins to establish a hegemony over nonwhite peoples both at home and abroad, it is also true that the assessments of the capabilities of nonwhites by Ward, Ross, and Sumner were truly dynamic.

In the writings of Lester F. Ward, one of the most progressive and dominant sociologists of the period, there was a shift from the skeptical position on the issue of racial intellectual differences, which reflected Franz Boas's influence, to a strenuous denial of intellectual differences, a position far more progressive than Boas ever assumed. In 1906, Ward argued from the typically Boasian, skeptical point of view: "Doubtless within each such race [yellow, red, black], for there are many, intellectual equality, in the same sense as it exists in the white race, can be safely affirmed." Yet the question of whether intellectual equality existed between the white and nonwhite races posed a problem. Although Ward favored Benjamin Kidd's argument that most of the apparent differences in intellectual capacity between the races were attributable to differences in "mental equipment," he believed the problem was "worthy of thorough scientific treatment based chiefly on the practical experience of the lower races." Nevertheless, he ventured to conclude that "it is . . . clear that there is no race and no class of human beings who are incapable of assimilating the social achievement of mankind and profitably employing the social heritage."[40]

Despite his cautious remarks in 1906, Ward's egalitarianism was manifest the next year. Thus, it is not surprising that he was an outspoken critic of the eugenics movement, a movement which by the early twentieth century had become international. Its proponents attributed the plight of alcoholics, criminals, the insane, and the poor to heredity, and advocated stringent controls on the propagation of those groups.[41] Ward believed that the human will was capable of directing history, and especially opposed the eugenicists' argument that there were inherent intellectual differences between the rich and the poor. In response to D. Collin Wells of Dartmouth College, a Congregationalist minister who suggested that socialism and trade unionism interfered with the natural selection process,[42] Ward contended that:

So far as the native capacity, the potential quality, the "promise and potency," of a higher life are concerned, those swarming, spawning millions, the bottom layer of society, the proletariat, the working classes, the "hewers of wood and drawers of water," nay even the denizens of the slums . . . all of these are by nature the peers of the boasted "aristocracy of brains" that now dominates society and looks down upon them, and the equals in all but privilege of the most enlightened teachers of eugenics.[43]

For Ward, the idea of class and racial equality was based on faith. He had neither training in anthropology nor any new evidence indicating that all people were intellectual equals. Yet because of his democratic sentiments, Ward assumed the equality of all persons.

Because the views of sociologists were dynamic did not mean that they necessarily evolved in the direction of belief in the equipotentiality of blacks: in the case of Ward's son-in-law, Edward A. Ross, they evolved from the Boasian skeptical position to a belief in the inherent intellectual and moral inferiority of blacks. During a period in which his career at Stanford was in jeopardy, Ross's uncertainty was obvious. In an article that appeared in the *Annals of the American Academy of Political and Social Science (Annals)*, entitled "The Causes of Race Superiority," Ross argued that the issue of racial differences was muddled because of the tendency of social thinkers to accept either the "equality fallacy . . . which belittles race difference and has a robust faith in the power of intercourse and school instruction to lift a backward folk to the level of the best," or "the counter fallacy . . . which exaggerates the race factor and regards the actual differences of peoples as hereditary and fixed."[44]

Nonetheless, he made a reference to blacks and whites when he argued that the "American average of energy and character is lowered by the presence in the South of several millions of inferior race."[45] Offering a more explicit statement of his view of black inferiority after he had gained tenure at the University of Wisconsin in 1907, Ross declared: "The theory that races are virtually equal in capacity leads to such monumental follies as lining the valleys of the South with the bones of half a million picked whites in order to improve the condition of four million unpicked blacks. I see no reason why races may not differ as much in moral and intellectual traits as obviously they do in bodily traits."[46]

The issue of racial intellectual differences to which Giddings, Ward, and Ross addressed themselves was not entertained by William G. Sumner. Despite his conservatism and his belief in the natural inequality of individuals, Sumner did not believe that races were necessarily unequal. Although Thomas F. Gossett has found racist stereotypes in Sumner's writing, Sumner knew that the question of racial determinism was muddled.[47] "Modern scholars," Sumner commented in *Folkways* in 1906, "have made the mistake of attributing to *race* much which belongs to the ethos, with a resulting controversy as to the relative importance of nature and nurture."[48] Sociologists, however, did not have to reject the idea of the inherent intellectual equality of blacks and whites in order to argue the idea that blacks *would not* become first-class citizens in the foreseeable future, for concepts such as "consciousness of kind" and "ethnocentrism" were extremely useful in rationalizing contemporaneous race relations.

THE DISCUSSION OF PREJUDICE

One of the toughest obstacles to overcome for those who studied race relations before the mid-1920s was the idea that prejudice was difficult, if not impossible, to remove from whites. Viewing prejudice as both an acquired and an inborn action-pattern, they could not envision a time within the foreseeable future when whites would be color-blind. Ironically, in the initial theoretical discussions of the fathers of sociology, prejudice did not have biological assumptions. According to Franklin H. Giddings, the existence of "consciousness of kind" made prejudice and discrimination a part of the natural order of society. "Consciousness of kind" referred to "a state of consciousness in which any being whether low or high in the scale of life, recognized another being as of like kind." This consciousness was "coextensive with potential society," and underlay racial as well as "ethnical and political groupings."[49] Although the concept of consciousness of kind had strong theoretical foundations, Professor George M. Fredrickson has pointed out that when Giddings raised the concept to "an inescapable law of human association, it became the perfect basis for a sophisticated defense of racial segregation."[50]

Like Giddings's concept of consciousness of kind, William G. Sumner's concept of "ethnocentrism" was a "view of things in which one's own group is the center of everything, and all others are scaled and rated with reference to it." Nonetheless, Sumner, who had opposed the entrance of the United States into the Spanish American War, was extremely critical of ethnocentrism when it degenerated into patriotism and chauvinism successively. When patriotism was reduced to chauvinism Sumner noted that: "It overrules personal judgment and character, and puts the whole group at the mercy of the clique which is ruling at that moment. It produces the dominance of watchwords and phrases which take the place of reason and conscience in determining conduct."[51] Sumner had the moral courage to admit that ethnocentrism, when manipulated by leaders, was not only irrational but also dangerous.

The depiction of society that emerged from the writings of the fathers, except Sumner, was one in which blacks would witness a slow and protracted change in their status. Although the present capabilities of blacks and the existence of consciousness of kind, "the mores," and ethnocentrism were viewed as temporary obstacles to immediate assimilation, the progressive evolutionists were certain that assimilation would occur—albeit in the distant future. The progressive evolutionists, in other words, ignored the immediacy of the necessity of scientific inquiry into the so-called Negro problem. As a consequence, they neglected the writing of W.E.B. DuBois— perhaps the most polemical yet "scientific" authority on the issues of race and race relations during the 1890s.

DUBOIS AND SCIENTISM

DuBois's ideological orientation was, no doubt, a result of his personal revulsion against his inferior status as an Afro-American in a British-dominated society. Born in Great Barrington, Massachusetts, in 1868, DuBois had experienced racism in his native New England, during his tenure at Fisk University in the South, and in Germany. Nonetheless, the social scientific basis of his position on race was, for the most part, a product of his academic training in both the United States and Germany. Although DuBois received his doctorate in history, he was not a stranger to the sociological theories of the 1890s. During his training at Harvard, he took many courses in the social sciences, and he would later adopt in his writings the advice of his mentor, the institutional historian Albert Bushnell Hart, and turn away "from the lovely but sterile land of philosophical speculation, to the social sciences as the field for gathering and interpreting the body of fact which would apply to my program for the Negro."[52]

In Germany, DuBois was influenced significantly by one of the leading figures in the German historical school, Gustav von Schmoller, who thought that empiricism was the key to the development of a social science capable of shaping public policy. Such faith in empiricism led DuBois to reject relativism and assume that the "observations of different persons always lead to the same results."[53] With this assumption in mind, it is not surprising that he attempted to delimit the goals and approaches of sociologists on the issues of race and race relations.

In an article, "The Study of Negro Problems," which was published in the *Annals* in 1898, DuBois admonished the leading race authorities for their "slip-shod" and "unsystematic manner" of approach to the problems confronting blacks. He appealed to the search for "scientific truth," and warned the charlatans that "if they dally with the truth to humor the whims of the day, they do far more than hurt the good name of the American people; they hurt the cause of scientific truth the world over, they voluntarily decrease human knowledge of a universe of which we are ignorant enough, and they degrade the high end of the truth-seeking in a day when they need more and more to dwell upon its sanctity."[54]

That the ideal of attaining "scientific truth" had not been achieved in the study of blacks stemmed from the fact that most intellectuals were involved in the progress–degeneracy debate. Liberal humanitarians, DuBois noted, tended to point to black progress, and thus assumed that the race problem would eventually be a thing of the past. The reactionaries, on the other hand, insisted that blacks, because of their inability to solve their social problems, would die out. DuBois believed those points of view were untenable: first, because they contained conclusions obtained "without carefully weighing evidence and testing it"; second, because social scientists usually studied blacks only from the perspective of their "influence on the white inhabitants"; and third, because the biases of the commentators demonstrated a lack of a "deep sense of the sanctity of scientific truth." Thus DuBois concluded that the works of these social scientists were "worthless as science."[55]

Indeed, DuBois was ahead of his time. In the 1910s, when social scientists began to stress their desire for a field in which broad conclusions were based on empirical data, sociology sought to shed its ties to moral philosophy and present an "objective" picture of society. Of course, recent sociologists have shown that value judgments impinge on all aspects of the social scientific enterprise.[56] Still, DuBois's insistence on a bias-free sociology was a necessary attack on those social commentators who approached the study of blacks as if the issues were clear-cut—as if detailed studies were not a prerequisite for their broad conclusions.

DuBois's *The Philadelphia Negro* was the epitome of the high standards of scholarship that he had set for scholars. In an appendix to his monumental study of Afro-Americans, *An American Dilemma*, Gunnar Myrdal praised DuBois's study. The distinguished Swedish social economist wrote in 1944 that: "We cannot close this description of what a study of a Negro community should be without calling attention to the study which is now all but forgotten. We refer to W.E.B. DuBois' *The Philadelphia Negro*, published in 1899."[57]

DuBois began by admitting that his goal of seeking scientific truth was an ideal which was unattainable on the controversial race issue. He was certain that "convictions on all great matters of human interest, one must have to a greater or less degree, and they will enter to some extent into the most cold-blooded scientific research as a disturbing factor." Yet DuBois was sure that his work, despite his sentiments, would supply the public with "a body of information as may be a safe guide for all efforts toward the solution of the many Negro problems of a great American city." The leading black scholar also admitted that his environmentalist beliefs ran counter to the hereditarian assumptions so commonplace in the social sciences.

He assumed that the "student must clearly recognize that a complete study must not confine itself to the group, but must especially notice the environment; the physical environment of city, sections and houses, the far mightier social environment—the surrounding world of custom, wish, whim, and thought which envelops this group and powerfully influences its social development."[58]

DuBois attempted to repudiate the assumption that blacks were a homogeneous group whose members did not differ in class or behavior. Anticipating the work of the "caste and class" school of race relations that emerged in the 1930s, DuBois insisted that "wide variations in antecedents, wealth, intelligence and general efficiency have already been differentiated within this group [the blacks]." But despite his emphasis upon differentiation in Philadelphia's major black community, DuBois brought forth ample evidence suggesting that the attitudes of the white population "limited and circumscribed" the opportunities of even "the better classes" of blacks. For DuBois, it was axiomatic that racial prejudice rather than supposed hereditary characteristics determined the status of blacks. "Negro prejudice," he argued unequivocally, "in cities like Philadelphia has been a vast factor in aiding and abetting all other causes which impel a half-developed race to recklessness and excess."[59]

DuBois's reference to blacks as a "half-developed race" demonstrates that he too lapsed into the racist thinking of the period, despite his desire for "scientific truth." DuBois's racial theorizing during this period is also obvious in an earlier essay, "The Conservation of Races," published in the *Occasional Papers* of the American Negro Academy in 1897. He defined race as "a vast family of human beings generally of common blood and language, always of common history, traditions, and impulses, who are both voluntarily and involuntarily striving together for the accomplishment of certain more or less vividly conceived ideals of life."[60] Like many scholars of the period, DuBois confused the terms "race" and "nation" when he argued that the "racial spirits" of the English, the Germans, and the Romance nations enabled them to make significant contributions to civilization. Criticizing DuBois's theory, Wilson J. Moses has stated that "the basis of DuBois's raciological theory was not rational, but mystical; it was not grounded in reason, but in something akin to faith."[61]

DuBois's call for an unbiased empirical approach to the issue of race was far more significant than his racial theorizing. Despite his contributions, most scholars were not impressed. An anonymous scholar who reviewed *The Philadelphia Negro* in the *American Historical Review* admitted that DuBois showed a "remarkable spirit of fairness." But the reviewer was not convinced that DuBois's argument, suggesting that the races did not intermix freely because of the low status of blacks, was correct. The reviewer believed that the "separation is due to differences of race more than of status."[62] Although DuBois continued to comment on race in sociological journals in the 1900s, his ties to the mainstream of sociology were weak. His series of poorly funded studies of blacks, *The Atlanta University Studies*, published during the 1900s and 1910s, received scant attention.

Ultimately, the loss of DuBois was irreparable, for he was one of the most original scholars of the period. The progressive evolutionists marched through the 1900s confident of gradual black progress, yet doubting the possibility of full black equality in the foreseeable future; unfortunately, their exclusion of DuBois inhibited the fruition of a theory of race relations that recognized the potency of the human will in dictating meaningful social change. Meanwhile, the fathers accepted uncritically the theories of Southern sociologists (most of whom were amateurs) eager to rationalize a castelike system in the South.

NOTES

1. Roscoe C. Hinkle, Jr., and Gisela J. Hinkle, *The Development of Modern Sociology: Its Nature and Growth in the United States* (New York: Random House, 1963), 1–17; Fred H. Matthews, *Quest for an American Sociology: Robert E. Park and the Chicago School* (Montreal: McGill-Queen's University Press, 1977), 90; Hamilton Cravens, *The Triumph of Evolution: American Scientists and the Hereditary–Environment Controversy, 1900–1941* (Philadelphia: University of Pennsylvania Press, 1978), 126–146; Robert M. Crunden, *Ministers of Reform: The Progressives' Achievement in American Civilization, 1889–1920* (Urbana: University of Illinois Press, 1984), 79–89.

2. Sterling D. Spero and Abram L. Harris, *The Black Worker* (New York: Columbia University Press, 1931; New York: Atheneum, 1972), 149–81. (Spero and Harris estimate that between 1870 and 1910, "the number of southern born Negroes increased at an average of about 67,000 in each ten-year period," 150–51.) William H. Harris, *The Harder We Run: Black Workers Since the Civil War* (New York: Oxford University Press, 1982), 52. John J. Halsey, Discussion of "Is Race Friction Between Blacks and Whites in the United States Growing and Inevitable?" by Alfred Holt Stone, *AJS* 13 (May 1908): 835.

3. W.E.B. DuBois, *The Black North in 1901* (1901; reprint, New York: Arno Press, 1969), 43; and *The Philadelphia Negro: A Social Study* (1899; reprint, New York: Schocken Books, 1967), 235–309. Recent historical accounts of the sordid conditions that fostered "social problems" among a large number of Northern blacks are: Gilbert Osfosky, *Harlem: The Making of a Ghetto, Negro New York, 1890–1930*, 2d ed. (New York: Harper and Row, 1971), 9–16; Allan H. Spear, *Black Chicago: The Making of a Ghetto, 1890–1920* (Chicago: University of Chicago Press, 1967), 11–20.

4. Ray Stannard Baker, *Following the Color Line* (New York: Doubleday, 1908), 106.

5. Halsey, Discussion of "Race Friction," 835.

6. August Meier, *Negro Thought in America, 1880–1915: Racial Ideologies in the Age of Booker T. Washington* (Ann Arbor: University of Michigan Press, 1963), 110–14; Louis R. Harlan, *Booker T. Washington: The Making of a Black Leader, 1856–1901* (London: Oxford University Press, 1972), 298–99, 302.

7. Van den Berghe, *Race and Racism*, 27–34. Van den Berghe describes "two ideal types" that are useful in analyzing race relations, types which he calls "paternalistic" and "competitive." Paternalistic race relations, which proceed from the aristocratic "master-servant" model, were characteristic of slavery (in both the North and South). Competitive race relations occur in urban-industrial societies, such as in the United States and South Africa, in which racism is psychopathological.

8. Booker T. Washington, "The Atlanta Exposition Address," in John Hope Franklin, ed., *Three Negro Classics* (New York: Avon Books, 1965), 147.

9. Washington, "Atlanta Exposition Address," 148–50.

10. Samuel R. Spencer, Jr., *Booker T. Washington and the Negro's Place in American Life* (Boston: Little, Brown, 1955); Saunders Redding, *They Came in Chains* (Philadelphia: Lippincott, 1950), 196; C. Vann Woodward, *Origins of the New South 1877–1913* (Baton Rouge: Louisiana State University Press, 1951), 323; Rayford W. Logan, *The Betrayal of the Negro* (New York: Collier Books, 1965), 312.

11. Franklin H. Giddings, *The Principles of Sociology* (New York: Macmillan, 1896), 329.

12. Giddings, *Principles of Sociology*, 328–29; George M. Fredrickson, *The Black Image in the White Mind: The Debate on the Afro-American Character and Destiny, 1817–1914* (New York: Harper and Row, 1971), 313.

13. Lester F. Ward, "Evolution of Social Structures," *AJS* 10 (March 1905), 601.

14. Ibid.

15. Ibid.

16. Ibid., 604.

17. Howard W. Odum, *American Sociology: The Story of Sociology in the United States through 1950* (New York: Greenwood Press, 1951), 86.

18. William G. Sumner, *Folkways* (Boston: Ginn and Company, 1906), 30.

19. Ibid., 78.

20. Gunnar Myrdal, *An American Dilemma*, 2 vols. (New York: Harper and Row, 1944), 2: 1048–50.

21. Edward A. Ross, *Social Control* (New York: Macmillan, 1901), 52, 330, 336.

22. Charles H. Cooley, *Social Organization* (New York: Charles Scribner's Sons, 1909), 215.

23. Ibid., 216–20.

24. Ibid., 220.

25. Ibid.

26. Steven J. Diner, "Department and Discipline: The Department of Sociology at the University of Chicago, 1892–1920," *Minerva* 13 (Winter 1975): 521. For a thorough treatment of the German historical school, see Jurgen Herbst, *The German Historical School in American Scholarship: A Study in the Transfer of Culture* (Ithaca, N. Y.: Cornell University Press, 1965).

27. Quoted in Diner, "Department and Discipline," 517.

28. Ibid., 516–28.

29. Hinkle and Hinkle, *Development of Modern Sociology*, 8–9.

30. Sarah E. Simons, "Social Assimilation," *AJS* 7 (January 1902): 543–48.

31. Simons, "Social Assimilation," 548.

32. Charlotte Perkins Gilman, "A Suggestion on the Negro Problem," *AJS* 14 (July 1908): 78–80.

33. Ibid., 81–85.

34. Ibid., 85.

35. Ibid., 79–80.

36. The attacks of Miller and DuBois on the degeneracy theories of Frederick L. Hoffman, Walter F. Willcox, and Joseph A. Tillinghast are found in: W.E.B. DuBois, review of *Race Traits and Tendencies of the American Negro*, by Frederick L. Hoffman, *Annals* 9 (January 1897): 127–33; Kelly Miller, *Race Adjustment: Essays on the Negro in America* (New York: Neale Publishing Company, 1908), 95; W.E.B. DuBois, review of *The Negro in Africa and America*, by Joseph A. Tillinghast, *PSQ* 18 (December 1903): 695–97; Monroe N. Work, "Crime among the Negroes of Chicago," *AJS* 6 (September 1900): 222–23.

37. Fredrickson, *Black Image in the White Mind*, 249–53; John S. Haller, Jr., *Outcasts from Evolution: Scientific Attitudes of Racial Inferiority, 1859–1900* (Urbana: University of Illinois Press, 1971), 60–68.

38. Giddings, *Principles of Sociology*, 328–29.

39. Ibid.

40. Lester F. Ward, *Applied Sociology* (Boston: Ginn and Company, 1906), 107–10.

41. Mark H. Haller, *Eugenics: Hereditarian Attitudes in American Thought* (New Brunswick, N.J.: Rutgers University Press, 1963), 8–20.

42. D. Collin Wells, "Social Darwinism," *AJS* 12 (March 1907): 702.

43. Lester F. Ward, Discussion of "Social Darwinism," by D. Collin Wells, *AJS* 12 (March 1907): 711.

44. Edward A. Ross, "The Causes of Race Superiority," *Annals* 18 (July 1901): 67.

45. Ibid.

46. Edward A. Ross, Discussion of "Social Darwinism," by D. Collin Wells, *AJS* 12 (March 1907): 715.

47. Thomas F. Gossett, *Race: The History of an Idea in America* (Dallas: Southern Methodist University Press, 1963), 154.

48. Sumner, *Folkways*, 74.

49. Giddings, *Principles of Sociology*, 18.

50. Fredrickson, *Black Image in the White Mind*, 316.

51. Sumner, *Folkways*, 13–15.

52. W.E.B. DuBois, *The Autobiography of W.E.B. DuBois* (New York: International Publishers, 1968): 148.

53. Quoted in Francis L. Broderick, *W.E.B. DuBois: Negro Leader in a Time of Crisis* (Stanford: Stanford University Press, 1959), 10–11.

54. DuBois, "The Study of Negro Problems," *Annals* 11 (January 1898): 11.

55. Ibid.

56. Alvin W. Gouldner, *The Coming Crisis of Western Sociology* (New York: Avon Books, 1970), 20–51.

57. Myrdal, *An American Dilemma* 2: 1132.

58. DuBois, *Philadelphia Negro*, 5–9.

59. Ibid., 350–51.

60. W.E.B. DuBois, "The Conservation of Races," in *The American Negro Academy Occasional Papers*, No. 2 (New York: Arno Press, 1969), 7.

61. Wilson J. Moses, *The Golden Age of Black Nationalism, 1850–1925* (Hamden, Conn.: Archon Books, 1978), 135.

62. "Review of *The Philadelphia Negro*," by W.E.B. DuBois, *AHR* 6 (October 1900): 164.

2

Southern Sociology Defends Jim Crow, 1900–1910

During the first decade of the twentieth century, the problems confronting blacks in both the North and South were exacting. In the South, a wall of containment—a direct product of political and legal factors and extralegal violence—subordinated blacks to whites. Disfranchisement, which began in Mississippi and South Carolina in the 1890s, spread to other Southern states. The Jim Crow principle, legitimized nationally by the Supreme Court's 1896 decision in *Plessy v. Ferguson*, was established in law. Thus, by 1910 most Southern states had laws requiring segregation in state welfare institutions, street and railway cars, recreational facilities, labor, and housing.

Despite those developments, lynching, which was usually a rural phenomenon, was declining in the South, for many blacks were migrating into the cities. Cities such as Birmingham and Atlanta experienced phenomenal growth. Black Southerners, however, met more violence in their new urban habitats. During the decade, race riots broke out in New Orleans, Atlanta and Statesboro, Georgia, and Brownsville, Texas. Summing up the situation in the New South, the distinguished historian of Afro-American history August Meier has written: "Piece by piece the patterns of disfranchisement, segregation, and racial subordination were brought to completion during the early part of the twentieth century."[1]

As the twentieth century opened, the discussion of the Negro problem started from a consensus among most students of race relations: they believed that blacks were at present inferior and unassimilable. The most domineering group was composed of Southerners, most of them amateurs. This diverse group of planters, historians, and political economists purveyed the conservative, paternalistic ideology of the planter class of the antebellum and post-Reconstruction South. Unlike their counterparts in the North, the Southern amateurs raised serious questions about the desirability of long-range assimilation. Unlike the Northern progressives, the Southern amateurs did not attempt to predict the future. Rather, they were intent on arguing that their Jim Crow system was at present as perfectly capable of resolving the Negro problem in the South as the defunct system of slavery, which, they argued, had been a humane and viable solution to the race problem. The transplanted African, they insisted, had differed from the white mentally, morally, and in his habits of work and thrift. In order to establish harmonious relations between the two fundamentally different races it had been necessary to provide blacks with the values that the white race held in esteem. This goal, they argued, had been attained through the institution of slavery. With emancipation, the black, without the close association and guidance of the white, relapsed into the barbarism that purportedly characterized his African heritage. Thus, blacks posed a serious "social problem" for the South, which could only be remedied by a system of caste and a strong dose of industrial education.

SOUTHERN AMATEUR SOCIOLOGY

In *The Political Economy of Slavery* (1961), Eugene D. Genovese has argued that Southern students of race—namely, Joseph A. Tillinghast and Jerome Dowd—led Ulrich B. Phillips astray in his assessment of African life. The present-day leading historian of slavery has accused Tillinghast and Dowd of applying untenable methods, making dubious assumptions, and publishing "work the anthropologists today consider of little value."[2] Genovese is indeed correct in pointing out the defective methodology and near worthlessness to contemporary scholars of Tillinghast's and Dowd's studies of African life. He obscures more than he reveals, however, by implying that turn-of-the-century social scientists who wrote about African life were simply crackpots. Although their work was certainly slipshod, Tillinghast and Dowd were considered the authorities on Afro-Americans and Africans in the 1900s; their work commanded the respect of many distinguished scholars in the social sciences in the United States.

When Ulrich B. Phillips wrote his classic *American Negro Slavery* (1918), numerous scholars based their interpretations of both West Africans and Afro-Americans upon the fundamental assumptions of a Southern-dominated group of amateur social scientists led by Tillinghast and Dowd. The so-called Negro problem was considered—and considered erroneously—to be a peculiarly Southern problem. And Southern social scientists, such as Tillinghast, Dowd, H.E. Belin and Walter Fleming, were regarded as experts because of their close proximity to a large number of blacks at early periods in their lives. Their depiction of the West African ancestors of Afro-Americans as mentally enervated savages emerged at a time when strong currents in both the North and South supported a smug racism.

Nevertheless, when the United States prepared for entrance into World War I and drew upon the reservoir of Southern black labor to work in Northern industry in the 1910s, a Northern-based group of skeptics began to question the empirical bases of the amateurs' arguments. Although the interpretation of the left-liberals was initiated in the early 1900s by Franz Boas, it made headway in sociology and anthropology only when large numbers of blacks began to inhabit the urban industrial North after 1910. Left-liberals succeeded in forging a depiction of West Africans as primitive people capable of achievements essential to progress. Their interpretation eventually triumphed in the 1940s, paving the way for the interpretation of African life developed by Melville J. Herskovits and mirrored in Kenneth Stampp's refutation of the Phillips thesis in his monumental work, *The Peculiar Institution* (1956).

Joseph A. Tillinghast's *The Negro in Africa and America*, published by the American Economics Association in 1902, was the seminal scholarly work on the relation between West Africans and Afro-Americans. Tillinghast was the son of a South Carolina slave-holder but had received an advanced degree from Cornell University. It is thus not surprising that he presented this work, the entire thrust of which reflected the conscious attempt of Northerners and Southerners to reconcile their differences over the moribund institution of slavery. For a Northern accommodationist such as Walter F. Willcox, the prominent demographer who wrote the preface to Tillinghast's book, the work indicated "how both sections and both races are coming more and more to cooperation of conclusions." Willcox, the leading authority on black crime, was, like Tillinghast, a Lamarckian. He praised Tillinghast for pointing out that the alleged characteristics of Afro-Americans were part of their inheritance from Africa, "bred into the race there in Africa through long generations." To Willcox, the proslavery argument was correct. "To realize," he declared, "that many faults often attributed to the debasing effects of American slavery, are faults which he shares with his African ancestors and contemporaries, may suggest a more just and impartial view of the merits and demerits of the economic system which crumbled as a result of the Civil War."[3]

For Willcox, Tillinghast's synthesis, which drew on the published reports about late-nineteenth-century Africa by European travelers and merchants such as Mary Kingsley, Paul Du Chaillu, and A.B. Ellis, centered in part on the most crucial question for the Spencerians: How long would it take primitive peoples to reach the plane of "advanced civilization?" Tillinghast's preoccupation with this question stemmed from his belief that blacks threatened the purported homogeneity of the South. Blacks constituted, he emphasized, a distinct racial group, and therefore could not be assimilated by the white majority. In order to demonstrate that blacks were unassimilable, Tillinghast analyzed the character and capabilities of their African ancestors. Because he adhered to Lamarck's doctrine of the inheritance of acquired characteristics, Tillinghast had to acknowledge the importance of both heredity and environment. He even conceded that "deliberate human action" influenced significantly the nurture—nature compound. For instance, he insisted: "Of two Negro infants, let one be brought up in the African jungle and the other amid the best American culture and very divergent results would certainly follow."[4]

Despite his concession that different environments had different effects on two individuals of the same race, he argued that heredity had a greater impact on the individual's character and capabilities. In fact, Tillinghast went on to assert that a race whose ancestors' innate abilities had been formed in an isolated environment could not radically elevate its abilities within the foreseeable future. Invoking an aspect of the proslavery defense, Tillinghast concluded that the "precarious position" of blacks in the South at the turn of the century was due not to their previous condition of servitude, but rather to the Afro-American's African ancestors.[5]

Tillinghast attempted to account for the alleged characteristics of blacks in typical Lamarckian fashion: the West African ancestors of Afro-Americans had been forced to live on the coastline by stronger tribes to the East, and lived in an environment that hindered the development of the high degree of "industrial efficiency" that the peoples of Northern and Western Europe had attained. West Africans occupied a transitional stage midway between the evolutionary stages of savagery and barbarism. Unlike the temperate and frigid climates Europeans confronted, the tropical climate in which they lived did not require West Africans to build "substantial dwellings." Nor did West Africa's climate, which provided abundant amounts of food, force them to spend much effort cultivating the soil. Since nature had not required West Africans to exercise foresight, Tillinghast believed that it had prevented them from developing the capabilities that accounted for civilized man's success.[6]

Tillinghast infused the Spencerian version of the "survival of the fittest" into his discussion of West African morals. West Africans, he asserted, did not inhibit their "sexual proclivities." These proclivities were supposedly a direct product of nature's efforts to counterbalance such forces as wars, slave raids, executions, witchcraft, pestilence, famine, the neglect of the young, and ignorance. Since selection, he argued erroneously, had produced in the race "exceptionally strong reproductive powers," the race thrived in the United States.[7]

Tillinghast, as could be expected, argued that the emphasis on education as a lever for black progress, rather than the slower process of evolutionary development, was ill-founded. He asserted, on the basis of old evidence, that all branches of anthropology had demonstrated the inability of primitive men to survive and thrive under civilized conditions, and drew on the conclusions of the leading Continental physical anthropologist, Paul Topinard, and the distinguished English cultural anthropologist Edward B. Tylor in order to demonstrate that the West African was inferior to the Caucasian. Drawing on travelers' observations, Tillinghast asserted that West Africans had "no great industrial system, no science, and art." Thus, he concluded without the slightest equivocation: "The consideration of the general laws of biological evolution would lead us, aside from the evidence above adduced, to believe the mind of a lower tropical race is unfitted to assimilate the advanced civilization of a strenuous and able northern race."[8]

In reply to scholars and reformers who wrote works praising the progress blacks had made since slavery, Tillinghast argued that slavery was directly responsible for that progress, because slaveholders had attempted to "uproot and destroy polygamy," and had introduced to blacks the values of monogamy, Christianity, and the institutions of civilized man. Nonetheless, Tillinghast believed that both physical heredity and social heredity militated against the successful implanting of those values. To him, the slaveholders' attempts were futile, for the process of "replac[ing] one stream of social heredity by another infinitely more exacting" could only occur when the physical heredity responded to the demands of modern life.[9]

Foremost among the deficiencies of blacks, in Tillinghast's view, was the absence of an industrial heritage. Without that vital heritage, blacks had no motive "to economize in consumption or handle with care." Tillinghast admitted that slavery "militated strongly against the sound improvement of race character." Yet he felt that the institution, which he labelled a "vast school," was responsible for the tremendous progress Afro-Americans had made in labor—especially when compared to the West Africa standard.[10] Finally, Tillinghast went to outrageous lengths to blame blacks for segregation. "The strain," he insisted, "required to maintain life on the level of whites is driving the Negroes to develop a society of their own, with easier moral standards, better fitted perhaps to their peculiar temperament."[11]

Tillinghast did not mention several factors that undoubtedly caused segregation in the South: the racial attitudes of whites, Jim Crow legislation, and forms of extralegal violence. His conclusions, in short, amounted to a rationalization of the survival of the fittest creed, and shared a spirit of skepticism concerning the future of blacks that pervaded Southern thought during the period.

The theme that the institution of slavery had enabled blacks to evolve from their barbarous West African background to some point of civilization was taken up by a North Carolinian who would emerge as the premier Southern amateur sociologist in the 1910s, Jerome Dowd. Although he received most of his academic training at Trinity College (now Duke University), Dowd, like Tillinghast, had spent some time in the Northern academic community. He taught at the University of Wisconsin from 1901 to 1906, and participated as a fellow in the prestigious department of sociology at the University of Chicago in 1903–1904.

Dowd's *The Negro Races*, volume 1 (1907) shared some of the same racial biases that permeated Tillinghast's work. Although Dowd drew sharper distinctions between the various peoples of West Africa than Tillinghast did, he nonetheless believed that West African societies were "abnormal or retrogressive." And despite his attempt to account for the various states of West African societies in materialistic terms, Dowd still incorporated biological arguments into his analysis: "His [the West African's] brain is so constituted that its sensorimotor activities predominate over his idio-motor activities; i.e., his passions and natural impulses are exceptionally potent and his inhibiting power exceptionally feeble."[12] Like Tillinghast, Dowd went on to develop the proslavery argument, suggesting that slavery compared favorably to European colonialism in providing for the educational needs of blacks. "The Negroes of America," he argued, "especially in the Southern United States were put through a course of training which corresponded more nearly to the natural evolution of things than the training which the black people have received in any part of the world." In slavery, blacks purportedly gained habits of industry and learned certain types of trades and crafts. Ignoring the fact that the vast majority of blacks during slavery were field hands, Dowd wrote in idealistic terms that: "When the time came for them to enter schools and colleges they had already gone through a period of training which gave them an industrial and moral foundation that saved them from many of the disintegrating effects, so conspicuous in Africa where education is begun too soon, at the wrong end."[13]

During the first decade of the century several articles appeared in the *American Journal of Sociology* that treated sympathetically the defunct system of black slavery and the castelike system which emerged in the South in the years following the abolition of slavery. Most of these writings have been ignored by historians of the social sciences because they were penned by minor figures whose contributions to major sociological developments seemed minimal, if not nonexistent, and whose connections with the newly developing discipline were tangential at best. I have found, however, that in the field of race relations, a field whose history is just beginning to be written, these writers' pieces form significant structures in the framework of argumentation that Robert E. Park and others had to take into account when they presented their new interpretations on the racial problems after 1915. That some of these writers were published in the country's major sociological journal attests to their contemporaneous significance.

The infiltration of the major themes of African inferiority, the civilizing effects of slavery, and the horrors of Reconstruction into the *American Journal of Sociology* was immediate. In contrast to the crass pessimist, Tillinghast, the Southerners who were published in the *Journal* tended to be paternalistic like Dowd. Although they promulgated the major themes of the proslavery argument, they still backed Booker T. Washington's program of gradual uplift through industrial education, for industrial education was purportedly an antidote to the transplanted African's retrogressive propensities.

Typical of the Southern amateur sociologists who felt that Southerners had to bear "the white man's burden" was H. E. Belin, a native of Charleston, South Carolina, who had fought for the Confederacy in the Civil War. Belin asserted confidently in 1908 that the institution of slavery was defensible on the grounds that it uplifted blacks "industrially, mentally, and even morally . . . to a higher level than that ever accomplished by his kinsmen in Africa." The slaveholder, he argued, provided adequately for the bondsman's physical and spiritual needs; he clothed, housed, and provided for the slave's physical well-being by maintaining a hospital, a day nursery, and a chapel with a clergyman. Belin admitted that discipline was harsh by early twentieth-century standards, but concluded that slaves were not "generally ill-treated," as evidenced by the "wonderful increase in their numbers" through "natural growth."[14] Slavery was essentially an institution used by the white to uplift the inferior

African so that the white could co-exist harmoniously with him. Suggestive of Belin's belief is this comment: "What the theory of evolution is to the scientist, that the institution of slavery was to the southern man. It might not be absolutely the true and perfect solution to the Negro problem, but it was at least the best 'working hypothesis' known to him for harmonizing the conflicting elements brought into compulsory contact in the South."[15]

Despite Belin's exaggeration of the benefits accrued to blacks by slavery, his emphasis upon slavery's ability to harmonize "conflicting elements" is an argument adopted by later sociologists. The prominent sociologist Robert E. Park, who felt that the rise of black consciousness threatened the social peace, often argued that the institution of slavery was a means of assimilating blacks.

Most Southerners who received their advanced academic training at Northern universities seemed intent on defending their historical traditions. At a time when Northern scholars had begun to believe that Reconstruction had been a mistake, the Southern defense of slavery and their credo of "white over black" were extremely hysterical. Walter L. Fleming, a history professor at West Virginia who had received his advanced academic training at Columbia University, was convinced that the plantation system of the antebellum South was "probably the most efficient plantation system the world ever saw." Like most Southern scholars, he defended slavery on the grounds that it trained blacks to be reliable and efficient laborers. Describing the functioning of the plantation and the activity of the blacks within it in idealistic terms, as most Southerners did, he wrote:

Clothes were cut out in the "big house" and made by the Negro under the direction of the mistress. There was much need for skilled labor, and this was done by blacks. Work was often done by tasks, and industrious Negroes were able to complete their daily allotment and have three or four hours a day to work in their own gardens and "patches." They often earned money at odd jobs, and church records show they contributed regularly. Negro children were trained in the arts of industry and sobriety by elderly Negroes of good judgment and firm character, usually women. Children too young to work were cared for by a competent nanny in the plantation nursery, while their parents were in the field.[16]

During the period of Radical Reconstruction, Fleming felt, the condition of blacks deteriorated ostensibly. The deterioration, he argued, occurred not only in the physical and mental spheres, but also in the moral. Believing that the plight of blacks was due to their inability to survive without the support of whites, Fleming contended that many blacks had reverted from civilization to the barbarism of their African ancestors: "The Negroes deteriorated much in personal appearance and dress; immorality increased, religion nearly died out; consumption and other diseases attacked the childish people who would not care for themselves; foeticide was common; there was a tendency to return to the barbarous customs of their African forefathers; witchcraft and voodoo were practiced, and in some cases human sacrifices were made."[17] Although Fleming's description of the conditions of blacks was a stereotype and was not documented, it did reflect the cruel circumstances that many blacks confronted in the post-Reconstruction South. Nonetheless, like Booker T. Washington, Fleming believed that the only hope for restoring blacks to their antebellum reliability and efficiency was the industrial education provided by schools such as Tuskegee, Normal, and Calhoun.[18]

Fleming's biases can be easily accounted for. An upwardly mobile white Southerner from rural Alabama, Fleming received his B.S. and M.S. from the Alabama Polytechnic Institute and worked as a librarian at the institution during the late 1890s. Then in 1900 he began graduate work in history at Columbia University, receiving his Ph.D. in 1904. He was appointed associate professor of history at West Virginia University and remained there until 1907, when he moved to Louisiana State University. Furthermore, Fleming was one of several Southern students who studied under William A. Dunning at Columbia University. These Southerners produced several works on Reconstruction that were filled with contempt for blacks, sympathy for the South, and criticisms of the North for its attempt to reconstruct the South. Exposing the biases of the Dunning school as a whole, and Fleming in particular, W.E.B. DuBois wrote in his revisionist study, *Black Reconstruction in America* (1935): "Fleming's *Documentary History of Reconstruction* is done by a man who has a thesis to support, and his selection of documents supports this thesis. His study of Alabama is pure propaganda."[19]

The claim that slavery effectively demolished the barbarous habits and customs of blacks and replaced them with the habits and customs of civilized people was, no doubt, a distorted one. Yet for many sociologists of the period it was an argument that was not to be questioned. Indicative of the fact that it was not merely the folklore of Southern sociologists is that some Northern sociologists held similar views. Carl Kelsey, a professor of sociology at the University of Pennsylvania, was a Northern advocate of the Southern amateurs' brand of racism. One of the younger professional sociologists writing during the 1900s, Kelsey was a Congregationalist minister who had received graduate training in both Germany and the United States. A native of Grinnell, Iowa, Kelsey had served as a minister of the Congregationalist church in Helena, Montana, and had spent a year in Germany, studying at the universities of Gottingen and Berlin, in the late 1890s. Upon returning to the United States, he entered the University of Pennsylvania and received his Ph.D. there in 1903. He joined the staff of the Wharton School of Finance and Commerce of the University of Pennsylvania as an instructor in sociology, remaining at the institution until his retirement in 1941.

The provincialism that characterized the Southern racial thought of the period also permeated Kelsey's early writing. In 1903, before his conversion to the Boasian skeptical perspective, Kelsey, influenced directly by Tillinghast, argued in Lamarckian terms that the blacks' primitive "inheritance from thousands of years in Africa" was the underlying cause of their alleged current difficulties as laborers. Although Kelsey believed that slavery had enabled the Afro-American to progress beyond the stage of his African ancestors, he felt that the institution had failed in some respects. Slavery, he argued, had not "trained the bulk of Negroes in any sense of personal responsibility away from the eye of the manager"; nor had the institution cultivated the "stable home life which was essential to the development of a race." According to Kelsey's firsthand observations, black free laborers were "still decidedly lacking." Kelsey concluded that the future progress of blacks would depend upon their ability to work "regularly and intelligently." Like the Southern sociologists, he believed that industrial education had the potential to play a vital role in the future of blacks.[20]

Clearly the commentators on slavery were led astray from a correct assessment of the institution by their uncritical acceptance of the assumption of African barbarism. By focusing on the purported inferiority of Africans as the cause of the black problem, they ignored the fact that the archaic institution of slavery encouraged malingering, carelessness, and the disruption of family life. All of them except Kelsey failed to mention that after slavery most blacks were forced to compete in a free labor system for which slavery had not prepared them. Suffice it to say that by viewing the purported traits of blacks as part of their racial inheritance that could only be altered by close contact with whites, sociologists did not come to grips with the evidence suggesting that slavery and the economic and social oppression so commonplace in the post-Civil War era were the major determinants of black life.

SOUTHERN PROFESSIONAL SOCIOLOGY

The Southern amateur sociologists had been concerned primarily with the past and present aspects of the race problem. Unlike such

Northern professional sociologists as Giddings, Ward, and Cooley, the Southern amateurs tended to avoid making predictions of the future outcome of race relations. Furthermore, they were far more conservative than the Northern amateurs, arguing that a caste system was perfectly capable of resolving the racial tension not only in their native region but also in the nation as a whole.

The task of articulating a theory of race relations that made such predictions was left to one of the most perplexing Southern professional figures in the discipline, Howard W. Odum. Odum's highly acclaimed *Social and Mental Traits of the Negro* (1910) was based on his firsthand observations of black communities in Oxford, Mississippi, and Covington, Georgia, and on the survey of conditions in the Southeast with populations under ten thousand. Odum viewed his book as "an effort to contribute something toward a scientific knowledge of the Negro . . . to describe the conditions of the Negro life in southern communities . . . not as a final treatment of the entire subject but just as a beginning, along with other special studies for a scientific but practical study of the Negro in the South."[21]

In his book, Odum argued that the most important step in the environmental adaptation of blacks was the development of viable relations with whites in economics, politics, and society. The economic relations with whites assumed prime significance since there was a "causal relationship" between the black's inherent negative traits and his economic condition. Odum's work dealt primarily with the cultural features of black life that prevented blacks from adapting to American civilization. While he felt that blacks had progressed beyond the stage of their African development, he insisted that blacks had not yet acquired the cultural values that would enable them to improve their present status in America. "In fine," he wrote, "the Negro has little social pressure, concentrated beliefs or definite conventions that control conduct in his own society, which demand the development of homes, the equipment for life, the faithful performance of duty or individual achievement."[22]

Yet in order to account for the inability of blacks to conform to proper behavioral patterns, he fell back on a list of inherent traits which he thought blacks possessed:

First, the Negro easily responds to stimuli, that is, he is *controlled by present impulses*. This results in almost complete *lack of restraint*, including both yielding to impulses and inertia. *Second*, this free response *tends always to pleasure*, sometimes the pleasure being more or less unconscious in the simple giving way to impulse and the breaking down of restraint or in negative feeling or non-exertion. *The Negro is therefore inactive. Third*, the Negro *tends to carry all responses to an extreme*. He loves plenty of stimuli. This exhausts and degenerates his vital powers. *Fourth,* the Negro has *little capacity for sustained control.* This applies to sustained efforts, conduct in general, morality, convictions and thought. He is therefore, *weak in social and self-control* and lacking in self-direction. *Fifth,* he does not, therefore, lend himself to the *development of permanent qualities through the working out of essential processes. Sixth,* he is, therefore, *superficial and irresponsible.*

Although Odum emphasized the negative inherent traits, he did point out that the black possessed some positive inherent traits. The "flexibility of his nature, his sympathetic adaptability and the plasticity of his consciousness," Odum thought, "may well be the basis of permanent ability."[23]

Odum believed that the alleged inherent negative traits were removable once the economic condition of the black changed. For him, the solution of the economic problem lay in the black's preparation as an efficient laborer (who willingly related to the white in that capacity), rather than in the acquisition of property. For by becoming an efficient laborer, he could eventually come to hold property. Odum conceded that while the black's prosperity was in a large part dependent upon his initiative, invariably "it was also largely in the hands of whites, in that he can only achieve results through the help and cooperation of the whites."[24]

Despite Odum's belief that the economic problem was "the only important problem in the Negro's environment," he did not hesitate to comment on the issues of political and social equality. Fundamental to Odum's position on those issues was his belief in the intellectual inequality of the races, for he thought blacks and whites had "different abilities and potentialities." It should be noted that Odum felt that blacks should not be allowed to participate in politics at that time because they were "incapable of intelligently using the ballot or in assisting in the direction of, and in the understanding of public policies." Nonetheless, Odum refused to assume a pessimistic outlook for the future. He predicted that "as the Negroes become qualified they will be given the opportunity to cooperate in the political workings of the South." Odum doubted, however, that the extension of social equality to blacks would take place, since that issue was bound inextricably to the issue of intermarriage. Socially, it was to be understood that "the races will develop separately." The refusal of the white to grant social equality to the black, however, did not mean that blacks would be denied channels of vertical mobility. Visualizing what Park would later describe as a "bi-racial organization of society," Odum thought the black would eventually occupy positions parallel to those of the white. "The Negro," he concluded, "has an unlimited field before him in the higher work of teaching, preaching, and professional work among his own people. There will be no competition there outside of his own."[25]

Odum's stand on economic, political, and social equality might tempt one to label him "conservative" or "anti-Negro," as some writers have done, and he was.[26] Yet it is necessary to remember that his ideas on these issues were similar to those of Booker T. Washington. Like Washington, Odum's main emphasis was placed upon economic mobility: the development of a yeomanry and of business and professional classes. The results of those developments were supposed to improve the quality of the lives of blacks.[27] Although this position did not suggest that blacks resign themselves permanently to their current inferior status, it did suggest that they should accommodate themselves to that status at present. That position did not come to grips with the fact that the presence of blacks in a lower status allowed whites to obtain certain "gains"—economic, sexual, and in prestige— and that those gains would not be discarded without a struggle.[28] In short, Odum's position did not challenge the status quo.

Odum's theory of race relations in the South, however, was significant, insofar as it showed the extent to which Southern racism impinged on racial theorizing. What is troubling about Odum's career is that during his advanced academic training he had been exposed to divergent points of view on the issue of race. The Georgian who held an M.A. from the University of Mississippi in English language and culture had received a Ph.D. in psychology at Clark University under G. Stanley Hall, one of the most extreme racists of the period, and a Ph.D. in sociology under Franklin H. Giddings at Columbia University. Yet he was also exposed to some of the most progressive thinking of his day. He had studied anthropology under Alexander Chamberlain, a disciple of Boas, at Clark, and he later attended Boas's lectures at Columbia. Although Odum would become one of the foremost spokesmen for Southern liberalism in the 1930s, his early position on race and race relations, like that of most of his Southern contemporaries, was tainted by his effort to rationalize the "Southern solution" to the Negro problem.

North—South Consensus on Prejudice

When sociologists during the 1900s looked for a defense of segregation, they often turned to the theories of an "instinctive prejudice." The foremost theoretician on prejudice was William I. Thomas. Thomas was a Southerner who was born in rural Virginia in 1863. He was brought up there and in Tennessee. Like many of the major early sociologists, he had an evangelical background; his father was a lay Methodist preacher. At the age of seventeen, Thomas entered the University of Tennessee and majored in literature and classics. He later pursued graduate studies there in English literature and modern languages, and received the first doctorate awarded by that university in 1888. Thomas went to Germany that same year to continue his studies in literature, and was introduced to folk psychology and ethnology—two fields that shaped his orientation in sociology. Returning to the United States the next year, Thomas was appointed professor of English and Comparative Literature at Oberlin College. He remained there until 1893, when, attracted to the Social Science department at the University of Chicago, he became a graduate student and instructor in that department.

Under the guiding hand of Albion W. Small, the sociology department of the University of Chicago had become the major center for the production of social workers and teachers interested in reforming American society. In his graduate program Thomas "selected what may be called marginal courses to sociology—biology, physiology . . . brain anatomy."[29] Receiving his Ph.D. from Chicago in 1896, he joined the faculty there, which included Small, Charles Henderson, and George Vincent. He remained there until 1918, when a newspaper scandal brought about his dismissal. A pioneer in social psychology, Thomas is best remembered for his multivolume study which he coauthored with Florian Znaniecki, *The Polish Peasant in Europe and America* (1918–1923).

Thomas's ingenious analysis of prejudice that appeared in the *American Journal of Sociology* in 1904 was a defense of the laissez-faire point of view. According to him, race prejudice was "called out primarily by the physical aspects of an unfamiliar people—their color, form and feature—and by their activities and habits in only a secondary way." Because race prejudice was an instinct, it could not be controlled. Thus, Thomas wrote: "It [race prejudice] is, too, an affair which can neither be reasoned with nor legislated about very effectively, because it is connected with the affective, rather than the cognitive processes." The association of persons of different races, however, dissipated prejudice; for example, white travellers who had associated with black Africans for a lengthy period of time became more accustomed to dark skin than light. It was also evident to Thomas that association militated against prejudice because Afro-Americans repudiated African standards of beauty, and because white men admired the Japanese for their successful struggle against Russia.[30]

For Thomas, who had spent long periods of time in both the North and South, the dominant types of white antipathy evinced towards blacks had distinct characteristics in those regions. He drew a distinction between "race prejudice" and "caste-feeling." Caste-feeling, which was a Southern phenomenon, developed as a "result of competitive activities." In the South, any badges of supposed inferiority were "aids to the manipulation of one class by another . . . and assumed such magnitude that they are difficult to eradicate." Unlike white Southerners, who had close associations with blacks and were not repelled by the skin color of blacks, Northern whites evinced "a sort of *skin* prejudice." The repulsion of Northern whites to "the external aspect of the Negroes" was due to the fact that they had "no contact with the Negro and no activity connections." Still, for Thomas, caste-feeling was far more insidious than race prejudice, for Southern whites invariably associated the skin color of blacks with inferiority so that "it was impossible for a southern white to think the Negro into his class." Although he was a native Southerner, Thomas did not attempt to justify the caste-feeling of whites. Yet, he did think race prejudice was an understandable and natural response to blacks. Thomas noted, however, that race prejudice diminished in significance "as increased communication brings interest and standards in common, and as similar systems of education and equal access to knowledge bring about a greater mental and social parity between groups, and remove grounds for invidious distinction." Furthermore, he predicted on an optimistic note that the ameliorative influences would create a society in which the individual's ability to get results give him an interest and a status independent of, in point of fact, quite overshadowing, the superficial marks of personality.[31] At that time, Thomas seemed to suggest that whatever residium of race prejudice that existed could be tolerated.

Although Thomas's theory was a lucid explanation of the supposed origins of racial prejudice and caste-feeling and the significant differences between them, it was not a straightforward attack on them as psychopathological attitudes. By viewing them as natural responses on the part of whites toward an alien black group, severe limitations were placed on his thought; so long as Thomas viewed the aforementioned attitudes as instinctive, there was a perfect rationalization for their existence. Furthermore, it implied that little could be done by the human will to eliminate those attitudes.

Articulate Afro-Americans, who believed that white attitudes could be changed, did not take the complacent position that characterized Thomas's scientific detachment. They therefore protested against the growing racial prejudice during the decade. One such protest, which took place in Boston in 1907, occasioned the writing of a controversial paper that was presented by Alfred Holt Stone at the American Sociological Society meetings in Madison, Wisconsin, that same year. Stone's paper was the most complete statement of the Southern doctrine of "no social equality." He was adept in his use of the idea of innate inferiority to demonstrate that blacks were not entitled to be treated as social equals, and he was also adept in using the doctrine of instinctive prejudice to demonstrate that prejudice was the universal attitude of whites. Stone's major arguments in 1907 could not be challenged effectively until the two doctrines were eroded by the ascendancy of an empirical worldview.

It should be noted that Stone had a vested interest in maintaining the status quo. Stone was born in New Orleans, Louisiana in 1870. Before the Civil War, his father was a professor of Latin and Greek at the University of Missouri, but when the war began, he volunteered to serve in the Confederate Army and was a captain for four years. After the war, the elder Stone moved to Washington County, Mississippi, and later became prominent in local and state politics. The younger Stone grew up in Washington County, graduating from the University of Mississippi in 1891. He practiced law in Greenville and Washington Counties, was a cotton planter, and served in the House of the Mississippi legislature until 1932. During this same period, Stone wrote a history of the Thirteenth, Fourteenth, and Fifteenth Amendments to the U.S. Constitution and lectured on history, economics, and the race problem at a number of universities and before numerous societies. In 1908, when Doubleday Page and Company published his *Studies in the American Race Problem*, he was considered to be an authority on that problem.

In a major article published in the *American Journal of Sociology* in 1908, Stone attempted to formulate a theory of race relations. He began by presenting a sophisticated theory of white prejudice which he called "racial antipathy." He explained prejudice in terms of its naturalness; what mattered to him was "the fact of racial difference." "It is the question," he argued, "of differences—the fundamental differences of physical appearances, of mental habit and thought, of social customs and religious belief, of the thousand and one things keenly and clearly appreciable . . . these are the things that at once create and find expression in what we call race problems and race prejudices." Unlike many sociologists, Stone did not believe that the presence of Southern and Eastern Europeans in the United States constituted a grave threat to the social order. The Southern and European immigrant problem was but a "temporary problem based upon temporary antipathies between different groups of the same race, which invariably disappear in one or two generations which form only a temporary barrier to physical assimilation by intermarriage with native stocks."[32]

For Stone, however, there were natural laws dictating the relationships between white and nonwhite races. He pointed out that "open manifestations of antipathy will be aggravated if each group feels its superiority over the other." Conversely, race relations were viewed as "milder when one race accepts the position of inferiority outwardly, or really feels the superiority of the other." The truth of these laws was evident to Stone in the different attitudes toward the Japanese and Chinese held by whites: whites felt that there was less racial antipathy between themselves and the Chinese, who outwardly accepted their inferior status, than between themselves and the Japanese, who refused to accept their inferior status. For Stone, the assertiveness of blacks was a source of problems. Interpreting Reconstruction in a manner similar to his Southern brethren, he argued that "*post-bellum* racial difficulties are largely the manifestations of friction growing out of the novel claim to equality made by the Negro after emancipation, either by specific declaration and assertion, or by conduct which was equivalent to an open claim, with the refusal of the white man to recognize this claim." Race friction was not the result of problems created during slavery, for Stone, like most Southern sociologists, believed that the peculiar institution minimized racial problems. Slavery, Stone declared unequivocally, "furnished a basis of contact which as long as it existed minimized the problems which resulted from racial contact upon a plane of theoretical equality." Slavery was an example of the simplest possible relation that could exist between diverse races, since the superordinate–subordinate relationship was mutually accepted by both races. Whites insisted upon their superiority and blacks accommodated and accepted their status.[33]

Turning to the conditions that facilitated race conflict and friction, Stone was convinced that demographic factors assumed primary importance, mainly because whites instinctively felt "pressure" when they were in the presence of a mass of persons of a different race. "In a certain important sense," Stone wrote, "all racial problems are distinctly problems of racial distribution." He buttressed this argument by pointing out that laws of the dominant white group were more proscriptive in areas where there were large numbers of a minority group than in areas where minorities were fewer in number. There was, in other words, a direct relation between the degree of proscription and the size of the minority group.[34]

It was axiomatic, for Stone, that the assertiveness of some blacks would cause race friction because the attitude of superiority of whites was universal. He argued that feelings of white superiority were "beyond question stronger in the so-called Anglo-Saxon than in any other" because in such countries as the United States, South

Africa, and Jamaica blacks were denied social, political, and economic equality. Stone felt it essential that blacks adapt to the situation and accept their inferior status. From his distorted interpretation of history, he was convinced that blacks had shown the
"marvelous power of adaptation to conditions." Resorting to a psychological explanation, based on an array of myths, Stone argued:
"His [the black's] undeveloped mental state made it possible for him
to accept conditions, and to increase and be content under them,
which a more highly organized and more sensitive race would have
thrown off, or destroyed itself in the effort to do so." The mass of
blacks in the South, who Stone admired, were therefore supposedly
content with their inferior status—as indicated by their lack of concern about suffrage, segregated schools and street cars, and social
equality. In essence, if all blacks accommodated themselves to their
inferior status, as most blacks in the South had supposedly done,
blacks could eventually occupy a section of the same territory as
whites with a minimal degree of friction.[35]

Despite his idealism concerning the docility of Southern blacks,
Stone noted that there were some blacks in the South and numerous ones in Northern cities protesting against existing conditions.
This group of educated blacks, many of whom were mulattoes, was
marked by its attempts through publications and organizations to
develop "a consciousness of its own racial solidarity." Indicative of
the ideology of this group was its celebration of the Japanese victory
over Russia. On the American scene, Stone noted that the group
insisted on complete social equality. Juxtaposing a passage from an
article published by W.E.B. DuBois in *The East and the West* in
1904, which called for the immediate abolition of the color line, with
a statement from Edward A. Ross's *Foundations of Sociology*,
which insisted that whites take "an uncompromising attitude" toward amalgamation with the "lower races," Stone concluded that
race friction would increase. For him, social equality held out the
possibility of intermarriage, which whites believed threatened An-
glo-American civilization. And with that recognition, whites would
refuse equality to an advancing group of blacks, thus creating an
atmosphere in which race friction would grow.[36]

Although the majority of social scientists who reviewed Stone's
paper at the Madison meeting of the American Sociological Society
in 1907 agreed with his decree of black inferiority, many of the
scholars offered significant criticisms of his causal explanations
and his prognostication. Typical of the conservative Northern position that did not envision a race war were the comments of the
distinguished demographer Walter F. Willcox. This pioneer demographer, who was a professor at Cornell University and served as

Chief Statistician of the United States, had predicted in 1900 that blacks would, like Indians, become extinct. Yet, surprisingly, he did not believe Stone's dire predictions. Willcox felt "that the two races at the South and perhaps in the whole country are unconsciously but, painfully, drifting toward a substitute for the slavery system." This system, which he labelled "caste," was supposedly in many respects like that of India, in that stratification was based on color. Like many Northern scholars who had witnessed the emergence of the caste system, Willcox exhibited the ethical schizophrenia that characterized the "American dilemma." He admitted that caste contradicted "at many essential points the political and moral ideals of the United States," but in the end, he felt that the contradictions could be countenanced, on the grounds that the caste system did "not menace the perpetuity of the country." Since black crime, which Willcox described as "a vent hole for the heat developed by race friction," was "no longer increasing in this country with great rapidity," it seemed probable to him that race relations were reaching a state of equilibrium.[37]

A conservative native of Newton, Indiana, Ulysses G. Weatherly, predicted that a race war would not take place because whites in both the North and the South would reach a consensus on the race problem. Weatherly's historical interpretation of race relations stressed the North's role in exacerbating Southern racial tensions. To Weatherly, blacks had never been primarily responsible for racial conflict, either during slavery or after their emancipation. Rather, they had been the "cause and center of a conflict between two opposing types of sentiment among the whites of the South and the North." Weatherly laid most of the responsibility for the antebellum conflict between the North and the South upon "militant abolitionism" which, "by arousing the hot passions of southern whites," gave to the slavery controversy a bitterness it would not otherwise have had. In a similar manner, Northerners had "injured" the interests of blacks after emancipation by making demands for their rights. Indeed, like most historians of the period, Weatherly thought Congressional Reconstruction had been a mistake: "The disastrous period of reconstruction fell with peculiar force on the Negro because, in giving him certain things which seemed of great value, it deprived him of that which he needed most of all—wise guidance and gradual initiation into his new position."[38]

Weatherly, who had received his doctorate in history under Andrew D. White at Cornell University in 1894, explained the post-Reconstruction treatment of blacks as a stand against "outside interference" on the race problem. The Southerners' stand was "not directed against the Negro himself, but rather against the idea of his social rights and privileges which he has acquired from sources outside the South." Weatherly felt that the Northern attitude on the race problem was changing and predicted that as more blacks moved into the North, the Northern white would become intolerant of the alleged "crime, unthrift, and political corruption" of blacks and recognize "the essential justice of the South's attitude on the Negro problem." For Weatherly, black assertiveness did not constitute a threat to racial harmony; he argued that when "whites of both sections definitely agree on a policy with reference to the Negro, that policy is likely to prevail and to be accepted by the Negro."[39]

Weatherly supported his belief that emerging black consciousness was no threat to white hegemony by arguing that blacks were little affected by their African heritage. The newly formed racial consciousness of blacks was thus "molded and held in check with this country and with the white man's institutions." Since that was the case, it followed that there was no need to fear a development similar to that in Austria-Hungary, where there existed "not only cultural differences between the races but in addition a sense of separate nationality based on divergent past histories."[40]

The Northern sociologists were not alarmed by the prospect or the threat of violence between blacks and whites. Confident in the eventual triumph of white supremacy in both North and South, they were certain that blacks would have no choice but to assent to the caste structure in which they occupied the lower stratum. The Southern commentators on Stone's paper, however, were critical of his use of race antipathy as a causal explanation of the development of racial strife and his belief in the inevitability of future violence.

James W. Garner, a Mississippian who had received his doctorate in political science from the University of Chicago in 1902 and who eventually became an authority in international law at the University of Illinois, concurred in Stone's belief that blacks were innately inferior to whites. Yet he went on to argue that economic and political factors were the primary causes of race friction. In the economic arena there had been an upsurge in competition between blacks who received encouragement from wealthy whites in the pursuit of land ownership and the poor white tenants who resorted to boycott and extralegal violence in order to prevent black economic advancement. Drawing on the census of 1900, which showed an increase in black employment in occupations outside of agricultural labor, Garner argued that economic inducements were attracting blacks to the cities of the South. Furthermore, Garner thought it was important to note that it was not the black elite that endangered smooth race relations, but the migration of blacks into the cities. In their segregated parts of the cities, Garner thought, blacks were "subject to an environment which breeds and increases criminality."[41]

In the political arena, Garner argued that the exploitation of the racial question by politicians, on issues in which it assumed no significance, was "one of the most serious obstacles in the way of maintaining harmonious relations" between blacks and whites. Although he agreed with James K. Vardaman (governor of Mississippi from 1904 to 1908) that black crime was too high, he could not perceive how the repeal of the Fifteenth Amendment and the denial of black rights to education and political participation could impede the increase in black crime. The solution to the problem of black crime, Garner concluded, was to subject blacks to the "rigid enforcement of the criminal law."[42]

Like Garner, John Spencer Bassett, a native North Carolinian who had received his Ph.D. at Johns Hopkins in history in 1894 and who taught history at Smith College, blamed Southern politicians for altering the social relations between blacks and whites. Presenting his interpretation of the history of Southern attitudes toward blacks, Bassett argued that the attitude of Southern whites toward blacks before 1830 had been one of benign paternalism: "Before 1830, the south considered the Negro an inferior who might possibly achieve civilization. It willingly saw him make the attempt and gave sympathetic attention to evidences of his success. Its attitude was but an outcome of a feeling of sincere esteem for unfortunate people who struggle against great obstacles." Thomas Jefferson's appointment of Benjamin Banneker to office, the absence of Southern protest when blacks were present at Andrew Jackson's inauguration, and the occupation of prestigious positions in North Carolina by blacks such as John Chavis, Ralph Lane, and Henry Evans, suggested to Bassett that the attitude of the pre–1830 Southerner was enlightened. "This older Southern attitude toward the Negro," he added confidently, "is essentially Anglo-Saxon."[43]

What happened in 1830, Bassett argued, was that "passion began to triumph over judgment" as a new group of young politicians led by John C. Calhoun began to gain the attention of the Southern voters, a process that eventually brought about the Civil War. Agitation by politicians continued after the war because blacks were given the vote, which Bassett believed they were unprepared to use judiciously. By giving blacks the vote, the North had caused them to view "equal social status" (which for Bassett did not mean "social intermingling") as a necessity. Although Southern politicians capitalized on the fear of social equality by rendering the Fifteenth Amendment void through restrictions on state voters, Bassett thought that this did not solve the racial problem—it only delayed the inevitable. "What will happen," Bassett asked, "when the disenfranchised Negroes, having become rich and intelligent, shall try to reconcile state suffrage restrictions with the Fifteenth Amendment to the United States Constitution?" For Bassett, the hope for the restoration of pre–1830 Southern attitudes lay with the "conservative force" of the churches. Symptomatic of the hypocrisy that pervaded the thought of many commentators on the race problem was Bassett's retreat from advocating a truly integrated society. Like Booker T. Washington, Bassett envisioned a society of "two great groups living side by side, distinct in all the ordinary affairs of life yet each enjoying the common privileges of the community, each tolerant of the other, each producing and trusting its own leaders and each willing to treat individual wrongs as crimes and not as 'race outrages' to be wiped out by 'race outrages' from the other party to the general struggle."[44]

Perhaps the most trenchant criticism of Stone was penned by W.E.B. DuBois. Taking Stone to task on the issue of slavery, DuBois argued that "slavery was a failure not because it mistook altogether the relative endowment of most of the men who were the enslavers and most of those who were enslaved, but because it denied growth or exception on the part of the enslaved and kept up that denial by physical force." DuBois looked forward to a "gradual emancipation in thought and customs." The whites of the South could not depend on the acquiescence of the mass of blacks; blacks in the South, though willing to ignore problems of "voting and freedom of travel," were nevertheless "pressing matters of wages and personal treatment, of housing and property holding." It was the growing protest of these problems that caused race problems. DuBois predicted that race friction would grow if the South assumed "that most human beings are to be kept in absolute and unchangeable serfdom to the Teutonic world," because blacks—like their oppressed brethren in Africa, the West Indies, Asia, and the Mediterranean countries— were "determined to contest this absurd stand to the death." But DuBois at this stage of his life was far more optimistic than in later years. Placing his faith in the rationality of whites on the racial question and on the patience of blacks, he argued that race friction "need not grow."[45]

Addressing himself to Stone's claim of black inferiority, DuBois placed his trust in the validity of the anthropological findings of Franz Boas, whom he interpreted to maintain that there was insufficient evidence to support the contention that blacks could not, because of mental or physical shortcomings, stand up to the rigors of modern life. DuBois contended that sufficient scientific evidence concerning blacks had not been obtained—mainly because scholars had not committed themselves to writing "unbiased" studies. Despite the absence of conclusive evidence, he believed that arguments such as Stone's, which suggested the incompatibility of blacks and whites on an equal plane, were untenable. These arguments reminded him of similar theories that sought "to prove that white men of a differing rank birth could not possibly exist in the same physical environment without similar subordination," and "that conflict between capitalists and laborers was an inevitable conflict which must lead to poverty and social murder of the masses." Arguments such as these had been proved untenable, and so would the theories of the racial supremacists, for in the modern world there would be "increasing contact of groups and nations and races." All of these groups would be essential to the "world's economy" and racial segregation could not survive. DuBois concluded that "what we ought to do in America is to seek to bind the races together rather than . . . accentuate differences."[46]

DuBois was both an excellent sociologist and a prophet. His emphasis on the similarity between the arguments used to rationalize the subordination of blacks and those used to rationalize serfdom was correct, insofar as it recognized the role of theory in justifying the rank order of societies.[47] Furthermore, DuBois's prediction of the increasing importance of the inextricable linkages between the economy of the United States and the economies of countries in what is now called the Third World was strikingly precise.

DuBois was not present at the Madison conference, however, and his paper was not received in time for Stone to reply to it. Stone did raise some objections to John Spencer Bassett's criticisms. The mild race relations between blacks and whites before 1830 to which Bassett referred, Stone argued, were "characteristic of many communities in which the number of Negroes is small compared with the white population, combined with a primitive social state." Such instances of simple race relations could, in the period before 1830, be found "in almost any southern community." As the population of blacks increased in an area and there was more contact between the races, Stone argued, the "Anglo-Saxon" assumed his natural antipathy toward blacks. As an indicator of the universality of his claim, Stone pointed out that the suffrage restrictions in the Pennsylvania constitution of 1790 changed when blacks began to increase in the state in the early part of the nineteenth century. Similar changes took place in North Carolina, Connecticut, and other states, and the Cape colony of South Africa. Introducing another indicator as conclusive proof of the universality of white racial antipathy, Stone argued that the uproar by British South Africans in 1896 concerning the reception of Prince Kharma by the Duke of Westminster was paralleled by that of Southern whites when Theodore Roosevelt received Booker T. Washington in 1901.[48]

Stone's contention that it was natural for whites to react nega-

tively to an increase in the black population was an important formulation, yet his assumption that prejudice and discrimination had
some bases in the racial character of the "Anglo-Saxon" was certainly suspect. It obviously masked, as both James W. Garner and
W.E.B. DuBois pointed out, the economic and political gains that
induced whites to subvert their own democratic value systems.
Stone's arguments, however, would permeate Southern social science circles for at least another decade. Typical of his influence was
an article published in the *American Journal of Sociology* by Walter
L. Fleming, a fellow Southerner, in 1910. In that piece Fleming argued that the migration of Pap Singleton and his followers to Kansas
in 1879–1880 resulted in a transformation in which "on the race
question a radical state became moderate; the change, if correctly
illustrated by newspaper comment, was ludicrously sudden." Revealing his belief that racial prejudice was a sectional attitude only
because blacks lived in the South in disproportionate numbers, the
Southerner wrote: "Could Singleton and others have succeeded in
bringing a large portion of the blacks to the North and thus have
somewhat equalized conditions and nationalized the Negro problem, it might have had some far reaching good effects. . . it certainly
would have relieved the 'southern situation.'"[49] Despite Fleming's
racism, he was astute, insofar as he did not underestimate the
strength of Northern prejudice.

As the decade came to a close, Southern social scientists had established their domination of the discussion of the Negro problem.
Basing their arguments on the theories of black inferiority and instinctive prejudice, the Southerners promulgated a conservative
philosophy of race relations which held that slavery, Jim Crow, and
industrial education had brought about the gradual evolution and
partial acculturation of a barbarous people. By developing these institutions, the white South had been preparing, as best it could, the
transplanted African for the occupation of his separate-but-equal
caste. Northerners passively accepted various aspects of the Southern argument because the Southern position supported their assumption of slow and protracted change. Their position on this
issue was tantamount to concurring in the Southern argument for a
separate-but-equal society in the foreseeable future.

Commentators on the sociological aspects of the race problem
were able to sustain such complacent attitudes at the turn of the
century because blacks were powerless. Disenfranchised and without strong economic foundations, blacks in the South had no voice
in the discussion of their condition and destiny. This condition
would change somewhat for many blacks once they migrated from

the industrially and culturally backward South, where they were the scapegoats for the region's ills, to the urban-industrial North, where their votes and economic influence would eventually have greater impact on the communities in which they lived.

NOTES

1. August Meier and Elliott Rudwick, *From Plantation to Ghetto* (New York: Hill and Wang, 1970), 186.

2. Eugene D. Genovese, *The Political Economy of Slavery* (New York: Pantheon Books, 1965), 72.

3. Walter F. Willcox, Preface to *The Negro in Africa and America*, by Joseph A. Tillinghast (New York: Macmillan, 1902), i.

4. Joseph A. Tillinghast, *The Negro in Africa and America*, 2.

5. Ibid., 2–5.

6. Ibid., 28–45.

7. Ibid., 64–65.

8. Ibid., 96.

9. Ibid., 104.

10. Ibid., 136.

11. Ibid., 225–26.

12. Jerome Dowd, *The Negro Races*, 2 vols. (New York: Macmillan, 1907–1914), 1:5, 432, 447–48.

13. Ibid., 447–48.

14. H. E. Belin, "A Southern View of Slavery," *AJS* 13 (January 1908): 517–20. See also Belin, "The Civil War as Seen Through Southern Glasses," *AJS* 9 (September 1903): 266.

15. Belin, "A Southern View of Slavery," 520.

16. Walter L. Fleming, "Reorganization of the Industrial System in Alabama After the Civil War," *AJS* 10 (January 1905): 498–99.

17. Ibid., 499.

18. Ibid.

19. W.E.B. DuBois, *Black Reconstruction in America, 1860–1880* (1935; reprint; New York: Atheneum, 1969), 720.

20. Carl Kelsey, "The Evolution of Negro Labor," *Annals* 21 (January 1903): 56–75.

21. Howard W. Odum, *Social and Mental Traits of the Negro* (New York: Columbia University, 1910), 18.

22. Ibid., 269.

23. Ibid., 274–75.

24. Ibid., 276–85.

25. Ibid., 286–91.

26. James R. Hayes, "Sociology and Racism: An Analysis of the First Era of American Sociology," *Phylon* 34 (December 1973): 334; Idus Newby, *Jim Crow's Defense: Anti-Negro Thought in America, 1909–1930* (Baton Rouge: Louisiana State University Press, 1965), 51.

27. An essay that points out the assimilationist undercurrents in Washington's thought is Howard M. Brotz's introduction to *Negro Social and Political Thought 1850–1920* (New York: Basic Books, 1966), 12–18.

28. John Dollard, *Caste and Class in a Southern Town* (New Haven, Conn.: Yale University Press, 1937).

29. Paul J. Baker, ed., "The Life Histories of W. I. Thomas and Robert E. Park," *AJS* 79 (September 1973): 247–48.

30. William I. Thomas, "The Psychology of Race Prejudice," *AJS* 9 (March 1904): 607–8.

31. Ibid., 608–11.

32. Alfred Holt Stone, "Is Race Friction Between Blacks and Whites in the United States Growing and Inevitable?" *AJS* 13 (March 1908): 676–79.

33. Ibid., 682.

34. Ibid., 680.

35. Ibid., 687–94.

36. Ibid., 694–97.

37. Walter F. Willcox, Discussion of "Race Friction," by Alfred Holt Stone, *AJS* 13 (May 1908): 820–23.

38. Ulysses G. Weatherly, Discussion of "Race Friction," by Alfred Holt Stone, *AJS* 13 (May 1908): 823.

39. Ibid., 824–25.

40. Ibid., 824.

41. James W. Garner, Discussion of "Race Friction," by Alfred Holt Stone, *AJS* 13 (May 1908): 828–31.

42. Ibid., 831.

43. John Spencer Bassett, Discussion of "Race Friction," by Alfred Holt Stone, *AJS* 13 (May 1908): 825–26.

44. Ibid., 826–28.

45. W.E.B. DuBois, Discussion of "Race Friction," by Alfred Holt Stone, *AJS* 13 (May 1908): 834.

46. Ibid., 835–38.

47. The legitimizing functions of theory in creating a race relations situation is discussed thoroughly in John Rex, *Race Relations in Sociological Theory* (London: Routledge and Kegan Paul, 1983), 136–61.

48. Alfred Holt Stone, Commentary on the discussion of his "Race Friction," *AJS* 13 (May 1908): 838–40.

49. Walter L. Fleming, "Pap Singleton, The Moses of the Colored Exodus," *AJS* 15 (July 1910): 82.

3

The Influence of Franz Boas,
1894–1910

During the 1890s American anthropology was based primarily in museums in major Eastern cities. The field was dominated by pre-academic pioneers such as Daniel Garrison Brinton, John Wesley Powell, and W J McGee. These anthropologists were the direct ideological descendants of such ethnologists as Edward B. Tylor, Lewis Henry Morgan, and John Lubbock, intellectual giants who had brought out major works within a few years of the publication of Charles Darwin's *Origin of Species* (1859), and who had developed the comparative method into a major analytical tool. Convinced that there was a pattern of cultural evolution, the nineteenth-century ethnologists posited three distinct categories by which cultures could be ranked: savagery, barbarism, and civilization. By assuming that their civilization was the most progressive—and the standard by which other cultures could be judged—the major Victorian ethnologists were extremely ethnocentric. As Idus L. Murphree has observed: "They suffered the excesses of enthusiasm for things close to home and for the familiar articles of nineteenth century life, including monogamous marriage."[1]

Typical of the onslaught of the early American anthropologists was Daniel Garrison Brinton's strident and dogmatic assertion in 1891 that "the abilities of a race must be based on accomplished results."[2] It was against Brinton's type of chauvinism, which preached the superiority of Anglo-Saxons, that Franz Boas, who would become the most influential anthropologist for the next four decades, rebelled.

Franz Boas's first major statement on the character and capabilities of Afro-Americans was presented in August, 1894, when he delivered an address, "Human Faculty as Determined by Race," to the anthropological section of the American Association for the Advancement of Science. In this attack on the racist orthodoxy permeating both European and American social scientific communities, Boas was expressing liberal convictions that flowed from a worldview that was unique in the United States. His convictions were a direct product of the remnants of liberal ideals in Germany, his scientific training, and his marginal status in the anthropological community.[3]

The patriarch of modern American anthropology was born in Minden, Westphalia, in 1858, a decade following the republican revolutions that swept Europe. By his birthdate, the revolutions which had been characterized by their emphasis on liberalism and the creation of democratic republican nations had failed. The young Boas nonetheless held firmly to the ideals of the "forty-eighters" throughout his entire life.[4]

As was the custom of the period, Boas attended several German universities: Heidelberg, Bonn, and Kiel. He was awarded the doctorate at Kiel in 1881, at the age of twenty-three. His dissertation, *Contributions to the Understanding of the Color of Water*, was in physics. He knew it was tinged by subjectivism. In his doctoral experiments, Boas had sought to determine the intensities of light that struck different types of distilled water. He was confronted by the problem of subjectivism when he had to distinguish between two lights that produced slight differences in the color of two different types of water. Boas recalled in 1939 that the experiments suggested to him that "there are domains of our experience in which the concepts of quantity . . . with which I was accustomed to operate, are not applicable."[5] Questions concerning the relativity of experience and the relationship between the physiological and the physical were two major philosophical problems he confronted frequently in his later works.

After a year in the German army and two years of studying and waiting for a teaching position, Boas went to Baffinland in 1883 on an expedition that was decisive in determining his gradual transition—which had begun in 1881—from a career in geography to one in anthropology. Although Boas's interest in geography matured after 1882, and though he continued to write articles for geographical journals until 1888, his experiences among the Eskimos sowed the seeds for his attempt to understand the laws of human nature.

The gradual transition from geography to ethnology continued in 1883–1884. While attempting to qualify for a teaching position, Boas studied ethnology under Adolf Bastian and anthropometry under Rudolf Virchow at the Royal Ethnographic Museum in Berlin. The transition was completed in 1888 when he published *The*

Central Eskimo, an ethnographic monograph based on his observations of the Eskimos in Baffinland.

The transition coincided with another turning point in Boas's life, for in January 1887 he emigrated to the United States. His emigration can be explained, for the most part, by his estrangement from the conservative, anti-Semitic climate of Bismarck's Germany. Scholars had to make a declaration of religious affiliation in order to hold a scientific post in Germany, and liberals were also being forced out of the universities.

For almost a decade after his arrival in the United States Boas confronted tremendous obstacles in securing and holding professional positions. He first served as geographical editor of *Science* from 1887 to 1888. After losing that job, he took a post as a docent in anthropology at Clark University, a position he held until 1892. He resigned this position and later became chief assistant of anthropology at the World's Columbia Exposition in Chicago. After his dismissal from that temporary position in 1894, Boas confronted eighteen months of unemployment. When he delivered "Human Faculty as Determined by Race" to the American Association for the Advancement of Science, he was in the midst of his eighteen-month employment crisis.

Boas's attack on the racist orthodoxy was bound inextricably to the so-called Negro problem in both the North and the South and the virulent anti-Semitism that pervaded the nation. Jews of German descent, who had begun to be affected by anti-Semitism as early as the 1880s, witnessed a further decline of their status. During the 1890s their opportunities in WASP-dominated institutions and housing were narrowed, as a direct product of the influx of large numbers of Eastern European Jews since the 1880s.[6]

Having confronted anti-Semitism in both his native Germany and the United States, Boas was especially troubled by the hatred of blacks in the United States. Liberal humanitarian sentiments were recurring themes in his 1894 address, in which he approached the problems of racial superiority and inferiority from the fields of history, physical anthropology, cultural anthropology, and psychology. Boas's position echoed the arguments of nineteenth-century writers of Afro-American descent.[7] Afro-American achievement literature, which had its origins in the attempts of blacks to change prevailing stereotypes of themselves during the antebellum period, stressed the historical advancement of blacks despite oppression. Boas summed up their argument graciously:

When . . . we consider the inferior position held by the negro race of the United States, who are in the closest contact with modern civilization, we must not forget the old race-feeling of the inferiority of the colored race is as potent as ever and is a formidable obstacle to its advance and progress, notwithstanding that schools and universities are open to them. We might rather wonder how much has been accomplished in a short period against heavy odds. It is hardly possible to say what would become of the negro if he were able to live with whites on absolutely equal terms.[8]

But Boas's assessments of racial determinist arguments in the various branches of the social sciences were divided. On the one hand, he demonstrated the primacy of cultural determinants in accounting for historical achievements and the psychological makeup of different races. On the other hand, he conceded to racists by insisting that physical anthropological assumptions of the direct relation between intelligence and brain weight or cranial capacity were relevant. Boas even thought bodily form might have certain influences on the psychological makeup of races.

The schism between the values of cultural determinism and the values of racial determinism was the major weakness in his philosophical position on race. The schism was a direct product of his methodological rigor. Although Boas's sentiments resonated with his penchant for emphasizing cultural determinism, he still could not reconcile those sentiments with physical anthropological assumptions about racial differences. The tension is evident in his analysis of racial determinism from the historical and physical anthropological perspectives.

From the historical perspective, the young Boas attacked the paradigm of the proponents of the comparative method. By assuming that there was a direct relationship between a race's achievements and the intellectual capacities of its members, the evolutionary anthropologists had essentially confounded achievement with an aptitude for achievement. Similarly they judged any deviation from the white type as "a characteristic feature of a lower type." Boas insisted that the superiority of Western civilization could be accounted for on grounds other than those which suggested the superiority of the white race's mental faculty. He argued that other races such as the Indians of Peru and Central America had evolved civilizations that were similar to that from which European civilization had its origins. However, European civilization, favored by the "common physical appearance, continuity of habitat and modern differences in modes of manufacture" of its inhabitants, spread rapidly. When European civilization came into contact with races outside its domain, assimilation of nonwhites was difficult because of "striking differences of racial types, the preceding and the greater advance in civilization." The advocates of Northern and Western European superiority, he stressed, had ignored that their civilization, which arose under favorable circumstances and spread rapidly, had "cut short" the development of non-European civilizations "without regard to the people whom it was developing." The evolutionists' historical explanation of the low status of nonwhites was wrong, because "historical events rather than race appear to have been much more potent in leading races to civilization than their faculty, and it follows the achievements of races do not warrant us to assume that one race is more highly gifted than the others."[9]

Boas's criticisms of the evolutionists had exposed the ethnocentric fallacy of ranking nonwhite societies according to these characteristics they shared with European and American civilizations, and revealed his cosmopolitan and liberal sentiments. But his evaluation of racial intellectual differences from the physical anthropological framework was infused with concessions to staunch racists. In the 1880s and early 1890s, Boas had been influenced significantly by the works of prominent Continental physical anthropologists such as Paul Broca and Paul Topinard, and directly by Rudolf Virchow, with whom he had contact at the meetings of the Berlin Anthropological Society in 1882. Furthermore, throughout his career Boas was certain that physical anthropological data could clarify important ethnological questions.[10] Working within the framework developed by Broca, who is often labelled the father of modern physical anthropology, Boas speculated in the early jargon of the discipline that "it would seem that the greater the central nervous system, the higher the faculty of the race and the greater its aptitude to mental achievement." According to Boas, there were two methods useful in determining the size of the central nervous system: one could either measure the weight of the brain (which provided the most "accurate results") or the size of the cranial cavity. He conceded that both the brain weight and cranial cavities of whites, on the average, were "larger than that of most other races, particularly larger than that of the negroes."[11] Boas's conclusions were not new. As early as the 1840s, the "American School" of anthropology, of which Samuel George Morton, Josiah C. Nott, and George R. Gliddon were among the members, had based a major part of its proslavery defense on the comparative measurements of the cranial cavities of blacks and whites.[12]

Despite Boas's physical anthropological assumptions, he exercised considerable restraint in interpreting the data that were based solely on the relatively simple mathematical techniques of means, medians, and percentiles. On a visit in England in 1889, he had become acquainted with Sir Francis Galton. He appropriated the eugenicist's techniques, and used them to demonstrate that the "frequency distribution" of the cranial cavities of blacks and whites overlapped. He pointed out that Topinard's measurements revealed that 55 percent of the Europeans, compared to 58 percent of "African negroes," had cavities in the range of 1450 to 1650 cubic centimeters; however, the range greater than 1550 cubic centimeters enclosed 50 percent of the whites and 27 percent of the blacks. His inference: "We might, therefore, anticipate a lack of men of high genius [among the Negroes] but should not anticipate any lack of faculty among the great mass of negroes living among whites and enjoying the leadership of the best men of the race."[13]

The statement reflects obvious tension between liberal humanitarian sentiments and the ideas of racism. On the one hand, he implied strongly that blacks would produce proportionately fewer men capable of shaping either the nation's or the world's higher affairs; on the other hand, he was arguing for the significance of individual differences regardless of a person's race. *All* blacks, in other words, were not intellectually inferior to *all* whites, yet disproportionately few had the mental faculty requisite to shape the course of history.

Boas's ambivalences concerning black capabilities were also extended to his discussion of their psychology. He admitted that the descriptive psychological evidence, on which Edward B. Tylor and Herbert Spencer based their generalizations about primitive peoples, had suggested that nonwhites were more fickle and passionate and less original than whites. To him, such arguments were not convincing "because causes and effects were so closely interwoven that it is impossible to separate them in a satisfactory manner, and we are always liable to interpret as racial characteristics what is only an effect of social surroundings."[14] Even on that issue, however, Boas infused physical anthropological assumptions into psychology and immediately genuflected to reactionary beliefs:

Based on these considerations we believe that in the more complicated psychological phenomena no specific differences between the higher and lower races can be found. By this, however, we do not mean to say no such differences exist or can be found, only that the method of investigation must be different. It does not seem probable that the minds of races which show variations in their anatomical structure should act in exactly the same manner. Differences of structure must be accompanied by differences of function, physiological as well as psychological, and as we found clear evidence of differences in mental structure between the races, so we must anticipate that differences in mental characteristics will be found.[15]

Then, in a feeble attempt to qualify those statements, Boas once again argued that there were variations in all races: "As all structural differences are quantitative, we must expect to find mental differences to be of the same description, and we found the variation in structure to overlap, so that many forms are common to individuals of all races, so we may expect that many individuals will not differ in regard to their faculty, while a statistical inquiry embracing the whole race would reveal certain differences.[16]

Boas was aware of the limitations of the physical anthropological explanations of psychological differences between whites and non-whites. He hoped, however, that experimental psychologists' investigations of the "physical processes of great numbers of individuals of different races who lived under similar conditions" would provide valuable insights into the psychology of those groups.[17] Much to the dismay of liberals like Boas, the discipline of psychology was dominated during the next thirty-five years by hereditarians who hindered its progress towards an environmentalist position on the issue of the intelligence of blacks and whites. When psychologists attacked that issue in the 1900s, they were not comparing "different races who lived under similar conditions." Rather than confronting the issue of significance of socioeconomic differences as factors in the determination of test scores, psychologists clung for the next twenty years to the argument that their tests indicated that blacks were clearly inferior to whites in intelligence.

The response of the proponents of Anglo-Saxon chauvinism to Boas's address was almost immediate. In the presidential address, entitled "The Aims of Anthropology," delivered to the American Association for the Advancement of Science in 1895, Daniel G. Brinton showed that he did not understand Boas's assessment of craniometric data and the cogency of his attack on the historical achievement argument. Revealing a reified view of white and non-white anatomical differences, Brinton argued, "The black, the brown and red races differ anatomically so much from the white, especially in their splanchnic [visceral] organs, that even with equal cerebral capacity, they could never rival the results by equal efforts."[18]

Boas's employment crisis ended in 1896, when Frederic Ward Putnam appointed him to the position of assistant curator at the American Museum of Natural History in New York City. He became the curator of that institution in 1901. In 1896 Boas was also appointed to the position of lecturer in physical anthropology at Columbia University, where he became professor of anthropology in 1899. Having obtained a relatively secure position, Boas, during the years 1900 to 1910, attacked the two pivotal theories of racial determinists: first, the intellectual and psychological inferiority of blacks as a whole; and second, the congenital inferiority of Africans.

Nevertheless, Boas's 1900 address before the American Folklore Society reflected the tension between his liberal humanitarian sentiments and the evidence from physical anthropology. He was willing to pursue the cultural determinist position to some extent. Boas argued that the mind of primitive man differed from that of civilized man not in its organization, as the advocates of the comparative method had proposed, but rather in the character of experience to which it was exposed. The mental functions—abstraction, inhibition, and choice—were all found among primitive peoples; thus, there was no justification for the Spencerian argument that primitive peoples occupied a lower evolutionary stage. In the same address, however, Boas retreated to the argument of black inferiority when he confessed: "A number of anatomical facts point to the conclusion that the races of Africa, Australia, and Melanesia are to a certain extent inferior to Asia, America, and Europe." Nonetheless, Boas argued that there was "no satisfactory evidence" available on whether differences in the size of the brains were "accompanied by difference in structure."[19]

In an article entitled "The Negro and the Demands of Modern Life," which appeared in *Charities* in 1905, Boas apparently tried to resolve the issues he had raised in 1894 when he argued that blacks would produce proportionately fewer "men of high genius" than whites. Although he once again pointed out that the "average" Negro brain was "smaller than that of other races," and that it was "plausible that certain differences of form of brain exist," he nevertheless cautioned that the data did not conclusively demonstrate differences in intellectual ability.[20] Modifying his 1894 position, which had suggested a direct relationship between brain weight and mental ability, Boas argued: "The inference in regard to ability is . . . based on analogy and we must remember that individually the correlation between brain weight and ability is often overshadowed by other causes, and that we find a considerable number of great men with slight brain weight." Although Boas admitted that causes other than brain weight "often" determined mental ability, he was still too committed to physical anthropological assumptions to dismiss those assumptions. Immediately contradicting his statement, which opened up the possibility of "causes" other than brain weight that affected mental ability, he penned a non sequitur: "We may, therefore, expect less average ability and also, on account of probable anatomical differences, somewhat different mental tendencies." Then, in an attempt to minimize the purported differences between the races, Boas brought forth the same argument that he had used in 1894: "We may, with the same degree of certainty, expect these differences to be small as compared to the total range of variations found in the human species."[21]

Boas attempted to give a favorable impression of Afro-Americans, despite the measurements indicating that the average cranial cavities of blacks were smaller than those of whites. In a passage that was a direct attack on segregation in the public schools, he wrote:

There is every reason to believe that the Negro when given the facility and opportunity will be perfectly able to fill the duties of citizenship as well as his white neighbor. It may be that he will not produce as many great men as the white race, and his average achievement will not quite reach the level of the average achievement of the white race, but there will be endless numbers who will do better than the defectives whom we permit to drag down and retard the healthy children of our public schools.[22]

Rhetoric aside, Boas was confronted by an irreconcilable dilemma. As a physical anthropologist, he adhered to the assumptions of his field. Furthermore, he insisted that he had always believed that there were fundamental differences between blacks and whites. "I do not believe," Boas stated unequivocally in *Science* in 1909, "that the negro is, in his physical and mental make-up, the same as the European. The anatomical differences are so great that corresponding mental differences are plausible." As a cultural anthropologist, however, Boas could minimize the differences between blacks and whites. Thus, his liberal humanitarian sentiments were obvious when he wrote: "This view [of blacks as persons with appreciable mental abilities] is supported by the remarkable development of industry, political organization, and philosophical opinion, as well as by the frequent occurrence of men of great will power and wisdom among the Negroes in Africa."[23]

Nevertheless, Boas's belief in fundamental mental differences between blacks and whites was a pitfall from which he was never able to fully extricate himself. His methodological rigor in the discussion of craniometric differences ran counter to his ethical commitment to undermine the argument of staunch racists. His belief in the remnants of nineteenth-century raciology gives credence to the argument of Frank H. Hankins that Boas thought "racial differences though real are less extensive and important than popular opinion has heretofore supposed."[24] Although Hankins underestimated the extent to which Boas's argument undermined the theories of many scholars, it is clear that Boas was less perceptive and open-minded than current scholars acknowledge.

Boas's ethical sentiments were far more obvious, however, when he attacked the issue of the purported innate inferiority of Africans. Although Boas was never involved in fieldwork in West Africa, his empirical approach to the issues raised by social scientists such as

Joseph A. Tillinghast, H. E. Belin, Walter L. Fleming, Jerome Dowd, Carl Kelsey, and Charles A. Ellwood, led him to argue that the status of Afro-Americans in the United States was determined by the experience of slavery and the persistence of white prejudice rather than by the purported hereditary traits of their African ancestors. He based his critique of African life on different aspects of African material culture that he had seen in European museums in the early 1900s. In a series of articles published between 1904 and 1911, Boas drew on that evidence, along with the work of the German Africanist Leo Frobenius, to refute the Tillinghast–Dowd thesis.[25]

Although Boas thought the current stereotypes of Afro-Americans were true, it is clear where he thought the responsibility for the conditions of Afro-Americans lay:

The essential point that anthropology can contribute to the practical discussion of the adaptability of the Negro is a decision on the question of how far the undesirable traits that are at present undoubtedly found in our Negro population are due to racial traits, and how far they are due to social surroundings, for which *we* are responsible. To this question anthropology can give the decided answer that the traits of African culture as observed in the aboriginal home of the Negro are those of a healthy primitive people with a considerable degree of personal initiative, with a talent for organization.[26]

In an article entitled "Industries of the African Negroes," published in the *Southern Workman* in 1909, Boas attacked three weaknesses in the argument of the proponents of black inferiority. First, he argued that the stereotypes suggesting that blacks were indolent and unable to defer gratification were fallacious. Describing the industrious life in the typical West African village, he wrote:

Village life is replete with activity. The extensive gardens of the village must be tilled; the loom is busy; in the hands of the women plastic clay is made into useful pottery ware; the wood carver makes dishes and other useful articles for the home and adorns them with fanciful carvings; the blacksmith's bellows are busy and his hammer may be heard. The produce of the fields and the work of the artisan are packed up and carried to the market which is held at regular intervals, and where distant tribes may meet to exchange their commodities.[27]

Second, he attacked the stereotype of blacks as lacking strong will power by presenting evidence that suggested that some African leaders had succeeded in organizing large "political and military empires that have endured for many generations."[28] Third, Boas undermined the proponents of the historical achievement thesis by arguing that it seemed "likely that the art of making iron implements may have been first invented on the African continent by the Negro race." The industrial and artistic works of black Africans led Boas to conclude "that the impression which we gain from the failure of the American Negro to manifest himself in any of these directions is due, not to native inability, but to the degrading conditions under which he has been placed for generations."[29]

Boas's indictment of slavery and post–Civil War racial oppression depended on the argument that Afro-Americans were unable to retain their African cultural heritage—an argument that produces controversy even today. His insistence that blacks lost their traditions when introduced into a new environment led him to a direct attack on the empirical aspects of the Tillinghast–Dowd thesis, which had suggested that blacks in the United States had retained their African heritage. In a 1908 review of Jerome Dowd's *The Negro Races*, vol. 1, Boas argued that Dowd's book was based on "an uncritical collection of data drawn from the superficial reports of travelers which cannot form the basis of safe conclusion." Dowd had obviously ignored the high artistic achievements of black Africans in Benin. Furthermore, Dowd's theoretical framework laid too much emphasis on "anthropogeographical considerations," and thus ignored the "historical relations" of the different racial groups in Africa. On the basis of Ankermann's and Frobenius's studies of the distributions of inventions in Africa, Boas argued "that the forms of culture of the African continent must be considered and interpreted in their mutual interrelations to Asia and Europe." For Boas, Dowd's emphasis on geographical considerations to "explain political and other conditions" in Africa was merely "an attempt to fit selected data to preconceived notions."[30]

Boas's attack on the Tillinghast–Dowd thesis was also ideological. Both sides could summon data to support their generalizations. While it is true that Tillinghast and Dowd had a preconceived model into which selected data were fitted, the Boasians were also purveyors of an ideology. As Marvin Harris has pointed out, "the Boasian program corresponds rather closely with the fundamental ideological outlook associated with left-of-center political liberalism."[31] Why the Boasians' deterministic culture concept emerged as the major defense for a multiracial democracy is an issue that will be treated in the next chapter.

SOCIOLOGISTS ON THE CAPABILITIES OF NONWHITES

The discipline of anthropology during the 1890s was dominated by conservative defenders of the American elite of British ancestry. The discipline of sociology, on the other hand, was controlled by progressive evolutionists of British descent who were intent on minimizing the argument for existence of natural inequality among men. These democratic sentiments led the progressives to attack the underlying assumptions that even Boas himself embraced. Midwestern-born Charles H. Cooley raised important issues that Boas had not resolved in his "men of high genius" hypothesis. Although he did not cite Boas, in a monumental article published in the *Annals* in 1897 the social theorist refuted Galton's thesis that fame was the prime indicator of genius and that the number of geniuses contained in a race was a means of ranking a race's ability. He demonstrated that historical and social conditions determined the number of geniuses who attained fame. Also undermining Boas's conclusions indirectly was Cooley's concession that Sir Francis Galton was correct in *Heredity Genius* (1869) in not comparing blacks and whites in the United States on the issue of genius— primarily because the two races did not "mingle and compete in the same order, and under conditions substantially the same."[32]

Cooley opened up a whole range of sociological problems that would not be fully discussed for three decades: Why did the two groups mingle and compete in different orders? Were the conditions under which blacks lived the result of inherent disabilities or historical and social conditions? And finally, what types of reform, if any, were necessary to correct the disparity of conditions that hampered blacks from competing with whites? Ironically, Cooley never attempted to answer these types of questions. It is perhaps tragic that one of the most influential social thinkers in the United States eventually abandoned his early liberalism and capitulated in the 1900s to a brand of racism that defended a castelike system of race relations.

In an article published in 1896 in the *American Journal of Sociology*, which was edited by Albion W. Small and other members of the department of sociology and anthropology at the University of Chicago, William I. Thomas argued that the field of craniometry erroneously attempted to demonstrate a direct relation "between intelligence and brain mass." The conclusions of physical anthropologists, Thomas held, were of negligible value, because "all organs and tissues which cooperate in forming an association are equally important with the brain" in the creation of intelligence. Nonetheless, Thomas's Southern biases impinged ever so sharply on his argument, for he provided a rationalization for the South's peculiar social order that would later be developed by both Southern and Northern sociologists. For Thomas, a race's temperament was of far more importance to its society than was its intelligence; temperament supposedly predetermined within certain limits the society's institutions, "the form and spirit of the art, literature, ethics and politics."[33] Attempting to provide a scientific basis for the purported temperamental difference between the races, Thomas utilized a biological analogy, arguing that differences in racial temperament were "due to the same causes as positive and negative heliotropism or chemotropism in plants and animals, namely chemical composition."[34] It is clear that in the late 1890s Thomas was a racial determinist. And although he would eventually adopt liberal environmental views on the issue of racial equality, he still held as late as 1912 that blacks had not made sufficient progress since slavery.

The attempt of Northern, professional sociologists to make a rational decision on the issue of the capabilities of nonwhites gained considerable headway during the 1900s. Typical of those sociologists who held to the belief that racial intellectual differences were obvious was Charles A. Ellwood. When speaking of blacks in an article entitled "The Theory of Imitation in *Social Psychology*," which appeared in the *American Journal of Sociology* in 1901, Ellwood fell back on William James's doctrine of instincts. Ellwood, who had been trained at the University of Chicago, took to task the theory of Gabriel Tarde and James Mark Baldwin that imitation was the determinant of the processes of personal and social development. Ellwood argued "that the process of imitation is at every turn limited, controlled, and modified by a series of instinctive impulses which have become relatively fixed in the individual through the process of evolution by natural selection." The character of these instinctive impulses, which included organic sympathy, antipathy, mental attitudes, and attitudes toward religion and morality, varied from one race to another. Had not those racial instincts been present, Ellwood contended, "we should expect children of different races, when reared in the same cultural environment, to develop the same general mental and moral characteristics." Since the racial instincts of blacks and whites differed, Ellwood argued that the black child, "even when reared in a white family under the most favorable conditions, fails to take on the mental and moral characteristics of the Caucasian race." Although the instincts of the black were modifiable by voluntary or enforced imitation, there was "always a strong tendency to reversion." Ellwood, who was a Quaker and an advocate of Christian sociology, argued unequivocally that, "the reappearance of voodooism among the Negroes of the South, though surrounded by Christian influences," was indicative of "the innate tendency of the Negro mind to take such attitudes toward nature and the universe."[35]

Despite the theories of scholars like Ellwood, objections were raised to the theories of black inferiority. In fact, numerous Northern, professional sociologists and one Southern-born sociologist were making a concerted effort to come to a rational decision on the issue of differences between blacks and whites. It is possible to perceive in the writings of many sociologists the adoption of a skeptical position in regard to the capabilities of blacks. They did not deny that there were differences between blacks and whites, but rather suggested that, on the basis of the best available evidence, the differences were not substantial. In other words, most sociologists could not speak unequivocally on the issue of mental differences between the races; they could only speak in terms of what they thought was "probable" or "plausible."

For Ulysses G. Weatherly, a prominent conservative who taught at Indiana University, blacks and whites differed in somatic character and temperament. Yet he wrote in 1910 that "with reference to total mental faculty the degree of difference is not so clearly established." Although he was unwilling to make a strong case for the absence of racial mental differences, he nevertheless followed Boas's lead and commented that it was "probable that some individuals of all races are capable of any level of achievement," and that any "ethnic group as a whole may acquire ability in some lines in which it is now deficient." Influenced by Boas's 1894 address to the American Association for the Advancement of Science, Weatherly paraphrased in a tone of agreement Boas's contention of the capacity of the "darker races" to enter upon the level of civilization occupied by the white races.[36]

The writings of William I. Thomas, who kept abreast of the developments in anthropology on the issues of the difference between the races, followed the lead of Franz Boas so closely that later sociologists often credited him, along with Boas, with developing the liberal environmentalist creed.[37] In 1905 Thomas was still emphasizing the importance of temperament in determining the behavior of races. "There is much reason to think that temperament," he argued, "as determining what classes of stimulation are effective, is quite as important as brain capacity in fixing the characteristic lines of development followed by a group, and there is more unlikeness on the temperamental than on the mental side between both individuals and races." Thomas was perhaps reluctant to develop an argument for racial mental differences at this date. He realized that one area in social psychology demanding further investigation was "the comparison of states of consciousness of different races, classes, and social epochs, with a view to determining what mental differences exist, and to what extent they are due to biological as against social causes." Taking into consideration the anthropological data accumulated on the mental abilities of the nonwhite races, he conceded that it was a possibility "that what have sometimes been regarded as biological differences separating social groups are not really so, and that characteristic expressions of the mind are dependent on social environment."[38]

After 1907 Thomas ceased to express belief in the temperamental differences between whites and nonwhites. Probably influenced by Boas, he seemed far more certain that social factors accounted for the differences in the mental abilities of races. "It is probable," he intimated, "that brain efficiency . . . has been on the average, approximately the same in all races and in both sexes since nature first made a good working model, and that differences in intellectual expression are mainly social rather than biological, dependent on that fact that different stages of culture present different experiences to the mind, and adventitous circumstances direct the attention to different fields of interest."[39]

Despite his vacillation between racial and cultural explanations of groups' behavior the following year, his assessments of blacks' intellectual abilities were primarily sociopsychological. He concluded that the present intellectual state of blacks was due to "a defect of copies" found within their culture "more than mental machinery."[40] Thomas's conversion from biological determinism to environmentalism was not brought to its completion, however, until the publication of his monumental article, "Race Psychology," which appeared in the *American Journal of Sociology* in 1912.

Of all the sociologists of the period, Carl Kelsey most thoroughly understood the implications of Boas's assault on the traditional racist orthodoxy. Abandoning the racist doctrine in 1907, he now drew an important distinction between the limitations of the concepts of heredity and environment. "The word heredity," he noted, "should be used to denote those physical characteristics which come to us through the germ cells of the parents." Once the life of the child began, "heredity ends and environment begins." The separation of biological processes from sociocultural processes amounted to a subversion of the Lamarckian doctrine of the inheritance of acquired characteristics, which served as the primary explanation for racial differences. By denying that a race's heredity was affected by the environment, Kelsey was undermining the Lamarckian doctrine that racial differences were a product of the environment reacting upon a race's heredity.

SOCIOLOGISTS AND THE PROBLEM OF RACIAL INTERMIXTURE

Boas was far more progressive for his time than most social scientists on the issue of race. His progressivism also stimulated him to make perceptive insights into white prejudices. According to most social scientists, the function of racial prejudice was to maintain "a distinct social status in order to avoid race mixture." Criticizing the argument that prejudice was a physiological expression, Boas argued that the existence of a large mulatto population in the United States indicated that "the so-called instinct" was "not a physiological dislike." He chose to believe that prejudice was "an expression of social conditions that are so deeply ingrained in us that they assume strong emotional value."[41]

Sociologists, in a quite different fashion, sought to harmonize long-range theories of ethnical integration with theories of racial capabilities and prejudice. This was evident in their views on miscegenation and intermarriage. Reviving the polygenist argument to accommodate the realities of the 1900s, sociologists put forth the following arguments: black male and white female unions were often sterile; white male and black female unions were as productive as intraracial unions; unions between mulattoes were generally infertile; mulattoes were mentally, morally, and physically inferior to whites but mentally superior to pure blacks. With those specious conclusions in mind, it is not surprising that most sociologists recommended that intermarriage should be avoided at all costs.

Sarah Simons, one of the more progressive of the Northern sociologists, made a futile attempt to harmonize her theory of assimilation with her theory of innate racial differences between blacks and whites by avoiding the fact that assimilation was impossible without intermarriage. Simons declared that the "attempt to assimilate through this means [intermarriage] could not be successful on account of the great racial difference between the Caucasian and the black."[42] The documentation for Simons's argument rested on the polygenist argument of Franklin H. Giddings, who himself was influenced by the proslavery advocate of the American School of anthropology, Josiah Nott, and the European anthropologists Karl Vogt and Paul Broca.[43]

A more elaborate, primarily psychological, argument, which stressed the grave problems resulting from the intermarriage or intermixture of widely disparate ethnic groups, was offered by Ulysses G. Weatherly in 1910. Writing in the *American Journal of Sociology*, Weatherly argued that "the degree of fecundity in race crossing . . . was generally clearly correlated with the degree of cultural difference between parent stocks." When individuals of widely different levels of culture intermarried, "fecundity and vitality" were lowered because of the "transition to an alien mode of life." Another cause of the "relative sterility of mixed unions" was the absence "of harmony in their intimate matters of personal life." Gathering data from Wackler's study of Christian and Jewish intermarriage in Germany, he pointed out that the average number of offspring in families in which the father was a Christian and the mother Jewish was 1.58, as opposed to 4.35 for Christian families and 4.21 for Jewish families. "The variation," he inferred, "is clearly due to psychological rather than physiological causes." In such mixed unions, he concluded, the partners were unable to enter sympathetically into each other's inner lives and this bred disappointment and ultimately discord.[44]

In writing about areas where racial intermixing had occurred between blacks and whites, as in Jamaica and the Southern states, Weatherly infused both psychological and racial determinist assumptions in an attempt to demonstrate that the half-caste was in a precarious position:

The consciousness of his [the mulatto's] superiority to the more primitive stock raises a barrier against sympathetic cooperation on that side, while on the side of the dominant race he finds no willingness to grant social equality. If he is not more depraved in morals than either of the parent races he at least has acquired the reputation of being so. Unless the two extremes continue to cross; the mixed breed tends to disappear, either by marrying back into the darker race or by approaching the whites through conscious sexual selection, lighter mates always preferred in successive generations.[45]

White prejudice prevented the amalgamation between mulattoes and whites, Weatherly believed, and, relying on Hoffman's statements on Jamaica and Bruce's research on the South, he thought that the number of mulattoes was declining because they were only able to mix with blacks.[46]

Weatherly's vacillation between attributing the problems of racial intermixture to psychological determinants, on one hand, and biological determinants, on the other, was never satisfactorily resolved. Of particular note is his belief that the normal "ethnic-instinct of self-preservation" prevented intermixture between the vast majority of blacks and whites. The term *ethnic-instinct* was typical of the many loose concepts in turn-of-the-century sociology; it was not clear at this date whether the concept of "instinct" referred to an inborn or an acquired action-pattern. Weatherly, for instance, argued that the "ethnic-instinct" was evoked by the white's "consciousness of long stretches of cultural advance which the darker race is deemed incapable of approximating."[47]

Arguments in favor of the desirability of black and white intermarriage, which Weatherly noted had emerged in the writings of Wendell Phillips in the antebellum abolitionist movement, were still offered by some Northern whites. Weatherly, however, discerned a relationship between the size of the black population and the Northern white attitudes toward black and white intermarriage. The conservative Northerner noted that views favoring intermarriage were held "in communities where the Negro never has been found in sufficient numbers to have been the cause of an aroused race consciousness." On the other hand, Southerners, cognizant of the mass of blacks in their midst, opposed intermarriage because they viewed it as a threat to white society. The insistence on the color line by whites, Weatherly conceded, was "often the outgrowth of prejudice and passion rather than scientific analysis." Despite his worry that prejudice and passion might "become a serious social danger," Weatherly felt such actions could be tolerated. It was obvious to him that "for certain societies and for limited periods it can hardly be disputed that the practical identification of racial solidarity with cultural solidarity furnished a wise principle of social action."[48]

The purported nexus between racial solidarity and cultural solidarity, which ignored the black contribution to Southern culture, was a theme that permeated Howard W. Odum's *Social and Mental Traits of the Negro*. Although Odum, like most proponents of the polygenist arguments, stated that "the intermixing of the races has been judged to work to the detriment of both, so far as scientific observations have been possible," he did not elaborate on that statement. He preferred to demonstrate that white attitudes toward social equality militated against intermarriage. Odum argued that the white Southerner felt "that all forms of equality at bottom are based on at least the possibility of intermarriage, which is an impossible admission." Since the "feeling against any forms of social equality" had been "established as strong 'mores,'" such feelings were "impossible to cover in a short period of time." This was the case, Odum contended, because the whole way of life that the white Southerner cherished seemed dependent upon the maintenance of a homogeneous communal existence. Describing that attitude, he waxed: "He that violates it [the social community] is without religion and state. In the keeping of it is the highest culture, religion and conduct; it underlies purity, virtue, traditions, ideals and is also intensified in the social emotions and conduct." Having described the Southern rationale for its bigotry, Odum concluded that "so long as attitude is thus, it is needless to inquire into the advisability of the mixing of the races."[49]

When not dealing explicitly with the polygenist argument, Weatherly's and Odum's writings contain a degree of truth—insofar as they correctly describe the Southern hostility to intermarriage. Their writings give credence to Gunnar Myrdal's "rank order of discrimination" hypothesis, which suggests: "Highest in this order stands the bar against intermarriage and sexual intercourse involving white women."[50] Neither Weatherly nor Odum was critical of the prejudice against intermarriage. They seemed to suggest that this prejudice was a natural part of the social order; consequently it was the *right* attitude. By assuming this uncritical stance they were neglecting what Howard M. Brotz, a recent sociologist, labelled in 1970 "the theoretically elegant solution to the Negro problem": biological assimilation.[51] It seems clear, despite the variability of race relations in the history of the United States, that as long as blacks remain in the country the hostility toward black and white intermarriage will persist. Thus biological assimilation, which would absorb the black population, is merely a theoretical solution. Although one might disagree with Weatherly's and Odum's attitudes toward intermarriage, they, at least, did not underestimate the strength of racial prejudice.

Although Boas did not convince sociologists that assimilation was inevitable and that prejudice would disappear, he anticipated their argumentation after 1920. Of perhaps more significance, he was influential in convincing the leading Northern, professional sociologists that there was an "approximate" equality of whites and nonwhites. This internal development would assume greater significance during the "Great Migration" of blacks to the urban, industrial North after 1915.

NOTES

1. Idus L. Murphree, "The Evolutionary Anthropologists," *Procs. APS* 105, no. 3 (June 1961): 226.

2. Daniel G. Brinton, *The American Race* (New York: N.D.C. Hodges, 1891), 323.

3. Although a solid study of Boas has not been written, there are good studies of his life and works in: Hamilton Cravens, *Triumph of Evolution*; George W. Stocking, Jr., *Race, Culture, and Evolution*, (New York: The Free Press, 1968); Alfred L. Kroeber, "Franz Boas: The Man 1858–1942," Mem. no. 61, AAA, *AA* 45, no. 3, part 2 (July–September 1943); Melville J. Herskovits, *Franz Boas: The Science of Man in the Making* (New York: Charles Scribner's Sons, 1953).

4. Gosset, *Race*, 418.

5. Quoted in Stocking, *Race, Culture, and Evolution*, 143.

6. Leonard Dinnerstein, *Ethnic Americans: A History of Immigration and Assimilation* (New York: Harper and Row, 1982), 37.

7. See, for example, George W. Williams, *History of the Negro Race in America* (New York: G. P. Putnam's Sons, 1882). Other works are listed in Earl E. Thorpe, *Negro Historians in the United States* (Baton Rouge, La.: Fraternal Press, 1958), 14–43.

8. Franz Boas, "Human Faculty as Determined by Race," *Procs. AAAS* 43 (August 1894): 307.

9. Boas, "Human Faculty as Determined by Race," 301–8.

10. Stocking, *Race, Culture and Evolution,* 163–64.

11. Boas, "Human Faculty as Determined by Race," 314.

12. The definitive study of the American School of anthropology is William R. Stanton, *The Leopard's Spots: Scientific Attitudes Toward Race in America, 1815–1859* (Chicago: University of Chicago Press, 1960).

13. Boas, "Human Faculty as Determined by Race," 316. Although Boas did not list the fields in which the men of highest genius reigned, Frank H. Hankins, who was a contemporary of Boas, has suggested in *The Racial Basis of Civilization* (New York: Alfred A. Knopf, 1926), 306–7, that science, philosophy, and artistic masterpieces were the quintessence of culture. George W. Stocking, Jr., admits in *Race, Culture, and Evolution* (193–94) that Boas made a concession to racists, but goes on to imply that by 1911 Boas had thrown aside his racist ideas. See Stocking, ed., *A Franz Boas Reader: The Shaping of American Anthropology, 1883–1911* (Chicago: University of Chicago Press, 1974), 219.

14. Boas, "Human Faculty as Determined by Race," 326.

15. Ibid., 323.

16. Ibid., 324.

17. Stocking, *Race, Culture, and Evolution,* 167–68.

18. Daniel G. Brinton, "The Aims of Anthropology," *Procs. AAAS* 44 (December 1895): 12.

19. Franz Boas, "The Mind of Primitive Man," *JAFL* 14 (January–March 1901): 1–11.

20. Franz Boas, "The Negro and the Demands of Modern Life," *Charities* 15 (7 October 1905): 86.

21. Ibid., 86.

22. Ibid., 87.

23. Franz Boas, "Race Problems in America," *Science,* 28 May 1909, 847–48.

24. Hankins, *The Racial Basis of Civilization,* 323–24.

25. Franz Boas, "What the Negro Has Done in Africa," *The Ethical Record* 5 (March 1904): 106–9; "The Negro's Past," *AUP,* 19 (31 May 1906); "Industries of the African Negroes," *The Southern Workman* 38 (April 1909): 217–29.

26. Boas, "The Negro and the Demands of Modern Life," 86.

27. Boas, "Industries of the African Negroes," 223–24.

28. Ibid., 225.

29. Ibid.

30. Franz Boas, Review of *The Negro Races,* by Jerome Dowd, *PSQ* 23 (December 1908): 729–30.

31. Marvin Harris, *The Rise of Anthropological Theory* (New York: Thomas Y. Crowell, 1968), 298.

32. Charles H. Cooley, "Genius, Fame and the Comparison of Races," *Annals* 9 (May 1897): 3.

33. William I. Thomas, "The Scope and Method of Folk-Psychology," *AJS* 1 (January 1896), 436–43.

34. William I. Thomas, "On a Difference in the Metabolism of the Sexes," *AJS* 3 (January 1897): 31.

35. Charles A. Ellwood, "The Theory of Imitation in Social Psychology," *AJS* 6 (May 1901), 735–36.

36. Ulysses G. Weatherly, "Race and Marriage," *AJS* 15 (January 1910): 438.

37. Ellsworth Faris, "The Mental Capacity of Savages," *AJS* 23 (March 1918): 603; Edward B. Reuter, "The Superiority of the Mulatto," *AJS* 23 (July 1917): 92–93.

38. William I. Thomas, "The Province of Social Psychology," *AJS* 10 (January 1905): 451–53.

39. William I. Thomas, "The Mind of Woman and the Lower Races," *AJS* 12 (January 1907): 438–39.

40. William I. Thomas, "The Significance of the Orient for the Occident," *AJS* 13 (May 1908): 741–42.

41. Boas, "The Negro and the Demands of Modern Life," 87.

42. Sarah Simons, "Social Assimilation, Part II," *AJS* 7:548.

43. Sarah Simons, "Social Assimilation, Part I" *AJS* 6: 803.

44. Weatherly, "Race and Marriage," 445–47.

45. Ibid., 444.

46. Ibid.

47. Ibid., 448–49.

48. Ibid., 447–48.

49. Odum, *Social and Mental Traits of the Negro*, 287–88.

50. Myrdal, *An American Dilemma*, 60.

51. Howard M. Brotz, *The Black Jews of Harlem: Negro Nationalism and the Dilemmas of Negro Leadership* (New York: Schocken Books, 1970), 122.

4

The Dynamics of Change, 1911–1920

During the 1910s, the rise of a naturalistic worldview in the social sciences coincided historically with internal conceptual stresses and social structural changes. These conditions stimulated reassessments of the capabilities of blacks, the analysis of prejudice, and the nature of race relations. The adoption of what historian Edward A. Purcell, Jr., has labelled a "naturalistic and empirically oriented world view" stimulated sociologists to take up the idea that scientific knowledge about man and society must be "objective and based on concrete, universally verifiable data." By embracing a naturalistic worldview, sociologists hoped to equal the achievements of the natural sciences, to justify and protect their position in academia, and to avoid being implicated with government, business, and reform groups for whom they performed important tasks.[1]

The emphasis on the use of empirical data as a basis for authoritative statements on the capabilities of blacks was liberating, insofar as it provided sociologists with a factual basis for their ethical beliefs. Yet it also precipitated a debate over the relative merits of the conflicting assessments of the capabilities of blacks by anthropologists and experimental psychologists, and created tension between Northern and Southern sociologists that had not existed hitherto.

PSYCHOLOGY AND ANTHROPOLOGY ON THE CAPABILITIES OF BLACKS

Since 1895 psychologists had taken interest in comparing the mental processes of blacks and whites. The experimental work on these groups before 1900, however, was crude. Thus the prominent psychologist George O. Ferguson noted in 1916 that the work suf-

fered from "the need of a careful technique in the quantitative hand-
ling of this question," and was "of practically negative value."[2] But
Ferguson was unable to avoid the pitfalls of his precursors. Born in
Leesburg, Virginia, in 1885, he had received his advanced training
at Columbia University under Edward L. Thorndike and James M.
Cattell, both of whom were pioneers in the racial intelligence testing
movement. During the mid-1910s, Ferguson and a group of fellow
Southern-born and Southern-residing men such as Marion J. Mayo,
H. E. Jordan, and Josiah Morse, joined with Northerners such as S.
L. Pressey and T. H. Haines and reached a consensus on the issue of
racial intellectual difference. Lacking any background in anthropology and sociology, they repeated the mistakes of an earlier group of
testers and concluded that blacks were not as intelligent as whites.
Ferguson went on to administer the culturally biased Army Alpha
and Beta tests during World War I and served as the chief psychological examiner in the Army at Camp Lee, Virginia.

Of all the experiments that purported to establish that blacks were
innately inferior to whites, perhaps the most ambitious was conducted by Ferguson. In 1914, he administered a series of psychological tests to 286 whites and 421 blacks in schools in three small
Virginia cities. He compared not only the scores of blacks and whites
on the Woodworth and Wells Mixed Relations Test, the Ebbinghaus
Completion Test, the Cattell and Farrand Cancellation Test, and the
Columbia Maze Test, but also the scores of "sub-classes" of blacks.
On the basis of this limited study, Ferguson concluded that "the
average performance of the colored population of this country in
such intellectual work as that represented by the tests of higher
capacity, appears to be about three-fourths as efficient as the performance of whites of the same amount of training." Even this estimate, he went on to conjecture, was probably "too high rather than
too low."[3]

In order to test the corollary to the argument of the inherent mental inferiority of blacks, the Virginian divided blacks into four subclasses—pure Negroes, Negroes three-fourths pure, mulattoes proper, and quadroons. His classifications were made mainly on the
basis of skin color, though he also took into consideration hair texture and cranial conformation. Ferguson found that, among the
students he tested, those who had the "greater amount of white
blood scored nearer to the white norm." He conceded that it was
certainly possible that the lighter Negroes had a higher social status
than the darker Negroes, but since he believed (and this was an
erroneous belief) that most blacks did not make "social distinctions
based on color," he was certain that the lighter Negroes had achieved
their social status because "of their greater capacity."[4]

To Ferguson, the fact that Negroes—even the lighter subclasses—on the average scored lower than whites on intelligence tests had definite implications for public policy. To attempt to "raise the scholastic attainment of the negro through literary education," the Southern psychologist argued, was futile, since "education cannot create mental power, but only develop that which is innate." Although a group of Negroes, which for the most part would be composed of mulattoes, were capable of pursuing a literary education, a more viable alternative for the mass of Negroes that would "avoid great waste" was industrial education.[5] Psychology was supporting Brooker T. Washington's position just as anthropology was beginning to undercut his position.

The psychological testing of blacks and whites, which was in its infancy, was flawed by methodological deficiencies. As his critics would later point out, Ferguson, in comparing the scores of blacks and whites, had completely negated the socioeconomic differences between the groups. Furthermore, his division of blacks into four subclasses was based on a commonsense assessment of dubious criteria—skin color, hair texture, and cranial conformation—rather than on a more reliable examination of genealogical data. And even if one accepted the validity of Ferguson's subclasses, it is still questionable whether the higher scores of the lighter Negroes were due to their higher socioeconomic status, rather than to the infusion of white blood. Pointing to an even more critical error that psychologists like Ferguson committed, the anthropologist Ashley Montagu has stated that "IQ tests were ethnocentrically structured, and therefore, unfair when applied to members of ethnic groups other than those of the cultures upon which they had been standardized."[6] Assuming that intelligence tests were valid indicators of inherent mental ability, psychologists and their followers in sociology were wedded to the racist argument until late in the 1920s. Describing the racial attitudes of scholars in psychology, Rhett S. Jones has argued cogently that "White psychologists . . . usually concluded that Blacks were lesser men than Whites. They cited a battery of experiments to prove these arguments. Results to the contrary were argued away."[7]

Fortunately, anthropologists such as Franz Boas and Alfred L. Kroeber presented assessments of race and culture that provided different explanations of behavior from those of psychologists. In 1911, Boas's *The Mind of Primitive Man* was published. It contained large segments of his major articles on race and culture. Thus, it is not surprising that his statements on genius and the probability of differences in the mental makeup of blacks and whites contain statements that explicitly indicate that the races did not

have identical aptitudes.[8] Nonetheless, his idea of the "approximate" equality of blacks and whites was a persistent theme in the
creed of most sociologists and anthropologists for the next twenty
generations.

Boas's confusion on the problem of the capabilities of blacks was
avoided by Alfred Kroeber, who was developing his reputation as one
of the leading American cultural anthropologists. Kroeber, a former
student of Boas, was of German Protestant ancestry. It is therefore
not surprising that in 1915, during the midst of pervasive anti-
German feeling in the United States, Kroeber saw the necessity of
casting aside racial dogma in order to protect members of his immigrant group. In a short article entitled "Eighteen Professions," which
appeared in *American Anthropologist*, Kroeber delineated the assumptions that distinguished history—a title that embraced history
proper, historical anthropology, and sociology—from psychology
and biology. Kroeber insisted that the historian had to assume "the
absolute equality of and identify of all human races and strains as
carriers of civilization." On an ideological level, he was transforming
the Boasian skeptical position into a credo that distinguished his
left-liberal position from those of mainstream Progressivism. Kroeber went on to argue that the equality of the races had not been
proved or disproved. Although hereditary and cultural factors were
so "closely intertwined," they had not "yet been sufficiently separated to allow demonstration of the efficiency of either." Thus, scholarly opinions on the issue of racial differences were mere "convictions falsely fortified by subjectively interpreted evidence." Biologists
necessarily had to assume "at least some hereditary difference." The
historian, on the other hand, could not assume they existed "until
such differences are established and exactly defined."[9]

What emerged from Kroeber's article was a worldview in which
scholars in "history" would assume that cultural explanations were
far more cogent arguments for differences in ethnic groups than the
concept of race. The culture concept, which emphasized the roles of
traditions and habits in determining human behavior, could explain human differences far more precisely than the biological sciences. On an ideological level, the culture concept emerged during a
period when Boas and Kroeber, both of whom were pro-immigrant,
extended to nonwhite peoples a compensatory explanation for their
status.

THE BOASIAN CRITIQUE IN SOCIOLOGY

On the issue of racial capabilities, progressive anthropologists
were opposed to psychologists. For sociologists, however, the problem was far more complex. The complexity of resolving the issue of

black capabilities stemmed from the ethnic and sectional backgrounds of the partisans, the movement toward naturalism, and social structural changes that affected blacks.

The adoption of an empirical worldview by sociologists certainly contributed to the infusion of the Boasian position on the capabilities of blacks into the sociology department at the University of Chicago. Founded in 1892, the Department of Sociology and Anthropology at Chicago had emerged by 1910 as the major center for the study of sociology in the United States. With the recruitment of Ernest W. Burgess, Ellsworth Faris, and Robert E. Park in the 1910s, Chicago had attracted scholars who would shape the study of race and race relations until World War II. Furthermore, such prominent scholars in race relations as E. Franklin Frazier, Charles S. Johnson, Oliver C. Cox, and Bertram Doyle received their advanced training at Chicago under Burgess, Faris, and Park.

William I. Thomas seemed to be the conduit between sociologists at Chicago and Franz Boas and his followers. As early as 1912, his writings reflected the influence of Boas. Thomas, a Southerner, believed that the concept of temperament was relevant in the discussion of the capabilities of blacks and whites. Yet he argued in an article in the *American Journal of Sociology* that "individual variation is of more importance than racial difference, and the main factors in social change are attention, interest, stimulation, occupational differentiation, mental attitude, and accessibility to opportunities and copies." And he appended a statement as a final dismissal of the discussion of racial mental differences: "Present-day anthropology does not pretend that any characteristic mental powers, such as memory, inhibition, abstraction, logical ability, are feeble in any race." When Thomas spoke of "present-day anthropology," he was referring to the work of Boas, whose article, "The Mind of Primitive Man," had appeared in the *Journal of American Folk-Lore* in 1901. That article, which Thomas quoted extensively in the footnotes in his text, was the foundation of his environmentalist beliefs.[10]

Robert E. Park also eschewed the idea of the total intellectual inferiority of blacks. This fact is evident in an article written for the *Publications of the American Sociological Society* in 1918, in which he asserted that the anthropological, ethnological, and theological literature emphasizing the intellectual inferiority of blacks was of value only because it revealed the "distortion of sentiment and opinion which the racial conflict has produced in the black man and the white." Even psychological tests, such as those administered by George O. Ferguson, were still highly speculative and on the whole inconclusive. Park therefore concluded that the "question remains where Boaz [sic] left it when he said that the black was little, if any, inferior to the white man in intellectual capacity and in any case, racial as compared with individual differences were small and relatively unimportant."[11]

An important question emerges from Park's comments. For whom were those "small" differences "relatively unimportant?" Surely blacks who aspired and had the ability to rise above the bulk of both the black and white populations could not find much comfort in such statements. Even more important than the fact that Park, like Boas, refused to raise the real issues that emerged from the "men of high genius" hypothesis was that he ignored or was not aware of Alfred Kroeber's charge to assume the equality of races.

Nevertheless, it is significant to note that Park was especially critical of the claims of psychologists. In a long review of George O. Ferguson's "The Psychology of the Negro," Park argued in the *American Journal of Sociology* in 1917 that "the fact is that the justification for segregation and separate education of the Negro is sociological and not biological. The principal reason for the separate education of the Negro is the existence of a racial prejudice which makes it difficult for the colored student, except in special cases, to act unrestrainedly to work without strain in the midst of a group of white students."[12] Although Park asserted that biological arguments were not relevant in the discussion of "separate but equal" schools, he still defended the practice of segregation on sociological grounds.

Despite his penchant for sociological arguments, Park could not escape the pitfalls of racial determinism. Park believed that blacks, like other races, possessed a distinctive racial temperament. For Park, "fundamental temperamental qualities" were the "basis of interest and attention," and acted "as selective agencies" that determined "what elements in the cultural environment each race will select; in what region it will seek and find its vocation in the larger social organization."[13] Describing the purported temperament that had persisted within the black race from Africa to America, Park asserted:

Everywhere and always it [the black race] had been interested rather in expression than in action; interested in life itself rather than its reconstruction or reformation. The negro is, by natural disposition, neither an intellectual nor an idealist, like the Jew; nor a brooding introspective like the East Indian; nor a pioneer and frontiersman, like the Anglo-Saxon. He is primarily an artist; loving life for its own sake. His *metier* is expression rather than action. He is, so to speak, the lady among the races.[14]

Although Park did not acknowledge that his concept of the black racial temperament had been delineated by W.E.B. DuBois, it is obvious that their concepts were quite similar; for DuBois had written in 1913 that "the Negro is primarily an artist. The usual way of putting this is to speak disdainfully of his sensuous nature. This means that the only race which has held at bay the life destroying forces of the tropics, has gained therefrom in some slight compensation a sense of beauty, particularly for sound and color, which characterizes the race."[15] However, unlike DuBois, who was attempting to extend to the Afro-American underdogs a racial explanation for their achievements, Park was attempting to make scholars aware of the need to study the "heritages and backgrounds" of American immigrant groups. Nonetheless, the appeal of a recent historian, Fred H. Matthews, to accept the validity of Park's stereotype of blacks cannot be easily rationalized, for it is obvious that Park had succumbed to racist sentiments.[16] It is true, though, that Park was convinced that the dissipation of the racial temperament would be inevitable once blacks were dispersed within the white population. "When . . . society grows and is perpetuated by immigration and adaptation," he predicted, "there ensues, as a result of miscegenation, a breaking up of the complex of the biologically inherited qualities which constitute the temperament of the race."[17]

Park had attempted to establish that the vast majority of blacks in the post–Civil War era, hampered by their lack of intimate contact with whites and their own temperamental qualities, failed to conform to the behavioral patterns of the white majority. Yet the black population exhibited—and Park noted this time and again—cultural heterogeneity. Edward B. Reuter, one of Park's graduate students, attempted to substantiate Park's point of view. In 1917, the Missourian Reuter observed:

While the bulk of the [black] race in America is as yet not many steps removed from the African standard, there has nevertheless arisen a considerable middle class, which conforms in most essential respects to the conventional middle class standards of American people, as well as a small intellectual group, some members of which have succeeded in coming within measurable distance of the best models of European culture.

On the basis of his empirical investigation of blacks in the arts, professions, business, and politics, Reuter concluded that the progressive group of blacks was composed almost entirely of mulattoes. Entitled "The Superiority of the Mulatto," Reuter's article, which appeared in the *American Journal of Sociology*, was devoted to determining the cause of the mulattoes' superior achievements.[18]

Reuter asserted that two possible explanations for the disparity between the achievements of the mulattoes and blacks emanated from the contemporary controversy over racial mental differences. On the basis of experimental psychological evidence suggesting that blacks were inherently inferior to whites, it could be argued that superiority of the mulattoes to blacks was attributable to the inherent mental superiority of their white ancestors. Reuter did not find those conclusions convincing. He felt that line of investigation was "still in its initial stage." Further refinement in the technique by which the studies are made, he surmised, "may show that all modifying cultural elements have not been eliminated." Even at present, "granting all that these studies seem to show," Reuter insisted, "the difference in capacity is not sufficient to account for the observed divergence in status and attainment between the yellow and black groups."[19] In contrast to the experimental psychologists, anthropologists and sociologists held the opinion that races, for the most part, were intellectual equals. From this point of view, it could be argued that mulattoes were neither superior to nor inferior to either of the parent races. The superiority of mulattoes to blacks thus had to be explained in terms of their greater opportunities.[20]

Although Reuter agreed that the races were intellectual equals, he thought that the argument overemphasized the opportunity factor. To Reuter, it was possible to argue for the essential mental equality of blacks and whites and still account for the inherent superiority of mulattoes if one took into account the sexual selection process that characterized black and white relationships. The original mulatto population came into existence as the result of the extramarital affairs of white males and black women. On the Caucasian side, the mulattoes' ancestry was mainly composed of lower class whites. On the Negro side, however, their ancestry was the "best of the race." What had happened when miscegenation began was that white males had mated with the "choicest" black females, and over time white males repeatedly mated with the choicest black and mulatto females. This purportedly resulted in the production of a "choicer and choicer type of female." Since Reuter thought a "correlation maintains between physical perfection and mental superiority," he argued that the mulattoes' mental superiority was inherited from their black female ancestry. In accounting for the perpetuation of this inherently superior group, Reuter emphasized the marriage selection process. Mulattoes, believing they were superior to blacks, attempted to avoid intimate contact with them. Although mulattoes generally tended to marry within their own group, a significant number of blacks with superior endowments, seeking the prestige of the mulatto group, succeeded in marrying mulatto women.[21]

Although Reuter had attributed the alleged superiority of mulattoes to their inheritance from the black side of their ancestry, one of the leading black sociologists of the period was still critical of his findings. In a review of Reuter's *The Mulatto in the United States*

(1918), Kelly Miller of Howard University raised important objections to that work which also had import for the 1917 article. Writing in the *American Journal of Sociology* in 1919, Miller pointed out the process by which Reuter separated mulattoes from blacks was "unexplained." Such a separation was perhaps impossible, he argued, because few blacks possessed the genealogical data that would verify claims of white ancestry, and also because there was "no scientific test of blood composition." Indeed, some men that Reuter classified as mulattoes, Miller was certain, were full-blooded Negroes. Also questionable was Reuter's attempt to minimize the significance of the opportunity factor in determining the mulattoes' social status. Miller argued that the mulatto "received every initiatory advantage over his black brother." Before the Civil War some mulattoes were educated and sent to the free states; numerous others obtained free Negro status. "Small wonder then," Miller concluded, "that they became the first leaders of the Negro race of the generation immediately following freedom."[22]

Although most Northern, professional sociologists thought that they had established the "approximate" equality of blacks and whites, there were still some in the North who held the reactionary beliefs that had characterized the racial thought of the 1900s. Representative of that group was Charles H. Cooley. As late as 1918, Cooley was mulling over the issue of whether there were mental differences between the races. "It is even possible to doubt whether there is any important physical difference among the several branches of mankind," he conceded. But he was certain that "spiritual differences" (the products of sociohistorical forces), separated the races. The existence of so-called spiritual differences between the races did not mean that there were no racial differences. Cooley contended it was possible to confuse the two: "And as race differences, when present, are always accompanied by historical differences, it is not possible to make out just how much is due to them alone." Cooley also admitted that racial theories stressing the unlikeness of temperament and capacity between whites and blacks were "the judgment of common sense . . . incapable of demonstration"; yet he assumed that the "divergence in cranial and facial type may reasonably be supposed to mean *something*, however unfair may be their interpretation by white people." Without sufficient data to establish his case, Cooley reasoned "from general principles" that since the races had "been bred apart for thousands of years" and had become differentiated physically, they were not "just alike as to innate mental traits." Indeed, Cooley's analogy was quite similar to that of Boas, yet he proceeded to ask: "Why should races be presumed equal in mental and moral capacity when family stocks in the same race are so evidently unequal in these respects?"[23] Although Boas would eventually undermine that analogy, it is clear that for the reactionaries such arguments purportedly refuted the environmentalist theory.

Most prominent sociologists, however, believed that the argument of black intellectual inferiority was untenable. Furthermore, they attacked one of the corollaries of the black inferiority argument—the idea of African inferiority. The myth of African inferiority had been under attack by Franz Boas in the 1900s; in fact, Boas's interpretation of African life set a precedent for the discussions that took place during World War I. The progressive scholars minimized the purported mental differences between West Africans and whites and uncovered evidence suggesting that the historical achievements of West Africans were both high and substantial. George E. Howard's statements concerning West Africans were typical of the views of the more progressive sociologists in the late 1910s on the issue of the capabilities of blacks. Although he did not document his sources, Howard insisted in the *American Journal of Sociology*, in 1917, that "the proverbs of the natives of the Guinea coast, the ancestors of so many of the southern freedmen, reveal a capacity for abstraction, for generalization equal to that of the Anglo-Saxon makers of the Shakespeare folklore."[24]

An influential Northern-based sociologist of Southern background who agreed, in part, with Howard's position was Ellsworth Faris. Unlike most sociologists who wrote about West Africans, Faris had lived in that region of Africa; from 1897 to 1904, the native Tennessean was a missionary to the Congo, where he observed the lives of the tribes of the Upper Congo River. While teaching at the State University of Iowa in 1918, the future chairman of the Department of Sociology at the University of Chicago published an article, "The Mental Capacity of Savages," in the *American Journal of Sociology*.

In the article, Faris pointed out that the works of J. R. Angell, Franz Boas, John Dewey, and William I. Thomas corroborated the results of his investigations of the tribes of the Upper Congo River. Despite his use of the pejorative term *savage*, Faris wrote:

The hypothesis that has been forming . . . in recent years concerning the mind of so-called primitive man, meaning the uncivilized races of the present day, is that in native endowment the savage child is, on the average, about the same in capacity as the child of civilized races. Instead of the concept of different stages or degrees of mentality, we find it easier to think of the human being, in its capacity, about the same everywhere, the difference in culture to be explained in terms of physical geography, or the stimuli of other groups, or the unaccountable occurrence of great men.

Nonetheless, like his fellow Southerner Howard W. Odum, Faris thought psychology could provide better insights into the issue of differences between blacks and whites. He believed that experiments that correlated the differences in brain weights with differences in mental capacities, and mental and physical tests—such as those given to the natives of the Torres Strait by the Cambridge University Expedition in 1898—had potential for establishing the existence of differences in the mental capacities of white and nonwhite peoples.[25]

Perhaps the fullest expression of the Boasian position on West Africans was put forth in W.E.B. DuBois's small volume, *The Negro*, published in 1915. DuBois explicitly acknowledged his debt to Boas in 1939, when he stated in *Black Folk: Then and Now*, "Franz Boas came to Atlanta University where I was teaching in 1906 and said to a graduating class: 'You need not be ashamed of your African past'; and then he recounted the history of the black kingdoms of the Sahara for a thousand years. I was too astonished to speak."[26] DuBois began with the assumption that he was writing about "a normal human stock, and that whatever it is fair to predicate of the mass of human beings may be predicated to the Negro."[27] Influenced by Boas's treatment of the African kingdoms in his address at Atlanta University in 1906,[28] DuBois depicted the evolution of the kingdoms of the Sudan. He based his accounts of the historical achievements of Ghana, Mali, Songhay, and smaller kingdoms of West Africa on the observations of the fourteenth-century Arab traveler Ibn Batuta and the German Africanist Leo Frobenius. Despite the historical value of these men's works, DuBois bitterly concluded, "most of this splendid history of civilization and uplift is unknown today, and men confidently assert that Negroes have no history."[29]

With the publication of DuBois's work, the foundations of the African inferiority argument began to quake. The proslavery and Jim Crow arguments that appeared frequently during the 1900s could no longer be based rationally on the assumption of the innate inferiority of West Africans. Boas's followers had taken the evolutionary anthropologists to task on their own terms. Where the evolutionists had assumed the primitiveness of African life, the Boasians had found substantial historical and ethnological evidence that contradicted the evolutionists' arguments. With the ascendancy of the liberal humanitarian argument after World War I—when doubts about the superiority of Western civilization were growing—the way was paved for the reinterpretation of African life.

Despite sociologists' flirtation with racism during the 1910s, their ideas on the intellectual capacity of blacks changed perceptibly. Some scholars assume that anthropology, through the diffusion of the culture idea, had created a new paradigm for the social sciences.

While such statements are somewhat true, they ignore the external factors that impinged on the issue of black capabilities. The movement towards empiricism not only resulted in an alliance between progressive anthropologists and sociologists, but it also stimulated interest in the social structural changes affecting blacks.

During the years 1911 to 1919, several forces pushed and pulled blacks out of the South into urban-industrial areas in the North where most competent sociologists taught. The push came from the oppressive and exploitative conditions in the South; not only was widespread legal and extralegal violence perpetrated against blacks, but they also felt the brunt of extreme economic discrimination. The chief force pulling many blacks into the North was the shortage of unskilled labor. Although the migration of blacks from the South to the North had increased steadily from 1870 through 1910, by 1915, when the World War began to impede the flow of cheap labor from Europe, and when many immigrants returned to their homelands to take part in the conflict, larger numbers of blacks were recruited to take the places left vacant in Northern industries. Even more blacks came North after 1917 when industries began expanding as the United States entered the conflict. The net increase in the black population in the North during the years 1910 to 1920 was 321,890. The effects of the migration of many blacks to the North after 1920 were to begin the nationalization of the so-called Negro problem, to precipitate black racial consciousness (as manifested in the Garvey Movement), and to stimulate the development of progressive sociological theories by Afro-Americans on race and race relations.

As early as 1913, the *Annals* devoted an issue to the study of blacks. Entitled "The Negro's Progress in Fifty Years," the issue's contributors included such black sociologists as George E. Haynes, R. R. Wright, Jr., W.E.B. DuBois, Monroe N. Work, and Kelly Miller, and such white Northern sociologists such as James P. Lichtenberger and Robert E. Park. In their articles the sociologists drew on empirical evidence to buttress their argument that blacks had made tremendous progress since emancipation. Their empirical worldview essentially reinforced their progressive evolutionist theory.

Black sociologists were especially fascinated by the progress brought about by the urbanization of blacks in both the North and the South. George E. Haynes, who had received his doctorate from Columbia University in 1912, worked for the National Urban League (an organization dedicated to finding labor for black migrants), and later taught economics and sociology at Fisk University, believed that tremendous obstacles confronted blacks in the cities. Nonetheless, he argued that the "successes . . . in both industry and trade are multiplying and with substantial encouragement may change the rule to exception in the teeth of excessive handicaps." He went on to assert that "judging from the studies of Negro enterprises made in Philadelphia and in New York City and from widespread attendance upon the annual meetings of the National Negro Business League, substantial progress is triumphing over unusual obstacles."[30]

Most blacks who were migrating to Northern cities were unskilled laborers, however. This did not daunt the optimism of the proponents of progress. R. R. Wright, Jr., an African Methodist Episcopal minister who had received his doctorate from the University of Pennsylvania in 1912, expressed optimism concerning the prospects for black unskilled labor in the Northern cities:

Unskilled Negro labor has invaded the Northern cities within the past fifty years, and while it has been with extreme difficulty that the skilled laborer has found a place, the Negro unskilled laborer has been a welcome guest. In nearly every large city, special employment agencies have been opened in order to induce Negro workers from the South to come North, where there is abundant public work to be done, on the streets, sewers, filter plants, subways, railroads, etc. Negro hodcarriers have almost driven whites out of business in some cities, while as teamsters, firemen and street cleaners, they are more and more in demand. In the hotel business, the Negro is in demand in the large cities, as waiter, bellman, etc., while the Negro women are more and more in demand as domestic servants.[31]

To Wright, the suggestion that the mass of black unskilled labor was stagnant was fallacious because of the "degree of respect given much unskilled work among Negroes." Indeed, he argued that "this group of unskilled workers has shared something of the progress of the group."[32]

The idea that black progress was not restricted to unskilled labor and business was documented in W.E.B. DuBois's article, "The Negro in Literature and Art." After surveying the achievements and progress blacks had made in literature and art, DuBois pointed to discrimination in those vocations, concluding: "So the sum of accomplishment is but an imperfect indication of what the Negro race is capable of in America and in the world."[33]

White Northern sociologists such as James P. Lichtenberger, Robert E. Park, and George E. Howard also thought that blacks had made tremendous progress since emancipation. Lichtenberger, the native of Macon County, Illinois, who taught sociology at the University of Pennsylvania, had transferred many of his moral concerns from the pulpit to the classroom; throughout his graduate training under Franklin H. Giddings during the 1900s, he had been an itinerant minister of Disciples of Christ churches in Illinois and New York.

In his article "Negro Illiteracy in the United States," Lichtenberger, who was a proponent of an objective sociology, noted that black illiteracy had declined significantly (from 95 percent to 30.4 percent) since emancipation. He believed that the decline was not due "solely to his [the black's] own desire, nor to his inherent capacity but must be regarded in the light of his imitative ability and the opportunities afforded for his advancement by the population in the midst of which he lives." Lichtenberger did not attempt to comment in detail on his stereotypes of blacks, and he refused to predict what the status of blacks would have been without the aid of whites. But he did conclude that when environmental conditions were taken into account to explain the differences in illiteracy between blacks and whites, "the supposed evidence of race difference disappears." The rate of black illiteracy was a function of the distribution of the group in various geographical regions and in urban and rural areas. Black illiteracy was ten times higher than white illiteracy because 89.5 percent of blacks, as compared to 32 percent of whites, were living in the South, where the educational facilities were inadequate for both groups. That opportunities for a quality education were of significance in determining the amount of illiteracy was revealed when he compared the illiteracy rate of Northern blacks with that of the white population of the South. The rate for the former was 10.5 percent; for the latter it was 7.7 percent. To Lichtenberger, it was "clear that if there was an equal distribution either of population or of educational opportunities, much of the differences in the rates between the races would disappear." Turning to the distribution of blacks and whites in urban and rural areas, he found that 82.3 percent of the blacks lived in rural areas, while the figure for the white population was 37.7 percent. Since rural educational facilities were inferior to those in urban areas, Lichtenberger believed it was "safe to assume . . . that if the distribution of Negroes in regard to urban and rural conditions approximated that of the whole population, or of the native whites of native parentage, that the differences in illiteracy would be considerably diminished." Despite the fact that inadequate facilities retarded the decline of black illiteracy, Lichtenberger contended that on the basis of the census data for the period 1880 to 1910, "it will require only a few decades more to bring the rate down to the level of that for the country as a whole at the present time and below that of foreign born." Taking to task the proponents of black degeneracy, he concluded that the intellectual achievements of blacks since slavery offered "little ground for complaint or discouragement but rather a just feeling of satisfaction and optimism."[34]

Robert E. Park tried to account for the improvement in home life and standard of living among blacks. Park drew distinctions between the different classes of blacks and insisted that in order to understand "the social standards, the degree of culture and comfort which the Negro peasant, the Negro artisan, business and professional man enjoy today," one had "to take account of those earlier, ante-bellum conditions out of which they sprang." For the vast majority of blacks, whose progenitors were field hands, conditions varied according to the locale in which they lived. Park described the homes of black peasants in Southwestern Virginia and the Sea Islands of South Carolina as "comfortable"; while those in the "up-country" of Alabama were depicted as "rude huts." Nonetheless, there was a group of black farmers in both the North and the South who had achieved a high standard of living. Typical of that group was one farmer in Edwardsville, Kansas, who had recently "erected a handsome modern house which has been described as 'twenty-two room palace overlooking a 503 acre farm.'" Typical of the "thrifty" black artisans, who were the descendants of the antebellum skilled workers, was a man who lived "in a neat five-room cottage" which he owned. The black middle class, which was descended from free blacks and privileged slaves in Charleston, Baltimore, Washington, D.C., Philadelphia, New York City, and New Orleans, lived in "comfortable" homes. Although Park admitted that in all large cities and in all small towns in the South the "multitudes of Negroes . . . live meanly and miserably," he still believed that there was cause for optimism. "The Negro," Park concluded, "has made great progress in many directions during the past half century, but nowhere more so than in his home, and nowhere, it may be added, do the fruits of education show to better advantage than in the home of the educated Negro."[35]

It is clear that Park had undermined not only the idea of the homogeneity of the black population, but that he had also, despite the stereotypes he often utilized, demonstrated that all blacks were not degenerates. But the task of enjoining the moderate antiracist argument emanating from the internal influence of Boasian anthropology, and the evidence of black progress, which was precipitated by external forces affecting the lives of blacks, was left to George E. Howard. In an article published in the *American Journal of Sociology* in 1917, Howard, who taught at the University of Nebraska, took one of the progressive positions. Influenced by the works of scholars such as Boas (to whom he oddly made no specific reference), the former lawyer and historian wrote: "People differ in their planes of cultural development, not in their inherent capacity for development." In other words, terms such as *high* and *low* were descriptive of a group's rank in a cultural hierarchy, rather than its inherent abilities. Holding that all groups had the capacity to attain the highest level of cultural development—i.e., civilization—he argued that the "existing differences in mental or moral status between brown and yellow, black and white, Oriental and Occidental, appear as the resultants of variations in environment, institutions, experience, opportunity." For Howard, the most conclusive proof of the abilities of blacks was provided by the evidence of their educational progress. Drawing on a quote taken from Monroe N. Work's article in the "Fifty Years of Negro Progress" issue that appeared in the *Annals* in 1913, Howard concluded: "Such a picture as that is surely good cause for pride and an eloquent assurance to the future."[36]

The arguments concerning the capabilities of blacks and whites were often determined, as they had been in the 1900s, by the commentators' region of birth. Despite the fact that Southern-born, professional sociologists such as William I. Thomas, Howard W. Odum, and Ellsworth Faris often admitted that cultural determinism was a sound alternative to hereditary determinism, they did not embrace the idea that the progress of blacks was sufficient to compel them to argue that blacks deserved first-class citizenship during this period. Perhaps their early experiences in the South, in which the idea of the superiority of whites was embedded at an early age, prevented them from accepting the obvious evidence of black progress at this early juncture.

Most Southerners tended to hold that there were significant mental differences between blacks and whites; yet despite this tendency, their writings reflected the tension between the hereditarian and environmental perspectives. Most revealing in this regard was an article by Howard W. Odum, who was teaching at the University of Georgia. His "Negro Children in the Public Schools of Philadelphia," published in the *Annals* in 1913, was an experimental study comparing not only the attendance and progress of white and black children, but also their scores on the Binet, Ebbinghaus, and Thorndike aptitude tests. Odum's assessment of his results clearly reveals the tension in his thought between strict environmentalism and the Lamarckian doctrine of the inheritance of acquired characteristics. As a strict environmentalist, he attributed the failure of black children to fare as well as white children in school attendance and academic progress to the influence of their home environments. This led him to comment that "injustice would be done to Negro children if harsh judgment be passed upon them because they do not maintain the standard of white children." But Odum felt that the influence of the different home environments could not account for the differences in the performances between white and black children on aptitude tests. As a proponent of the Lamarckian doctrine, he argued that because blacks had lived under a different environment "for many generations," the mental aptitude that black children inherited was lower than that of white children. "Apparently the Negro children," he assumed, "found it difficult to go beyond their inheritance of simple mental processes and physical growth." For Odum, this did not suggest that black children were not capable of improving their performances on aptitude tests; the performances of some black children, along with the "theory of the plasticity of human types"—a theory for which he found support in the writings of Franz Boas—suggested "great possibilities in the development of the Negro." Odum concluded that the development of the mental capacity of black children to its fullest could be brought about by the construction of an environment in which the simple mental processes would be "coordinated," which would "lead to a higher degree of intellectuality."[37] Curiously, Odum avoided the issue of whether blacks would reach the aptitude level of whites.

Even William I. Thomas, who held liberal views on racial mental differences, did not think that blacks had made sufficient progress since emancipation. Like his fellow Southern sociologists, Thomas believed that emancipation was a crisis that blacks failed to turn to an advantage. Thomas admitted that blacks "had not been properly prepared for freedom." Such preparation would have required time for the education of blacks. "This education," Thomas insisted, "was not necessarily a matter of schooling, but rather of general opportunity." Furthermore, he argued that the habits of slavery limited the present effectiveness of blacks as laborers. Since blacks in slavery, he claimed, had "never worked at a high rate of energy even under the lash," during freedom they had been unable to develop the "pace" of other competitive groups. The condition of blacks was aggravated because they had also acquired the "worse qualities" of their former masters. They had, Thomas suggested, "imitated the leisure, drink and classical learning of the white rather than his working habits." Making an obvious reference to the strategy of Booker T. Washington, Thomas concluded: "The best Negro schools are now working out for the masses of the race, at least, a system which includes only those elements of the white culture which the Negro can use in his life as he will probably lead it."[38]

Despite the Northern–Southern split over the issue of whether blacks had made sufficient progress since slavery, it is clear that most prominent sociologists in the last decade of the Progressive Era had adopted the Boasian idea of the "approximate" equality of blacks and whites. For these sociologists, the idea of black intellectual inferiority was overstated and as a consequence, the capabilities of blacks were no longer viewed as permanent obstacles to their assimilation.

NORTHERN AND SOUTHERN THEORISTS OF RACE RELATIONS

The idea that "social equality" should not take place in the South permeated the writings of most Southern social theorists during the 1910s, despite the looming demise of racist theories. They did not think it was necessary at all times to use the argument of black inferiority to justify the perpetuation of their traditional social order. Although theories of black inferiority were interwoven ever so subtly, the Southern social theorists were content, for the most part, to view white prejudice as the key factor in determining the nature of race relations, for white prejudice was viewed as a natural reaction to a fundamentally different race. In view of the fact that prejudice was assumed to be natural, they argued that the system of segregation, despite the restrictions it placed on blacks, was a justifiable and necessary substitute for slavery. The alternative to segregation or caste was threatening, since it raised the possibility of social equality. Social equality opened up the possibility of intermarriage, a possibility that Southern social theorists hoped to avoid, for they believed their civilization was somehow built and sustained by homogeneous group life.

Jerome Dowd thought it was necessary to defend the Jim Crow system that arose in areas where blacks concentrated in large numbers. Dowd believed demographic factors determined the attitudes of whites and the system that emerged to dictate the relations between the races. In a review of Sir Harry J. Johnston's *The Negro in the New World* that appeared in the *American Journal of Sociology* in 1911, Dowd defended the Southern racial policy on the issue of social equality. Johnston's work contained sections critical of the Southern treatment of blacks. Dowd remarked that it was "now out of fashion to condemn the South for proscriptions against the Negro which obtain throughout the North and West wherever the Negroes are found in considerable numbers." It seemed obvious to Dowd

that if only a small number of Negroes lived in the South, they would be objects of curiosity, as they are in London, Paris, and Boston, and southern men would no more hesitate to sit in banquet with an African prince than did King Edward; and, having nothing to fear or suffer from such social freedom, all proscriptive laws and customs would be abolished and the southern people could then facilitate themselves on their superiority to the rest of the world.[39]

The idea that whites had something to "fear or suffer" by treating blacks as social equals in areas where they constituted a sizeable part of the population, which was suggested by Dowd, was supported by Lafayette College's John M. Mecklin. The Mississippian, a professor of philosophy who was an ordained Presbyterian minister, was the chief spokesman for the perpetuation of the *Herrenvolk* democracy in the South; he was an ardent defender of individual freedom for whites, and, at the same time, an advocate of black subjugation. In his article "The Philosophy of the Color Line," published in the *American Journal of Sociology* in 1913, Mecklin analyzed English attitudes toward blacks from a comparative perspective. He concluded: "Wherever the white of English stock has been brought into contact with masses of Negroes and however the geographic, economic, or political conditions have differed, we find . . . the stubborn opposition to group fusion and the strenuous insistence upon the supremacy of his group ideals." The attitudes of Southern whites and those of the British toward their colonial subjects, especially in South Africa, convinced him of the truth of that generalization.[40]

The nature of race relations in the various white-controlled areas differed, however, depending on the type of government instituted. Race relations were smoother in Jamaica, where the British had implanted a "paternalistic regime," than in the Southern United States and South Africa, where the races coexisted "under democratic institutions." Mecklin insisted that the nature of race relations in Jamaica was mild because throughout most of its history whites were the "complete and undisputed masters of its destiny." In response to British paternalism, Mecklin thought, blacks had accepted white domination "as part of the eternal order of things." Since there was no conflict over status, friction between the races was minimal. Indeed, Mecklin went so far as to argue that a situation similar to Jamaica existed on the plantations in the Black Belt of the South, despite the egalitarian pronouncements of the Constitution.[41]

Race relations in the United States differed from those in Jamaica, Mecklin argued on historical grounds, because of the North's efforts during Reconstruction to imbue blacks with social and political ideals. The color line was thus a means of remedying the purported adverse effects of the Reconstruction period; it was an "effort of the ruling group to make the black constantly aware of his subordinate status and actually restrict him in the absence of legal means." Mecklin asserted that the "real motive . . . was not so much to humiliate the black or to perpetuate the social habits of slavery; the determining factor was the practical necessity of finding and maintaining a *modus vivendi* between a race with long training in the exercise of democratic liberties and another without training and forced by disabilities of its own to occupy indefinitely a subordinate place in the social order." Since Reconstruction, Mecklin thought, the nation as a whole had come to view the "dominance of the white group as the prerequisite of anything like satisfactory relations between the races."[42]

Mecklin believed that the South was destined to be a divided society in which the black occupied a lower social status than the white because of the necessity of maintaining the social order. In a society where groups with different social values live together, Mecklin hypothesized, a "permanent social order is only possible where one or other of the two sets of social values represented by the two groups secures and maintains supremacy, or where there is a fusion of the two groups through intermarriage, which alone makes it possible for all members of the social order alike to attain that similarity of selfhood necessary to complete social solidarity and common loyalty to common group ideals." The whites of the South were faced with the alternative of intermarrying with blacks or segregating them and insisting upon their "recognition of the supremacy of the white group." Mecklin thought that it was unfortunate that the "Negro should be required to attain selfhood as best he can outside the higher cultural possibilities of the white group"; yet he asked, "what other alternative would the social philosopher offer us?" For Mecklin, it was understood that the social philosopher "would not ask of the white group the supreme sacrifice of its ethnic purity which is the bearer of its social heritage and therefore the ultimate guarantee of the continuity and integrity of its peculiar type of civilization."[43] Mecklin's emphasis on the dubious relationship between white endogamy and the South's social heritage was no more than a sophisticated defense of the old "no social equality" credo. The idea that the South's social heritage was not influenced significantly by blacks was false. Ignoring the pervasiveness of miscegenation in the South, Mecklin exhibited the arrogance of the proponents of Jim Crow.

Northern sociologists rarely commented on contemporary American race relations. They felt that race relations were mainly Southern problems and a field on the periphery of the discipline. Yet when they discussed the nature of race relations, they usually subordinated racial to environmental factors as the cause of the race problem. Representative of their point of view were Charles H. Cooley's comments in 1918 that racial problems were the result of "biological and social factors working together" to "produce lasting differences sufficient to keep the groups apart." In racial problems the biological factors were not of primary importance. "The ruling factor," Cooley remarked, "is not the precise amount of strictly racial difference, as distinct from social, but the actual attitude of the groups toward each other." The immigration of such Southern and Eastern European immigrant groups as the Italians, Slavs, and Jews, who differed from the older groups of Northern and Western European heritage, did not create a racial problem. The collective attitudes of Northern and Western European groups did not militate against the possibility of assimilation of Southern and Eastern Europeans in the near future. Unlike the Southern and Eastern European immigrant groups, blacks were a problem because the assimilation of blacks was deemed "undesirable" by whites. Furthermore, Cooley believed that the immigration of a large Asian population to the Pacific Coast "would create an enduring race question." Desiring to avoid the creation of a caste system similar to that in the South, he wrote, "I see no reason why America and Australia should not avoid the rise of an unnecessary caste problem by restricting Oriental immigration."[44] Despite Cooley's reactionary tendencies, his concern with the attitudinal aspects of those problems was perceptive; it was the orientation that most sociologists adopted after 1920.

Of all the Northern sociologists commenting on the racial problem, none was more critical of race relations in the South than George E. Howard. In 1917, Howard attempted to expose the manner in which racial prejudice distorted the Southern mind. Offering statistical data demonstrating that blacks had made substantial "progress materially and spiritually" after emancipation, despite an inefficient school system, he found no evidence to support the Southerners' contention that blacks had degenerated since slavery. In regard to the morality and crime rates of blacks, he noted that Southerners offered biological explanations where environmental explanations were more sufficient. And finally, he noted that the idea of the inherent "moral uncleanness" of blacks was a myth. In fact, he asserted, the Southern white man "has been far more guilty (of rape), because the relative helplessness of Negro women has exposed them to his lust."[45]

Unlike the Southern sociologists, who believed that white prejudice was a natural reaction to blacks, Howard thought that prejudice was the result of the dogma of white supremacy. "A perverse psychology," he was certain, "is costing the South very dearly. The tremendous power of the mass of suggestion presented to consciousness through the daily and hourly repetition of the vicious phrases giving expression to the dogma of race-inferiority could not fail to have a harmful effect. It has caused mutual distrust and antagonism between the races." Essential to the destruction of the dogma, which had hindered Southern progress in general, Howard felt, was the education of white youth. Although it was important that black youth be educated, he argued that it was even more important that whites, "because of their greater responsibility . . . be properly trained for their just share of the world's work." For Howard, the goal of educating white youth pertained "to the social, cultural assimilation of the races." Drawing on the work of Sarah E. Simons, Howard held that social assimilation was "psychic fact" which was not to be confused with amalgamation by intermarriage. It referred primarily to "the sharing of the same cultural idea." Besides, there was no reason to believe, as Southerners did, that blacks desired intermarriage. The black's "race consciousness and race pride are raising before the Negro's vision a quite different goal."[46]

Howard clearly evaded the problems stemming from the possibility of intermarriage between blacks and whites. Nonetheless, it is certain that he could not have supported the polygenist argument. For an egalitarian like Howard, the polygenist argument had been refuted by Carl Kelsey in 1916. The thrust of Kelsey's attack was launched against the polygenist argument of Frederick L. Hoffman. Hoffman had inferred from anthropometric studies of black and mulatto soldiers during the Civil War by S. B. Hunt and B. A. Gould that there were significant mental, moral, and physical differences between the full-blooded black and the mulatto; he had held that the mulatto was physically and morally inferior, but intellectually superior, to the full-blooded black. Kelsey did not understand how Hoffman could make such inferences from anthropometric data, and he suggested that "possibly certain differences in social conditions may account for the varying results." He found no evidence to support the contention that mulattoes, because of their alleged physical inferiority, were declining in numbers. Kelsey argued that the "number of Negro—White cross-breeds in the country today cannot be far short of the whole number counted as Negroes at the close of the Civil War, or from one-fourth to one-third the total." Furthermore, Kelsey pointed out that teachers did not find great differences in intellectual ability between full-blooded blacks and mulattoes and that the leadership of black Americans contained both mulattoes, such as Booker T. Washington and W.E.B. DuBois, and full-blooded blacks, such as R. R. Moton and Kelly Miller. Closing his refutation of the polygenist argument, Kelsey wrote: "Whatever the future may disclose there is no evidence worthy of credence to show that intermarriage of even the most widely separated races results in physically inferior offsprings."[47]

Attempting to deal realistically with the country's racial problems,

Kelsey described two solutions: one was amalgamation; the other was a "caste system much like that of India with its denial of opportunity to the lower caste, the consequent destruction of democracy, and downfall of Christianity as now understood at least." Arguments against intermarriage that stressed the maintenance of racial purity were equally as superficial as those that advocated it as a means of extending social equality. What was of central importance to Kelsey was that "two individuals of two races must be considered in the light of their own qualities just as if they were of one group." Kelsey cautioned, however, that mixed marriages in which one of the partners was "socially inferior" and distinguishable by some "physical trait like color" were not advisable because of the difficulties that it would create for the children. Thus he insisted that "no thoughtful person, then, it seems to me can today advocate the intermarriage between whites and blacks by law," since it was "perfectly possible that in years to come such intermarriage will seem both natural and desirable."[48]

The contradiction that Kelsey pointed to, between the country's democratic and Christian principles and a racial caste system, had been acknowledged by Southern theorists, but they appealed to a higher principle than the principles of Christianity and democracy: the sanctity of the social order. For Kelsey, this appeal was too hysterical. The practice of intermarriage did not involve a threat to the social order. Kelsey preached a higher tolerance. Yet, tolerant as Kelsey was, even he was forced to concede that this was not feasible or desirable at the time.

None of the white commentators on the issue of race relations before 1920 had been more intimately involved with blacks than Robert E. Park. Born in Harveyville, Luzerne County, Pennsylvania in 1864 and brought up in Red Wing, Minnesota, the erstwhile newspaper reporter received a doctorate under Georg Simmel in Germany in 1904 and taught at Harvard the following year. In 1905, Park became affiliated with the Congo Reform Association and met Booker T. Washington. That same year, he was appointed press secretary for Tuskegee Institute, where he served as a ghostwriter for Washington and undertook studies of blacks in the South. He published the Washingtonian philosophy in various periodicals, wrote most of Washington's *The Story of the Negro* (1909), and collaborated with the Great Accommodator in the writing of *The Man Farthest Down* (1912). So intellectually profitable was Park's overall experience at Tuskegee that he later wrote: "I probably learned more about human nature and society in the South under Booker Washington than I learned elsewhere in my previous studies." Convinced that he had had the opportunity to observe a significant sociological process, Park wrote: "I was interested in the Negro in the South and in the curious and intricate system which had grown up to define his relations with white folk. I was interested, most of all, in studying the details of the process by which civilization, not merely here but elsewhere, has evolved, drawing into the circle of its influence an ever widening circle of races and people."[49] In 1913, William I. Thomas persuaded Park, who was financially hard-pressed, to come to the University of Chicago, where he remained until his retirement in 1933.

Gunnar Myrdal noted in 1944 that although Robert E. Park was "much less conservative than Sumner, he was still bound by a similar fatalism." In attempting to account for Park's adherence to a naturalistic philosophy, Myrdal suggested that Park's "keen observation of social conditions—and, perhaps, also disillusionment from his reform activities—have made him realize the tremendous force exerted by 'natural' influences. Not observing much in the way of conscious and organized planning in his contemporary America except that which was bungling and ineffective because it did not take due account of natural forces, he built up a sociological system in terms of natural forces." Myrdal concluded that Park had helped to perpetuate the "do-nothing" or "laissez-faire" tradition in the field of race relations.[50]

The question of whether or not blacks could be assimilated was indeed significant. The problem of the assimilation of blacks and other nonwhite groups would become one of Park's primary concerns for the next thirty years. His earliest definition, which appeared in the *American Journal of Sociology* in 1914, was stated in terms of a biological analogy: "Assimilation, as the word is here used, brings with it a certain borrowed significance which it carried over from physiology, where it is employed to describe the process of nutrition, somewhat similar to the physiological one, we may conceive alien peoples to be incorporated with, and made part of, the community or state." The assimilation of blacks and Asians in secondary groups posed a problem. Park insisted that the "chief obstacle" to the assimilation of those groups was "not mental but physical traits." In other words, those groups were prevented from sharing the social life of white Americans because they were "distinguished by certain external marks," which furnished a "permanent physical substratum upon which and around which the irritations and animosities, incidental to all human intercourse, tend to accumulate and so gain strength and volume."[51]

Park's earliest conception of the assimilation process was, in many respects, similar to that of Jerome Dowd. In 1911, Dowd had written that "the American Negro under slavery, especially the domestic slaves, developed in some respects a very high degree of morals." During slavery, Dowd argued, blacks "had the opportunity to be molded by emotions, ideas, and habits of their masters and mistresses because of the close and prolonged association with them."[52] Like Dowd, Park was certain that assimilation had taken place—at least to a limited extent—during slavery. "Slavery has been, historically, the usual method," Park stated, "by which peoples have been incorporated into alien groups." He went on to argue that "when a member of an alien race is adopted into the family as a servant, or as a slave, and particularly when the status is made hereditary, as it was in the case of the Negro after his importation to America, assimilation followed rapidly and as a matter of course." Primary group relations—that is, intimate relations between the master's family and the slave—nurtured assimilation. Thus, the black, "particularly when he was adopted into the household as a family servant, learned in a comparatively short time the manners and customs of his master's family. He very soon possessed himself of so much of the language, religion, and the technique of the civilization of his master as in his station, he was fitted or permitted to acquire." The domestic slave even held the same sentiments and interests as his master's family. On the other hand, the assimilation of the field hand was less complete because the contact between the field hand and his master's family was "less intimate." In determining to what extent the white influenced the cultural life of blacks on any plantation, Park thought the "size of the plantation, the density of the slave population, and the extent and character of the isolation in which the master and his slave lived are factors to be reckoned with." On small plantations, such as those that had existed in Virginia and the border states, where there were intimate relations between the master's family and the slave, blacks "gained relatively more of the white man's civilization." Blacks on these small plantations were far more assimilated than those who lived on the large plantations, such as those located on the Sea Islands off the coast of South Carolina. So great was the impact of the type of plantation upon blacks that even during the 1910s it accounted for the cultural heterogeneity of the black population. Indeed, Park thought that "an outline of the areas in which the different types of plantations existed before the War would furnish the basis for a map showing distinct cultural levels in the Negro population in the South today."[53]

With the end of slavery, Park argued, the assimilation process was terminated. In the postbellum period, the black became mobile and left the plantation, thus severing "the personal relations which bound him to his master's people." Relations between the races that had been "direct and personal became more and more indirect and secondary." Although black mobilization brought about the demise of intimate relations between blacks and whites, at the same time it nurtured more intimate ties within the black group. Thus, the system of segregation, though "fostered by the policy of the dominant race," actually "began as a spontaneous movement on the part of both" races. The segregation of the races affected the black population significantly, for it ensured the development of a "common interest among all the different colors and classes of the race." Park believed that the sentiment of solidarity among blacks, which facilitated the development of a nationality, was a "response and accommodation to changing internal and external conditions." In that stage of accommodation, the nationalist movement that emerged served an important function: it substituted "for those supplied them by aliens, models based on their individuality and embodying sentiments and ideals which spring naturally out of their own lives." Once a race had attained its "moral independence" through nationalism, Park speculated, it would remain loyal to the state "only insofar as the state incorporates as an integral part of its organization, the practical interests, the aspirations and ideals of the nationality." That the emergence of separate churches, schools, libraries, hospitals, and towns was affecting social conditions in the South, Park thought, was evident in the fact that the "races seem to be tending in the direction of a biracial organization of society, in which the Negro is gradually gaining a limited autonomy." Still, he was hesitant to predict the "ultimate outcome of this movement."[54]

In his discussion of race relations, Park departed from the Southern line of argument. Although he was in substantial agreement with the Southern position in regard to the assimilative effects of slavery, Park did not embrace the view that the mental abilities of blacks affected the nature of race relations. For Park, the nature of race relations between blacks and whites was determined by the types of contact between the races. Despite Park's tendency to utilize the concept of racial temperament, he had accepted the Boasian point of view on the issue of racial mental differences. In that respect, he was progressive.

Park's analysis of prejudice, however, was in many respects similar to the Southern position. Like William I. Thomas, Park thought that racial prejudice was instinctive. Yet whereas Thomas viewed the physical appearance of an alien group as the fundamental stimulus to prejudice, Park believed the main stimulus was competition. Park wrote in 1917: "Race prejudice may be regarded as a spontaneous more or less instinctive defense reaction, the practical effect of which is to restrict free competition. Its importance as a social function is due to the fact that free competition, particularly between people with different standards of living, seems to be, if not the original source, at least the stimulus to which prejudice is the response." For Park, it was a universal law that racial prejudice was "present in every situation where the fundamental interests of races and peoples are not yet regulated by some law, custom, or any other *modus vivendi* which commands the assent and the mutual support of both parties." Racial prejudice, however, could be assuaged "by the organization of . . . conflicting interests and by the extension of the machinery of cooperation and social control." Such "natural" solutions to the problem of racial prejudice were slavery and the caste system; since racial competition was restricted in both cases, racial prejudice disappeared, and there was "no obstacle to racial cooperation."[55]

Despite the fact that the caste system ensured smooth race relations, Park thought it was objectionable. Although Park conceded that the caste system might be "politically desirable," he argued that it was "economically unsound." "A national policy of national efficiency demands," he stated unequivocally, "that every individual have not merely the opportunity but the preparation necessary to perform that particular service for the community for which his natural disposition and aptitude fit him, irrespective of race or 'previous condition.'" Furthermore, the restriction of economic opportunity, though not contradictory to American traditions, did conflict with the country's political principles. Since that was the case, Park believed that there would "always be an active minority opposed on grounds of political sentiment to any settlement based on the caste system as applied to either the black or brown man."[56]

The idea that racial prejudice toward blacks was a natural response on the part of whites placed severe limitations on Park's thought, for as long as he viewed prejudice as instinctive, there was no way in which racial equality could be achieved. However objectionable Park found the caste system, he was unable to precisely define the forms of racial cooperation that could develop in a democratic system which might eliminate prejudice. The caste system remained for Park the only viable alternative to a social order torn by racial antagonism and conflict.

At this juncture, Park's evaluation of black culture was as biased as his analysis of prejudice. As it has been observed, Park discerned "distinct cultural levels" within the black population. The cultural level that any group of blacks occupied was determined by the extent to which it conformed to the behavioral patterns of the white population. Arguing along the same line, Edward B. Reuter drew a distinction between the culture of the mulattoes, which conformed to middle-class white standards, and that of the vast majority of blacks, which he referred to as a "lower" or "inferior culture." Undoubtedly these scholars, by demonstrating that blacks under the proper conditions were capable of conforming to white behavioral patterns, were intent on undermining the idea of black inferiority. But by constructing a cultural hierarchy in which white middle-class culture was the evaluative standard for judging black progress in that area, they had made a significant departure from the Boasian ideology, for one of the central elements of the concept of culture that emerged from Boas's writing was relativism.[57] Boas had emphasized in 1900 that the "student must endeavor to divest himself entirely of the opinions and emotions based upon the peculiar social environment into which he is born." While Western man's penchant for valuing his own civilization was understandable—due to the fact that he participated in that civilization and that it had controlled all his actions since birth—Boas still insisted that it was "certainly conceivable that there may be other civilizations, based perhaps on different traditions and on different equilibrium of emotion and reason, which are of no less value than ours."[58] That the Chicago sociologists ignored or were unaware of the virtues of Boas's cultural relativism was unfortunate, because their lead was followed by sociologists like E. Franklin Frazier and Charles S. Johnson, who developed fully the idea of the inferiority of the culture of lower-class blacks.

Considerable progress towards infusing the Boasian point of view into sociology was made during the period 1911 to 1919. On the issue of racial mental differences, the studies of Northerners such as Howard, Kelsey, and Lichtenberger, and those of Southerners, such as Thomas and Faris, based on the empirical data at hand, led sociologists to accept Boas's statements on the approximate mental equality of blacks and whites. Although there was some opposition to the Boasian position, it came from sociologists who had been publishing prior to 1911 and whose post–1911 statements were either based on commonsense judgments, as were Cooley's, or on the results of psychological testing, as were Odum's. Furthermore, and perhaps of greater significance, most black and many Northern white sociologists uncovered empirical data indicating that blacks were making considerable progress. That argument was definitely fueled by the external changes affecting black life and would become the most potent argument for liberals in the 1920s.

In the area of race relations, the idea that blacks would eventually achieve first-class citizenship was slow to gain acceptance—mainly because of the stubborn opposition of the Southern amateurs, who felt that white prejudice toward an inferior black race was instinctive. On the other hand, Northern professionals such as Cooley and Howard tended to subordinate biological explanations of race relations to social factors. Robert E. Park played an important role in changing the arguments in race relations by establishing it as a field of central significance in sociology. Park took a position on segregation midway between the Southern amateurs and the Northern professionals: while he was willing to concede to Northern professionals that it was not the mental but the physical traits of blacks that evoked white prejudice, he still agreed with the Southern amateurs that prejudice was instinctive. Obviously, Park ignored or was not familiar with Alfred Kroeber's position on the necessity for the separation of the biological from the social and cultural processes. For as long as leading sociologists, such as Park, continued to mix biology and sociology, the static view that the races could not mix and mingle freely would persist.

The 1910s ended on a violent note. In the summer of 1919, race riots broke out in twenty-five cities in the nation. The most serious incident occurred in Chicago, where thirty-eight persons were killed. The violence exacerbated the heated debate between the various authorities on race relations. At the annual meeting of the American Sociological Society in December 1919, Jerome Dowd, the premier Southern amateur sociologist, presented a paper beginning with the thesis that "all forms of life upon the earth have a natural tendency to segregate." Dowd, who was both an outspoken racist and a nativist, saw "nothing to be gained by legal segregation of races within the nation," for he believed that the races that were "notably opposite . . . will naturally form segregated groups." Nonetheless, he argued that it was not in the best interest of the nation to "permit the unrestricted immigration of the yellow, brown, and black races." Concluding with a direct attack on the issue of racial amalgamation, Dowd held that the "more probable outcome of blending would be an increasing segregation, a confusion of traditions, and the postponement to some indefinite future of the development of a unified tradition and the flowering of a distinct culture."[59]

Robert E. Park, who believed like Dowd in the instinctiveness of prejudice, nevertheless raised significant objections to the Southerner's theory. He argued that Dowd was seeking to "justify a political policy with regard to segregation" and therefore did not question whether instincts were as "impervious and unequivocal" as they might seem. In fact, Park's analysis of race relations in the South, where blacks and whites were "more completely segregated than elsewhere," suggested that different classes tended to "come together across the racial barriers and unite for their common welfare."[60] Like many other Northern sociologists during the latter years of the Progressive Era, Park had begun to draw a line (albeit a thin one) between himself and the reactionary Southern sociologists.

E. Franklin Frazier, who was one of Park's students at the University of Chicago in the late 1920s, suggested in 1947 that the threat to social peace that blacks posed in Northern urban areas stimulated his mentor to develop "the most comprehensive and systematic theories of race relations developed by American sociologists":

[The] migration of Negroes to the metropolitan areas of the North had destroyed the accommodation that had been achieved to some extent following the racial conflict during and following Reconstruction. The publication of *Introduction to the Science of Sociology* by Park and Burgess coincided with the study of the race riot in Chicago in 1919. The impact of the Negro problem on American life undoubtedly helped Park as much as his experience in the South in the formulation of a sociological theory.[61]

During the next decade Park saw racial conflicts in both the North and the South as the result of progressive changes in the status of blacks rather than as a clash of race and instincts. Furthermore, professionalization engendered the movement towards empiricism, resulting in a more rigorous analysis of prejudice. Park would go on to provide the "orientation for empirical studies of race relations."[62] The stage was set.

NOTES

1. Edward A. Purcell, Jr., *The Crisis of Democratic Theory: Scientific Naturalism and the Problem of Value* (Lexington: University of Kentucky Press, 1973), 15–27.

2. George O. Ferguson, "The Psychology of the Negro," *AP* 25 (April–June, 1916): 11.

3. Ibid., 46–83.

4. Ibid., 84–122.

5. Ibid., 125–26.

6. Ashley Montagu, ed., *Race and IQ* (New York: Oxford University Press, 1975), 6.

7. Rhett S. Jones, "Proving Blacks Inferior: The Sociology of Knowledge," in *The Death of White Sociology*, ed. Joyce A. Ladner (New York: Random House, 1973), 131.

8. Franz Boas, *The Mind of Primitive Man* (New York: Macmillan, 1911), 271–72, 268.

9. Alfred L. Kroeber, "Eighteen Professions," *AA* 17 (April–June 1915), 283–86.

10. William I. Thomas, "Race Psychology," *AJS* 17 (May 1912): 726–27.

11. Robert E. Park, "Education and Its Relation to the Conflict and Fusion of Cultures: With Special Reference to the Problems of the Immigrant, the Negro and Missions," *PASS* 13 (December 1918): 40–41.

12. Robert E. Park, "Review of George Oscar Ferguson's, *The Psychology of the Negro*," *AJS* 22 (March 1917): 685.

13. Park, "Education and Its Relation to the Conflict and Fusion of Cultures," 59–60.

14. Ibid., 59.

15. W.E.B. DuBois, "The Negro in Literature and Art," *Annals* 49 (September 1913): 233.

16. Matthews, *Quest for an American Sociology*, 172.

17. Park, "Education and Its Relation to the Conflict and Fusion of Cultures," 62.

18. Reuter, "Superiority of the Mulatto," 83–85.

19. Ibid., 85–92.

20. Ibid., 92–94.

21. Ibid., 94–106.

22. Kelly Miller, "Review of Edward B. Reuter's *The Mulatto in the United States*," *AJS* 25 (September 1919): 218–24.

23. Charles H. Cooley, *Social Process* (New York: Charles Scribner's Sons, 1918), 274–75.

24. George Elliott Howard, "The Social Cost of Southern Race Prejudice," *AJS* 22 (March 1917): 580.

25. Faris, "Mental Capacity of Savages," 603, 618.

26. W.E.B. DuBois, *Black Folk: Then and Now* (New York: Henry Holt and Company, 1939), vii. DuBois later wrote: "I did not myself begin actively to study Africa until 1908 or 1910. Franz Boas really influenced me to begin studying this subject." Quoted in Harold R. Isaacs, *The New World of Negro Americans* (New York: Viking Press, 1964), 207.

27. W.E.B. DuBois, *The Negro* (New York: Home University Library, 1915), 7.

28. J. A. Brigham, ed., *AUP* 20 (Atlanta: Atlanta University Press, 1916), 84.

29. DuBois, *The Negro*, 27–45.

30. George E. Haynes, "Conditions Among Negroes in the Cities," *Annals* 49 (September 1913): 24.

31. R. R. Wright, Jr., "The Negro in Unskilled Labor," *Annals* 49 (September 1913): 114.

32. Ibid., 22.

33. DuBois, "Negro in Literature and Art," 233.

34. James P. Lichtenberger, "Negro Illiteracy in the United States," *Annals* 49 (September 1913): 177–85.

35. Robert E. Park, "Negro Home Life and Standards of Living," *Annals* 49 (September 1913): 147–63.

36. Howard, "Social Cost of Southern Race Prejudice," 580–83.

37. Howard W. Odum, "Negro Children in the Public Schools of Philadelphia," *Annals* 49 (September 1913): 205–7.

38. Thomas, "Race Psychology," 745.

39. Jerome Dowd, "Review of *The Negro in the New World* by Sir Harry H. Johnston," *AJS* 19 (November 1913): 343.

40. John M. Mecklin, "The Philosophy of the Color Line," *AJS* 19 (November 1913) 343.

41. Ibid., 344–47.

42. Ibid., 347–48.

43. Ibid., 355–56.

44. Cooley, *Social Process*, 276, 278–80.

45. Howard, "Social Cost of Southern Race Prejudice," 587–89.

46. Ibid., 589–91.

47. Carl Kelsey, *The Physical Basis of Society* (New York: D. Appleton and Company, 1916), 297–300.

48. Ibid., 301–2.

49. Robert E. Park, "An Autobiographical Note," in *Race and Culture* (New York: The Free Press, 1950), vii–viii.

50. Myrdal, *An American Dilemma* 2:1049–50.

51. Robert E. Park, "Racial Assimilation in Secondary Groups," *AJS* 19 (March 1914): 607–10.

52. Jerome Dowd, Discussion of "The Racial Element in Social Assimilation," by Ulysses G. Weatherly, *AJS* 16 (March 1911): 633–34.

53. Park, "Racial Assimilation in Secondary Groups," 611–13.

54. Ibid., 614–23.

55. Robert E. Park, Introduction to *The Japanese Invasion*, by Jesse F. Steiner (Chicago: A. C. McClurg, 1917), xiii.

56. Ibid., xv.

57. Stocking, *Race, Culture, and Evolution*, 228–30.

58. Boas, "Mind of Primitive Man," 1, 11.

59. Jerome Dowd, "Race Segregation in a World of Democracy," *PASS* 14 (December 1919): 189–202.

60. Robert E. Park, Discussion of "Race Segregation in a World of Democracy," by Jerome Dowd, *PASS* 14 (December 1919): 203.

61. E. Franklin Frazier, "Sociological Theory and Race Relations," *ASR* 12 (June 1947): 269.

62. Ibid., 271.

5

The Triumph of Liberal Environmentalism, 1920–1929

The northward trek of blacks continued in the 1920s. With the passage of the immigration restriction acts of 1921 and 1924, blacks found work as unskilled laborers in positions that had once been held by immigrants, and increasingly became a part of the regular element in the labor force in nearly every basic industry. Yet despite the widespread economic prosperity of the 1920s, blacks continued to be relegated to a low socioeconomic status. Furthermore, violence against blacks in the form of white-initiated race riots and an upsurge in lynching exacerbated the problems. In this atmosphere of disillusionment, an estimated two million blacks in the North and South were attracted to Marcus Garvey's racial chauvinist program. Garvey's Universal Negro Improvement Association began to collapse in 1923, when Garvey was convicted of using the mails to defraud in raising money for the shipping line he had created. It was, however, a significant movement. As John Hope Franklin writes: "Its significance lies in the fact that it was the first and only real mass movement among Negroes in the history of the United States and that it indicates the extent to which Negroes entertained doubts concerning the hope for first-class citizenship in the only fatherland of which they knew."[1]

Coinciding with Garvey's tremendous popularity was the outpouring of group literature by black writers involved in the Harlem Renaissance, including Zora Neale Hurston, who was one of Franz Boas's students. The rise of black consciousness in literature did not escape the attention of Robert E. Park. After surveying the poetry of writers such as Claude McKay and Walter Everette Hawkins, Park concluded in 1923 that the "poetry of the renaissance was characteristically the poetry of rebellion and self-assertion." He believed that two factors—international events and the urbanization of blacks—contributed to the development of the new racial consciousness. "The unrest which is fermenting in every part of the world," Park asserted, "has gotten under the skin of the Negro. The Negro is not only becoming radical, but he is becoming Bolshevist, at least in spots." Furthermore, he believed that urbanization shattered the traditions and habits of slavery which "vanish as soon as the Negro enters into the vivid, restless, individualistic life of cities."[2]

The increasing migration of large numbers of blacks from the South into Northern urban-industrial areas after 1920 coincided historically with the rise of anti-black, anti-Semitic, and anti-Catholic feelings among Americans of British ancestry. Furthermore, nativism was being reinforced by some intellectuals. Among them was the amateur anthropologist Madison Grant. In *The Passing of the Race* (1916), Grant argued that Northern and Western Europeans and Americans of "Nordic" ancestry should not intermix with "Alpines" and "Mediterraneans" of Southern and Eastern European ancestry. Nordic theory also received a timely reinforcement from psychology. As we have observed, psychologists and cultural anthropologists in 1917 held dissimilar views on the issue of the inherent capabilities of blacks. During World War I, psychologists under the direction of Robert M. Yerkes, president of the American Psychological Association, administered "intelligence tests" to 1.7 million American servicemen, thus strengthening the opposition to anthropology. As George W. Stocking has written: "The Army Alpha and Beta tests provided the most important single scientific buttress for the racism of the 1920s."[3]

The net effect of "tribalism" in the 1920s was to exacerbate the conceptual stresses between anthropology and psychology in regard to the racial capabilities of Afro-Americans. Sociologists witnessed that debate and, in turn, divided into conservative and liberal camps. By 1930, however, when even the most conservative psychologists capitulated to Boasian anthropology, sociologists dismissed the argument of the conservatives. By that time, they espoused a belief not only in black progress but in the inevitability of assimiliation.

REACTIONARY PSYCHOLOGY AND PROGRESSIVE ANTHROPOLOGY

One of the influential psychologists who put forth the views of his fellow psychologists during this period was Carl C. Brigham of Princeton University. The New Englander, who had received his doctorate in psychology at Princeton in 1912, had administered and analyzed the results of the Alpha and Beta tests during World War I. Brigham is best remembered for his pioneering work in developing scholastic aptitude and achievement tests for the College Entrance Examination Board. In his book *A Study of American Intelligence* (1923), Brigham drew on the Army Alpha and Beta tests to demonstrate that "Nordics" were intellectually superior to blacks as well as "Alpines" and "Mediterraneans." He went so far as to assert that "in a very definite way, the results which we obtain by interpreting the army data by means of the race hypothesis support Mr. Madison Grant's thesis of the superiority of the Nordic type."[4] Brigham found even greater differences between blacks and whites than George O. Ferguson's 1916 study indicated. He thought that the variations in the results of psychological investigations "as to the *amount* of difference" between the races was due to methods by which whites and blacks living in the same neighborhood with the same educational opportunities were compared. The differences between whites and blacks were smaller "than those obtained by comparing samples of the entire white and negro populations." Nevertheless, he pointed out, in both cases, on the average, blacks scored lower than whites.[5]

Some commentators on the Army tests had held that differences between the scores of blacks and whites were attributable solely to differences in educational opportunities. Their argument was based on the fact that Northern blacks, who on the average had succeeded in finishing higher grades than Southern blacks, scored higher than Southern blacks. In his response to that criticism, Brigham argued: "That the difference between the northern and southern negro is not entirely due to schooling but partly to intelligence is shown by the fact that groups of southern and northern negroes of *equal schooling* show striking differences in intelligence."[6]

Although educational opportunity was one factor that enabled Northern blacks to score higher than their Southern brethren, Brigham contended that other factors—namely, "the greater amount of admixture of white blood," and "the operation of economic and social forces, such as higher wages, better living conditions, identical school privileges, and a less complete social ostracism" that drew the more intelligent blacks from the South to the North—deserved consideration. Brigham's propensity for minimizing the influence of education and the environment on test scores was also evident in his criticism of scholars who sought to compare only those blacks and whites with similar educational and environmental opportunities. "If intelligence counts for anything in competition," Brigham commented, "it is natural to expect that individuals of superior intelligence will adjust themselves more easily to their physical and social environment, and that they will endow their children not only with material goods but with the ability to adjust themselves to the same or a more complex environment." Brigham concluded by asserting that whites with educational and environmental backgrounds similar to blacks were not typical of their race; rather they were individuals with an "inferior hereditary endowment."[7]

The idea of the innate intellectual inferiority of blacks had widespread acceptance in psychology throughout the greater part of the 1920s.[8] But by 1930 the idea was undergoing a perceptible erosion, primarily because the assumptions and methodology of racial testing were being subjected to negative criticism by cultural anthropologists.

Franz Boas, whose own ethnic group was being subject to abuse by businessmen such as Henry Ford, proponents of 100 percent Americanism, and the Ku Klux Klan, was especially disturbed by the upsurge of both nativist and racial ideologies and practices that gained momentum during the 1920s.[9] In an article, "The Problem of the American Negro," which was published in *The Yale Quarterly Review* in 1921, Boas attacked racists by criticizing their interpretations of concrete data. Although he reviewed the findings of physical anthropologists, he did not draw invidious distinctions between blacks and whites. Also, his "men of high genius" hypothesis was conspicuously absent. And although he willingly admitted "that, on the average, the brain of the negro is slightly smaller than the brain of the European," his inferences suggested the possibility of functional similarities: "the response on the part of brains of different structure and size to the demand of life may be very much the same."[10]

When speaking of the Afro-American problem and its relation to issues in the field of heredity, Boas was critical of some of the psychological experiments. In 1894, Boas had hoped that experimental psychology would clarify the issue of racial mental differences. He was dismayed to discover, after twenty-seven years, that the investigations into the mental abilities of black and white children were biased. "I am not convinced," Boas wrote, "that the results that have been obtained are significant in regard to racial ability as a whole. The variability of the results is also very marked and there is an overlapping of racial traits." He was even more intent on pushing the liberal environmentalist argument as far as possible. Responding to a study by M. R. Trabue which was based on the culturally biased Army Alpha and Beta tests, Boas argued that Northern blacks were not inherently superior to Southern blacks. He asserted that it was not true that only "the gifted Southern negroes emigrated."[11] In a lucid passage, he continued:

in the absence of sound proof this [inherent intellectual] superiority may just as well be explained by the assumption that Northern negroes are exposed to a wider range of experience than Southern negroes. Anyone who knows the abject fear of the Southern negroes who are put under the control of an unknown white officer in foreign surroundings, anyone who knows the limitations of early childhood and general upbringing of negroes in the South, will accept these findings, but will decline to accept them as a convincing proof of the hereditary inferiority of the negro race.[12]

To prove that cultural factors were more significant for an understanding of the plight of Afro-Americans than the study of heredity, Boas idealized the achievements of black Africans. He found striking differences between the "African industrial and political conditions among our poor negroes." Boas believed that Africans were industrially more advanced than other primitive peoples and that their "native arts," such as weaving, carving, pottery, blacksmithing, metal casting, and glass blowing, were "excellent." Furthermore, the political organization of black Africans was like the political organization in Medieval Europe, for African states in the Sudan, Congo, and South Africa had "negro rulers whose genius for organization has enabled them to establish flourishing empires."[13]

The article that marked the end of Boas's evolving thought on race, "What Is Race?" appeared in *The Nation* in 1925. In that piece he sought to delimit the boundaries of the nature versus nurture controversy. Although he mentioned blacks only once, the implications for the discussion of the so-called Negro problem were clear. Taking Madison Grant to task, Boas argued that "racial heredity" referred to "certain characteristics in which all members of a race partake." The different skin colors of whites and blacks were examples of "hereditary traits, because they belong to all members of each race." But it was wrongheaded to try to "judge" an individual "by the size of his brain" or by his physiological or mental functions, mainly because those forms and functions "vary enormously in each race, and many features that are found in one race are also found belonging to other races." Indeed, it was "impossible to speak of hereditary racial characteristics because the traits characterizing any individual occur in a number of human races." Although Boas believed that there were obvious differences in the appearance and behavior of certain "social groups," this did not "imply that these characteristics are hereditarily determined." But it was obvious to him that "racial strains, when subject to the same social environment, develop the same functional tendencies."[14]

Finally, when addressing himself to the controversial issue of racial mental differences, Boas pointed out correctly that the "occurrence of hereditary mental traits that belong to a particular race has never been proved." Thus, for him, it was safe to infer that the "behavior of an individual is therefore not determined by his racial affiliations, but by the character of his ancestry and his cultural environment." One could only "judge the mental characteristics of families and individuals, but not of races."[15] It would be an over-statement, however, to assert that Boas completely expurgated himself of racist anthropological assumptions. His "men of high genius" hypothesis appeared in the highly revised 1938 edition of *The Mind of Primitive Man.*

To view Franz Boas's position on the issue of differences between blacks and whites during the years 1894 to 1925 as "equivocal" or as that of a liberal humanitarian is to oversimplify the views of this complex man. Yet it is true that Boas's position up until 1920 was indeed uneven. His attempt to draw a direct relation between brain size and intellectual ability led him to infer that blacks could not produce a proportional number of "men of high genius." This position, which was a concession to racists, severely undercut his liberal humanitarian sentiments. But Boas's views on the character and capabilities of Afro-Americans and Africans were not static. Although my analysis is somewhat inferential, it seems that Boas was conscious of the growing impact that Afro-Americans were having upon the nation's economic, social, and cultural life. After 1920, he used the liberal environmentalist argument to dispel the idea of "racial hereditary characteristics." Like so many original minds, Boas was able, through the rigorous examination of his world and his beliefs, to adapt to the ebb and flux of history.

THE TRIUMPH OF BOASIAN CRITICISM

As noted earlier, both anthropologists and psychologists had taken empirical approaches to the issue of racial mental differences, and the empirical worldview masked the dissimilar ideologies of the disputants in anthropology and psychology. With this in mind, it is not surprising that the struggle for the ascendant position on the issue of racial mental differences was marked by the tendency to argue about the relative merits of the methodology of intelligence testers. In 1921, Boas had attacked the empirical bases of the conclusions of intelligence testers. By 1926 his position was reinforced by two of his prominent students, when both Margaret Mead of Barnard College and Melville J. Herskovits of Columbia University offered trenchant criticisms of studies by George O. Ferguson and Carl C. Brigham. In so doing, they proved conclusively that the results obtained from such tests were suspect.

Herskovits, who was completing a three-year project on the anthropometry of Afro-Americans (and who went on to found the first university program in African studies in the United States at Northwestern University), attacked the work of George O. Ferguson in *Pedagogical Seminary.* In order to test the argument put forth by Ferguson, which asserted that blacks with greater amounts of white blood were inherently superior to those with greater amounts of black blood, Herskovits conducted a study in 1926 in which he collected the anthropometric measurements, the test scores, and genealogies of a combined total of 539 black males attending Howard University and in New York City.

From his study, Herskovits concluded that the attempt to divide blacks into subclasses on the "bases of anthropological data such as skin color," without using genealogies, was futile "because of the large overlapping in any traits which may be selected as criteria." For Herskovits, the assumption that discrimination within the black group against those with Negroid traits did not create environmental differences that would account for differences between the social status of the various subclasses of blacks was also questionable. Herskovits concluded that the "basic hypothesis of White superiority in general social efficiency and innate intelligence" was "to be gravely doubted" because of the inability of its proponents to verify its logical corollaries.[16]

Like Herskovits, Margaret Mead, who had received an M.A. in psychology, also presented a convincing refutation of the methodology and conclusions of the leading intelligence testers. While reviewing the state of nationality testing in the *American Journal of Sociology* in 1926, Mead was especially critical of the Army Alpha and Beta tests that Carl C. Brigham had drawn on in substantiating his case for black, "Alpine," and "Mediterranean" inferiority. "No discussions today which pretend to scientific caution," she argued, "quote the army tests without explicit reservations." The deficiencies of the Army tests, she believed, were characteristic of those found in most racial and nationality testing. On the bases of evidence gathered from the few experiments that were "suggestive methodologically," Mead argued that it was apparent that social status and language disabilities affected test scores. To Mead, it was also probable that the "environment may determine the [subject's] attitude toward the test and profoundly affect his score." Experiments such as those performed by Ferguson, which attempted to equate test scores with the amount of racial admixture, were "subject to modification" because the language and social status factors had been ignored and also because of "the inherent weakness of the method in the present state of ignorance concerning the laws regulating the inheritance of mental traits." Emphasizing the need to take environmental factors into account, Mead concluded that "all these considerations should suggest extreme caution in any attempt to draw conclusions concerning the relative intelligence of different racial or nationality groups on the basis of tests, unless a careful consideration is given the factors of language, education, and social status, and further allowances made for an unknown amount of influence which may be logically attributed to different attitudes and different habits of thought."[17]

Psychologists were apparently receptive to the criticisms of Mead and Herskovits. Indeed, some of them were in the process of offering criticism of their own. In summarizing these criticisms, Carl C. Brigham remarked in 1930: "A far-reaching result of the recent investigations has been the discovery that test scores may not represent unitary things." Since some psychologists had demonstrated that the Army Alpha test was "internally inconsistent," it was a mistake—which he acknowledged having committed—"to go beyond this point and combine alpha, beta, the Stanford-Binet, and the individual performance tests in the so-called 'combined scale,' or to regard a combined scale score derived from one test or complex of tests." Brigham's recognition of the methodological limitations of intelligence tests led him to concede that "comparative studies of various national and racial groups may not be made with existing tests." Forced to reject his own previous conclusions, Brigham wrote that "one of the pretensions of these comparative racial studies—the writer's own—was without foundation."[18]

In establishing that intelligence tests were defective, many psychologists were destroying the foundations upon which the argument of innate black inferiority had been built in their discipline, and were helping to undermine racism in sociology and anthropology as well. An empirical study conducted in the fall of 1929 by Charles H. Thompson, professor of education at Howard University, which polled the majority of psychologists competent in the field of racial mental differences, indicated that the skeptical position was the most widely held point of view. When asked: "Do you conclude from recent investigations that Negroes are inherently mentally (inferior to) or (equal to) Whites," 64 percent of the seventy-seven psychologists who responded to the question thought that experimentation had not proved that blacks were inferior to whites; 11 percent thought that blacks were equal to whites; and 25 percent contended that blacks were inferior to whites.[19] Although a sizable minority of psychologists were content to view blacks as mentally inferior to whites, it is clear that by 1930 the Boasian skeptical position in psychology had at least triumphed at that particular juncture. By the 1970s, however, there would be a revival of hereditarian thinking in that discipline.

REACTIONISM AND PROGRESSIVISM IN SOCIOLOGY

Most prominent sociologists in the 1910s embraced the Boasian skeptical position on the issue of the inherent mental capabilities of blacks. Yet until 1930, because of the negative evaluations of psychologists, the sociologists' position was controversial. With the capitulation of most psychologists to Boasian thought, however, the viewpoint of sociologists was vindicated. It would be an overstatement to argue that racism disappeared completely from sociology and that students of that discipline could claim that they were morally superior to psychologists. As could be expected, some sociologists in the 1920s still believed in hereditarian concepts of racial differentiation and rejected the Boasian argument that the traits of blacks were attributable to the cultural environment. In his *Society and Its Problems* (1922), Grove S. Dow, a second-rate sociologist who had received an M.A. from Brown University in 1911 and had gone on to teach at Baylor University in Waco, Texas, brought forth arguments in favor of the inequality of the races.

In accounting for differences in the behavior of blacks and whites, the Missourian Dow attempted to avoid a strict hereditarian argument. The differences in the characteristics of blacks and whites, he argued, could be explained adequately when one took into consideration "the influences of natural selection and environment." When one notes that Dow's argument was based on the works of the Southern social scientists Jerome Dowd and Joseph A. Tillinghast, one is not surprised by his reactionary stance. Like Dowd and Tillinghast, Dow contended that natural selection and the environment had operated in Africa in the distant past, causing blacks to inherit certain behavior patterns that were unlike those of whites. Dow's treatment of the characteristics of blacks as if they were "racial" characteristics and his insistence that blacks were inefficient laborers led him to conclude that the industrial schools could correct the problems.[20]

The themes that Dow developed, however, had dropped out of favor among most competent sociologists. Nonetheless, Dow, who had received his advanced academic training before the publication of Boas's *The Mind of Primitive Man*, was content to ignore the change in the orientation in the social sciences and the inexorable change in the lives of many blacks. It was much easier and safer to reinforce the prejudices of the popular audience, to whom his work was addressed, than to take part in a scientific revolution that would alienate the readers of his popular work. Furthermore, Dow was not engaged in valid research to test his theory, and if he read Boas and Kroeber, he never showed it.

Dow had held that blacks were inferior to whites, if not in their indigenous environment, then certainly in the modern civilized world. He did not elaborate critically on the theory of racial equality, as did the Southern amateur sociologist Jerome Dowd. Dowd, who taught economics at the University of Oklahoma, stated in his major work, entitled *The Negro in the American Life* (1926): "The term race equality involves a good deal more than a general ability to learn." For him, racial equality meant that races responded alike to the "same stimulus," possessed the "same propensities, the same emotional temperament, and the same general aptitudes." Ridiculing the theory of racial equality, which he mistakenly attributed to Boas, he argued that there were no grounds "for assuming the races are alike in these respects if dogs are not." It was obvious to Dowd that even if the Red Indian and the black African were "equally endowed mentally," they still differed "strikingly in temperament." Conjuring up stereotypes that had been promulgated by Franklin H. Giddings in the 1890s, Dowd asserted that "the Indian is stolid and obstinate; the Negro plastic and rollicking." Dowd nonetheless conceded that the theory of racial equality was "in a certain limited sense" defensible—insofar as there was "reason to believe that all races of men have the same mental faculties and that in general ability to learn they differ in no important degree."[21]

Despite this concession to the Boasians and their proponents in sociology, the reactionary Southerner thought it was necessary to add that because of the influence of natural selection, the races did not have "equal capacity to adapt themselves to the same environment, nor to attain to the same accomplishment." Dowd certainly understood the implications of Alfred L. Kroeber's position on the separation of the biological from the social processes; yet he was obstinate and argued that proponents of that position necessarily had to deny the significance of too many biological and social factors. These theorists had negated the role of heredity, natural selection, sexual selection, and history in differentiating races. Such a philosophy, which rendered eugenics to the status of "bunk," Dowd thought was "a complacent philosophy which no man of the first order of ability has ever believed in." While it was true that the proponents of racial equality were reacting against the extremism of the racial determinists, the controversy between the two groups of disputants had led to extremism on both sides. Dowd believed—and in a certain limited sense he was correct—that the controversy was bound to reach an impasse; for it was apparent to him that the "line of demarcation between heredity and environment can never be exactly determined."[22]

Despite the fact that Dowd gave attention to the controversy over the issue of the superiority and inferiority of blacks and whites, he did not feel that this issue bore directly on the "Negro problem." The race problem, he insisted, "would be essentially the same if all races were in fact equal." For the sake of discussion, Dowd was "willing to assume that all races are equally capable of the highest culture." Yet it was obvious to him that races differed in physical characteristics, in psychological traits, in traditions, and in general culture. "These differences," he concluded, "give rise to the race problem, no matter what may be the facts as to the superiority of one race over another."[23]

Because the question of racial superiority and inferiority was fraught with extremism, Dowd assumed a relatively safe position by insisting that the question of differences in physical, psychological, and cultural traits was paramount. A far more sophisticated attempt to undermine the Boasian position on the racial capabilities and character of blacks, which avoided the polemics that characterized some of Dowd's statements, was penned by Frank H. Hankins, a professor of sociology at Smith College. The native Ohioan, who had received his doctorate under Franklin H. Giddings at Columbia University in 1908, is often labelled a significant figure in the development of demography in the United States. Hankins has also often been called a strict scientific determinist—mainly because of his reductionist tendencies. He used his empirical approach to the issue of racial differences to mask a highly sophisticated racist position.

Unlike Dow and Dowd, Hankins professed in his book *The Racial Basis of Civilization* (1926) a belief in the common humanity of all races. For him, "every comparison of races must be made on the basis of racial norms or averages and the range of variation there about." Racial differences were "those of relative quantitative frequency in a statistical distribution, rather than differences of kind." Thus racial differences were "differences in degree only." When Hankins spoke of the superiority of one race to another in respect to a particular trait, he meant that the "race manifests a given trait with greater frequency or in more extensive development." With those assumptions in mind, Hankins resuscitated the Lamarckian doctrine of the inheritance of acquired characteristics and argued that the presence of physical differences between the races, which had resulted from life in different climates and different "selective conditions," was significant. For the presence of those purported differences provided grounds for the inference that mental powers and character and traits have undergone differentiation comparable to that of physical traits."[24]

By arguing that inferiority and superiority were primarily "statistical concepts," Hankins escaped the pitfall of Aryanism—that of attributing superiority or inferiority to an individual simply because he or she belongs to a particular race. It was evident to Hankins that an individual could "be superior in his own group but still inferior to the average of another group." And conversely, one could belong to an inferior group and still be superior to most of the members of a superior group. For example, though it was probable that blacks were inferior to whites in intelligence, some blacks were obviously superior to "most whites" in intelligence. Hankins, in essence, agreed with the Boasians' liberal position, for he proceeded to argue that the "treatment of individuals on the basis of individual merit requires that they be considered as individuals rather than as undifferentiated members of a group."[25]

If Hankins was cautious to draw a distinction between the traits of certain individuals and the group to which they belonged, he was nonetheless intent on demonstrating that actual differences between groups existed. Although the Boasians had found comfort in the fact that the traits of races overlapped, Hankins insisted that the overlapping was merely the "expression of the underlying humanity of all races of men." Such a finding, Hankins asserted, should have been "obvious and taken for granted." According to Hankins, many people were attracted by the arguments indicating that individual men were similar because those arguments supported liberals' faith in the "democratic theory" and the "social ideals and policies growing out of egalitarianism" which had "been conspicuous in the evolution of western culture during the past century and a half."[26] But individual differences were still obvious to him:

> In spite of heroic effort to equalize objective conditions, inequalities of individual achievement are as great as before; they are in some respects much greater. Moreover, and this is the main point, if one is considering relative achievement whether in intellectual or artistic eminence, political power or financial accumulation and prestige, he must give a large, and in fact a predominant role, to inborn differences among men. . . . All men are alike in being human, but no two are alike as regards the whole complex of qualities—intellectual, emotional and physical—which determine reactions to and their utilization of environmental conditions.[27]

Like many of the sociologists previously mentioned, when Hankins spoke of racial superiority and inferiority, he was primarily concerned with racial intellectual differences. For him, racial intellectual differences were the "crux of the whole problem of racial equality or superiorities or inferiorities." As I have demonstrated, Boas stressed the fact that blacks did not produce a proportional number of great men as the white race. Although that hypothesis did not seem to detract from Boas's belief in the ability of blacks to participate fully in modern civilization, Hankins felt that the issue of genius was crucial in evaluating the abilities of races.

> The frequency of superior individuals born within the group is of the greatest significance for the role of that group in cultural evolution. These individuals are the natural leaders of the group. They represent its genius, its originating, pioneering, ruling, crowd-swaying individuals. It is their ability which solves the primary problems of practical arts, their statesman-ship which holds the group together and enables it to meet the great exigencies of the intergroup struggle for domination and their creative genius which produces those rare flowers of culture—scientific discovery, philosophical generalization and aesthetic masterpiece.[28]

The inability of blacks to produce a proportional number of great men, Hankins argued, accounted for the fact that, even while living in "contact with centers of culture," they had "lagged behind the general levels of such cultures." Although the purported backwardness of blacks could be explained in part by "climatic resistance" and "social repression," Hankins felt that these factors did not fully explain why their responses differed from those of the Japanese and the Jews. Despite the fact that the Japanese had had contact with the Western world for a short time, Hankins argued, they had made great contributions to civilization. Furthermore, the Jews, though not a race, had made "remarkable contributions" to civilization, despite being hampered by anti-Semitism. Hankins was unwilling to attribute the backwardness of blacks to their "lack of social opportunity" because he felt that "had he [the Negro] been sufficiently gifted he would have made his opportunity somewhere in the mist of the existing milieu." Thus, like many writers influenced by biological theories on race, Hankins stated that the cause of the predicament of blacks was to be "sought in differences of body and brain structure."[29]

Although Hankins believed that there were many significant morphological differences between the races, he felt that the differences in the size and structure of the brain bore most directly on the differences in "cultural aptitudes." Drawing on the antiquated Civil War studies of Sanford B. Hunt and Ira Russell and the more recent studies of Robert B. Bean, Wingate Todd, and R. Crewdon Benington, Hankins argued that there was a "neurological basis for racial

differences in behavior and characteristic roles in cultural history."
Confirmation of the significance of neurological differences, Hankins felt, was supplied by experimental psychological data. Drawing
on a study by Joseph Peterson which argued that blacks were approximately "75 to 80 percent as intelligent as whites," Hankins
asserted that the "negro as a race is confronted by a severity of
competition that under any circumstances will relegate the majority
of his numbers to positions of inferior social status." Hankins was
aware of the fact that racial testing was marred by methodological
problems, but he minimized the significance of those problems.
Hankins dogmatically concluded that "it does not seem probable
that the fact of difference can be altered by any improvement in the
tests or any discounting of results on account of inferior home and
school environments, differences in cultural stimulation, great social repression, hookworm or other environmental factor."[30]

It was necessary to argue that blacks differed from whites physically, intellectually, and emotionally, Hankins thought, because the
"Boas School" had "succeeded in conveying the impression that it
believes the races are equal in inherited capacity." Hankins interpreted Boas's arguments in *The Mind of Primitive Man* to mean that
"racial differences though real are less extensive and important than
popular opinion has heretofore supposed." The distinguished demographer then took a quote from Boas's article, "Race Problems,"
which had appeared in *Science* in 1909. In that article (quoted earlier), Boas had magnified the supposed differences between blacks
and whites. Hankins felt that Boas had vindicated his point of view,
and he went on to state: "That average differences between the races
may be small in comparison with the total range of variation within
either race, does not make them any less real, nor any less significant for social theory."[31]

Indeed, Hankins had exposed some skeletons in the closet of the
Boas School on the question of both the average capacity of blacks
and the issue of genius. But he had not come to grips with Kroeber's
article, "Eighteen Professions," in which Kroeber had insisted that
because the social and biological factors were so closely intertwined,
it was impossible to establish differences between the races. For this
reason, social scientists had to assume the "absolute equality" of the
races. The absolute equality of the races was an assumption; yet it
was a necessary one as long as the biological sciences had not established the inequality of the races. In essence, Hankins's arguments
rested on shaky foundations, on works that purported to bridge a
gap between the assumptions of both the biological sciences and the
social sciences.

The use of statements by Dow, Dowd, and Hankins is not meant to convey the impression that the majority of sociologists still clung to the idea of the innate inferiority of blacks; rather, they have been cited in order to illustrate the persistence of racism in a discipline that had reshaped its assumption on the issue of human differences. In accounting for this reactionary thinking, I agree with Thomas S. Kuhn's argument that to claim to have solved a crisis-provoking problem is rarely sufficient to cause scientists to change their allegiance from an older paradigm.[32]

The Thompson study, which was conducted in 1929, had surveyed social scientists on the question: "Do you conclude from recent investigations that Negroes are inherently mentally (inferior to) or (equal to) whites?" Because Thompson placed sociologists and anthropologists in the same category, it is impossible to determine the exact distribution of the responses of sociologists to that query. Taken as one group, of the thirty sociologists and anthropologists whose replies were usable, 57 percent held that the data of human differences was inconclusive; 38 percent believed that blacks were equal to whites; and 5 percent thought blacks were inferior to whites. Thus it can be concluded in the light of the survey that the majority of sociologists and anthropologists who were authorities on the issue of racial differences had taken the Boasian skeptical position, while a sizable group had asserted that blacks and whites were equals.[33] The following outline of the thought of two sociologists will give some insight into the positions on racial differences held by most sociologists after 1920.

Of the sociologists who were skeptical of the claims of intellectual differences between the races, none was as cautious as the conservative Midwesterner, Ulysses G. Weatherly. Weatherly, who began his career in the 1900s, was typical of the sociologists who believed that racial differences were real. In fact, he asserted in his book *Social Progress* in 1926: "That racial differences are real is fairly well established despite the frenzied denials of emotional champions of racial equality." But he qualified his position somewhat when he conceded that "until the ethnic explanation of intellectual levels is more thoroughly demonstrated it is safer, as William I. Thomas suggests, to take the individual rather than the race as the real variable."[34] The above statement was sufficient to satisfy both liberal Boasians and reactionaries such as Frank H. Hankins.

For younger sociologists who were just entering the discipline, a far more cogent explanation of the issue of racial differences was needed. That task was left to James M. Reinhardt, an instructor in sociology at the University of North Dakota. Reinhardt was a graduate of Berea College, a Kentucky college which had been integrated until the Supreme Court decision of 1908 forced it to close its doors to blacks. His article, which was published in the *American Journal of Sociology* in 1927, was entitled "The Negro: Is He a Biological Inferior?" It exhibited the caution characterizing the works of scholars who believed that the results of investigations of racial differences were inconclusive. The native Georgian, who represented the young liberal Southerners of the period, stated clearly that he was "not saying here that no racial inferiorities and superiorities exist"; but rather he was "simply saying that the arguments for their existence have always been made by peoples who happen to occupy, for the time, a favorable position; and that these arguments have had an emotional rather than a scientific and rational background." The assumption that whites were inherently superior to blacks, Reinhardt felt, was a "natural one" for whites who occupied a superior position in society. It was not surprising to Reinhardt that scientists supported the assumption of black inferiority because "scientists, like other men—though perhaps not in the same degree—are not free from purely emotional influences."[35]

Reinhardt attacked the argument of innate black inferiority on three levels. First, on the basis of his survey of the physical anthropological literature on black and white differences, Reinhardt thought it was "impossible to make any reliable statement of inferiority" when discussing "purely anatomical differences." Nor was it possible to find "significant differences" in physiological actions of blacks and whites "living under similar environments." Second, equally as untenable as the arguments based on anatomical and physiological differences between the races was the argument that the high mortality rate and the pervasiveness of diseases among blacks was attributable to their racial equipment. Reinhardt argued that "environmental influences as conditioning factors would have to be eliminated before any claims based upon susceptibility to disease are worth anything."[36] Third, he argued that intelligence tests which indicated that blacks were mentally inferior to whites, such as those administered by the Army during World War I, did not give the environment the "weight it deserves." Reinhardt proceeded to argue that the effect of opportunity factors on test scores was borne out by the fact that Northern blacks not only scored higher than Southern blacks on the Army tests, but also higher than some Southern whites. In response to the position taken by Carl C. Brigham in 1923, which asserted that Northern blacks were the highly gifted blacks who had left the South to enjoy the opportunities in the North, Reinhardt contended that the argument was a "mere assumption and nothing more." And he added as a rejoinder: "It might be logically assumed that the superior Negroes would most likely remain in the South, since they would be the ones to have acquired property and thus have some permanent attachment to that region." To Reinhardt, the evidence indicated that "superiority of opportunity rather than superiority of inborn race equipment" determined intelligence test scores.[37]

In addition to his criticism of racist theories, Reinhardt offered the viewpoints of the leading progressive racial theorists, as he drew on the theories of the biologist Franklin Mall of Johns Hopkins University and the distinguished anthropologist Franz Boas. Mall's comparison of blacks and whites had shown that "there were individual differences in both races of approximately equal extent, but no racial differences of significance." As could be expected, Reinhardt, who kept abreast of the more progressive interpretations, also drew support for his position in Boas's article which had appeared in *The Nation* in 1925. In that article, Boas had stressed the overlapping of the brain sizes in the members of different races.[38]

Nevertheless, the most conclusive proof of the capabilities of blacks was the progress they had made, despite oppression, since emancipation. Drawing on Monroe N. Work's *Negro Year Book*, Reinhardt noted that "in spite of these handicaps, and in the short period of sixty years he has made an increase in literacy of 80 percent. He has acquired by his thrift and toil property running into the billions." He also noted that blacks had "pushed into practically every line of business and professional activity." The argument that blacks were mere imitators was untenable to Reinhardt, for the "records of Negro inventions in the patent offices at Washington" demonstrated that the "accusation" was false. Finally, he concluded that the "store of folk lore and legend and song" would "give rise to some of the richest melodies and finest literature of the future."[39]

In short, the ideas of achievement and progress that had been used as compelling evidence of black equality by black and liberal white sociologists since the 1900s had become the most cogent argument in the liberal environmentalist creed of sociologists in the 1920s.

SOCIOLOGY AND RACE MIXTURE

The fascination of social scientists with mulattoes had begun as early as the emergence of the American School of anthropology in the 1830s. And, as demonstrated earlier, the polygenist theory had been used as late as the 1900s to support the anti-amalgamation argument. The polygenist argument had come under attack in the 1910s by such prominent sociologists as Carl Kelsey, George E. Howard, and Edward B. Reuter. But it was not until the 1920s, when many social scientists were imbued with the anti-racist ideol-

ogy, that they began to raise significant alternatives to the hereditarian explanations that rationalized the assignment of mulattoes to
the same caste as their darker brethren. Despite the fact that social
scientists reached a tentative conclusion on the issue of the biological effects of racial intermixture, other issues continued to perplex
them. What were the sociological implications of racial intermixture? Was the mulatto inherently superior to the full-blooded black?
Was racial intermixture the solution to the race problem? The an-
swers to those questions were far more sophisticated in the 1920s
than in earlier decades.

Grove S. Dow held in 1922 that there were hereditary differences
between blacks and whites; nonetheless, he did not embrace the
polygenist argument. In fact, the Southern-based sociologist argued
that "biologically the crossing of the strains as a rule has a beneficial
effect, and the mixing of the colored and the white is no exception."
Black and white crossing, however, presented social problems: the
mulatto, Dow argued, tended to be "less submissive" than the full-
blooded black. The mulatto, because of his peculiar temperament,
was unwilling to accept his social status; he combined the "nervous
energy of his white father with the physique of his colored mother."
Furthermore, and of even greater significance for Dow, was the fact
that most mulattoes caused problems; they were the illegitimate
offspring of the "reckless and immoral element of the white population." Like most Lamarckians, Dow vacillated between hereditary
and cultural determinants. Thus he asserted that the mulatto's
"heredity" was "not conducive to good morals." Dow concluded that
the mulatto was a problem for his black brethren because his color
was the source of class distinctions, jealousy, and social ostracism.[40]

Fortunately, the problem of racial intermixture, like many other
social scientific problems of the period, was the subject of inter-
disciplinary scrutiny: in 1924 the American Sociological Society
published papers representing the viewpoints of biologists, anthropologists, and sociologists on the capabilities of mulattoes. In
an article entitled "A Biological View of Race Mixture," L. C. Dunn, a
biologist employed at the Storrs Agricultural Experiment Station,
concluded from his survey of the "general characteristics of hybrids"
that mixed races were not "in any biological sense inferior to purer
types." According to Dunn, "the kinds of deterioration which are
often alleged to follow race-crossing may be shown to follow many
interracial matings, and to be due to social and environmental factors." He could "see scant comfort for any hypothesis of racial deterioration based on hybrid inferiority as a biological postulate."
There was evidence, however, demonstrating "that mixed races even

of recent origin may be biologically quite as successful as unmixed types which have undergone a longer period of selection in a given environment."[41]

The anthropological view of race mixture reinforced Dunn's position—to an extent. When dealing with the issue of mixture, Ralph Linton, who was a curator of ethnology at the Field Museum of Natural History, emphasized the emotional biases of American students who dealt with the problems of racial equality and racial mixture. The Philadelphian, who would eventually succeed Franz Boas as chairman of the department of anthropology at Columbia University, pointed out that American students of the problem had greater difficulty maintaining a "spirit of scientific detachment" than Europeans because they lived in a country where the color line had a long history. Of significance also, he asserted, was that "we all received impressions during our formative years which can hardly fail to give us an emotional bias." Nonetheless, Linton was intent on reviewing those issues as objectively as possible. In regard to settling the issue of the desirability of racial mixture, Linton thought it was first necessary to attack the issue of racial equality, for these issues were "inextricably bound." He investigated the issue of racial equality from the viewpoints of biology, anthropology, psychology, and sociology. From the viewpoints of biology and physical anthropology, the theory of black inferiority was suspect, for studies of the physical characteristics of different races had indicated that "no one race shows a significant preponderance of simian traits." The conclusions of such studies suggested that the "various human breeds are simply the color phases and varieties which are to be expected in any mammalian species of very wide distribution."[42]

From a psychological standpoint, the issue of the relative mental ability of different races was an "open one" because of the scarcity of data. Although intelligence tests were the only valid approach for settling the issue, Linton felt that intelligence tests in their present stage of development were inadequate. The results of the Army tests, Linton asserted, indicated that scores were "more dependent upon education and social opportunity than race, and that the differences revealed cannot be adduced as a proof of racial inequality." Such tests were in their infancy, and most did not "differentiate successfully between innate mental ability and that which is the result of training." Although Linton thought it was possible that "further work may prove the existence of racial differences in intelligence," it seemed more "probable that in these, as in physical traits, inferiority in one respect will be compensated for superiority in another, so that the final result will be an approximate equality."[43]

Some psychologists, anthropologists, and sociologists believed

that temperamental differences between the races were real. Proponents of this theory held that the distinctive temperament of a race
determined the type of culture for which it was best suited. It followed that since hybrids did "not completely inherit the psychological traits of either" of the parent races, they were "less fitted to carry
on the culture of either than individuals of pure stock." Yet there
was evidence, Linton pointed out, undermining that theory. It could
be shown that individuals of a particular race, when brought up
among members of another race, became completely acculturated.
There were instances in which "white children adopted and reared
by Indians . . . became thoroughly Indian in culture and refused to
return to their own kin." It could also be shown that there were often
cultural differences between members of the same race; profound
differences, for example, existed among the cultures of American
Indians.[44]

Despite the vulnerability of his argument concerning the mental
ability of races, Linton thought he had established that there was
not sufficient proof for the claims of racial inequality. Thus he went
on to state that there was "no reason to conclude a priori that racial
hybrids will be inferior to pure individuals of either parent-stocks."
Indeed, the achievements of hybrids indicated to him that they attained a high mental status. Revealing his assimilationist sentiments, he wrote: "All great civilizations of which we have record
appear to have been the work of thoroughly mixed groups." Pushing
his assimilationist argument to its limit, Linton pointed out that
there were "probably no pure races in existence at the present time,"
and although there were "relatively pure strains," they were "nearly
always backward in culture." Thus it could be argued that "racial
hybridization has not interfered with the perpetuation of culture,
while cultural contacts entailed by the process have stimulated the
development of civilizations." It could, of course, be argued that
most racial mixing had occurred between closely related stocks, as
had been the case with the three European races. Yet Linton noted
that the Polynesians, an admixture of the Negro, Mongol, and
Caucasian races, were an example of a hybrid group of diverse
strains that was physically and mentally capable of adjusting to
modern civilization. "There is nothing to indicate," Linton stated,
"that they are inferior to any of their parent stocks or that hybridization has been other than beneficial in this instance." Furthermore,
in view of the fact that the hybrid was "as capable of perpetuating
and improving culture as the full-blooded individual," the progressive anthropologist thought the issue should be faced "with equa-
nimity." "There is no reason to suppose," Linton concluded, "that
the United States of one hundred or five hundred years hence will be

any worse for the gradual absorption into its white population of the present Mongol, Indian, and Negro minorities."[45]

The arguments of Linton and Dunn were mainly intended to be conclusive refutations of the aspect of the polygenist postulate that the hybrid was inferior to one of the parent stocks. Another postulate of the polygenist position, that the hybrid was inherently superior to one of the parent stocks, was attacked by Edward B. Reuter in an article entitled "The Hybrid as a Sociological Type."

This early pioneer on the issue of racial intermixture, who taught at the University of Iowa, noted that "in biracial situations comprising two racial groups of unequal culture, the hybrids tend to occupy an intermediate social and cultural status and to produce a markedly higher percentage of men of prominence and leadership than does the ethnically mixed group." The popular explanation that attributed the superior achievements of the mulatto to one of the parent stocks stressed the inequality of the races. Reuter felt that the popular explanation emphasized that the hybrid was the product of an inferior race and a superior race, and that as a result, the hybrid would naturally occupy an intermediate position between the parent races. He pointed out that the popular view on the issue of racial differences was contradicted by scholarly opinion: "At present practically all sound scholarship in social phenomena assumes an essential equality in the native mentality of racial groups and, before a scholarly audience, this sort of explanation may be dismissed without extended discussion." That Kelly Miller's criticism of Reuter's book *The Mulatto in the United States* had caused Reuter to change his mind is evident; he even conceded that it could not be said that the hybrid had a "selected type of ancestry" which provided him superior endowments. "From the known facts in regard to racial intermixture in this and other countries," Reuter asserted,

There appears to be no sufficient evidence to justify the belief that the mixed blood populations are descended from mentally superior persons or groups. If there be any correlation between social position and native ability, the hybrid groups in their origin were probably below rather than above an average . . . there appears to be no adequate ground for a belief in a native superiority of the individuals of biracial ancestry that would account for their superior intellectual and social status.[46]

For Reuter, social rather than biological factors accounted for the differences in the achievements of the hybrid and one of the parent stocks. The social factors were the relative degree of isolation and the differences in mobility and opportunity. In order to substantiate that argument, Reuter drew on historical data pertaining to the mulatto in the United States. Once again the influence of Kelly Miller, although unacknowledged, was obvious. Before the Civil War, Reuter argued, mulattoes had enjoyed advantages over full-blooded blacks. As a favored group, mulattoes were trained as mechanics and house servants and therefore had close contacts with the master class. Mulattoes had also constituted a considerable portion of the free black population. As free blacks, they had the advantage of receiving an education before emancipation. Reuter thus argued unequivocally: "Throughout the period of slavery the rational as well as the sentimental judgments of whites operated to make the mulattoes superior men and to make the superior groups in the Negro population mulatto groups." In essence, the superior achievements of the hybrid could not be explained in terms of his mental capacity, but must rather be attributed to the superior opportunity he had been granted.[47]

The argument that social rather than biological factors accounted for the superior achievements of mulattoes depended upon the validity of the argument that the races were essentially equal. Psychologists during the 1920s were certain that their intelligence tests proved that blacks were inferior to whites. Thus it is not surprising that Kimball Young, a professor of psychology at the University of Oregon, was critical of Reuter's paper.

Kimball Young, one of Brigham Young's numerous grandsons, had been trained in both sociology and psychology. He had received an M.A. in sociology at the University of Chicago in 1918 and a Ph.D. in 1921 from Stanford University under one of the pioneers of the intelligence tests movement, Lewis M. Terman. Young was not dogmatic, however. He admitted that social scientists had "great difficulty in segregating the factors of innate ability from those of learning." For him, "learning capacity, with its central features of attention and imagination, is really what is meant by intellectual ability." Like Frank H. Hankins, Young also admitted that social scientists possessed "no adequate criterion of racial differences except the statistical evidence based on percentages of members of culturally comparable racial groups who reach or exceed the median performance of another group." However, since "statistical criterion" would perhaps be the only means for determining racial differences that social scientists would ever have, Young thought it should be utilized to provide insights into the problem. In an attempt to show the importance of psychological tests that measured learning capacity to the discussion of racial mental differences, Young drew on the findings of Joseph Peterson. In a "rational learning test" administered to white, mulatto, and black children, Peterson had found that there were differences between the scores of the different groups; he also found a "high correlation . . . between the results of his learning problem and tests of general intelligence." Like the Southern psychologist George O. Ferguson, Peterson had found a "close correlation between the percentage of white blood in Negro-white crosses and tests."[48]

That mulattoes scored higher than pure blacks on rational learning tests, Young argued, could not be fully explained by pointing to the mulattoes' superior opportunities in the past. At present it was evident, as even Reuter had suggested, that mulattoes were excluded from participation in the culture of whites. With that in mind, Young argued that psychologists had "some point in asserting that the superiority of the mulatto over the pure-blood Negro is at least in part due to superior strains of white blood as well as cultural factors." By attributing the mulattoes' superior achievements to the presence of superior strains of white blood, Young contradicted Reuter's assertion that the mulattoes' ancestry of the white side was composed of inferior men. Despite the fact that he presented no evidence to substantiate his argument, Young asserted that the mulattoes' white ancestry was not made up of inferior men. "Certainly, up to a generation ago, this was not so," he added. Young also felt that the inadequacies of the cultural theory were most noticeable in the inability to account for the greater occurrence of men of high intellectual ability among the mulattoes than among the pure blacks while at the same time holding that they had the same social and economic status. When one considers that Young believed that there were differences between blacks and whites, it is not surprising that he assumed that mulattoes occupied an intermediate position between pure blacks and whites.[49]

Proponents of the anti-amalgamation argument did not necessarily have to assert that there were intellectual differences between blacks and whites in order to rationalize their biased points of view. For an old holdover from the 1900s like Ulysses G. Weatherly, the fact that social problems arose "from the crossing of highly alien stocks" was sufficient to justify his position on racial intermixture. In his book *Social Progress* Weatherly argued as late as 1926 that the mixed groups "vary decisively from the parent kinds and are not adapted to either, for they not only have different physical traits, but cannot claim a definite social status in either group." Although Weatherly did not mention the mulatto specifically, the implication for black-white crosses was perfectly clear, for he stated that "crossbreeds" were "usually unwilling to be classed with the group which has the lower prestige, and are denied admission to full standing with superiors." Furthermore, it was obvious to him that "in psychic type" the crossbreeds were "unstable and often exhibited the worst qualities of both races."[50] From those statements, it is apparent that Weatherly's point of view on racial intermixture was consistent with the one which he had held in 1910, and represents the reactionary tendencies that were still present in sociology as late as the early 1930s.

It is somewhat ironic that Frank H. Hankins advocated "white-negro crosses." He accepted uncritically the arguments that the mulatto's intellectual ability ranked "intermediate between white and negro norms." But unlike some commentators who believed that infusion of white blood was the determinant of the mulatto's intellectual ability, Hankins thought it was the "blood of the immediate ancestral strains rather than of race that is of primary importance." Stating his sophisticated position clearly, he argued: "Average mulattoes are doubtless superior to pure negroes while high grade ones are distinctly superior to average whites." Hankins had clearly departed, to some extent, from the old polygenist argument; he argued unequivocally that there were "no sound biological arguments against them [white-black crosses]." And he added that despite the fact that sociological arguments against racial mixture were "weighty," there were equally strong sociological arguments in its favor. Asserting that the mulatto was generally "superior in intelligence to his darker brother and less diverse in physical appearance from the general American population," Hankins thought that the mulatto had a "larger opportunity in the white world." When one considered that many mulattoes were "undoubtedly superior in their biological inheritance to millions of white citizens," this enlargement of the mulattoes' social opportunities, Hankins concluded, "must be looked upon as social gain."[51]

Regardless of whether scholars like Dow, Young, Hankins, and Weatherly viewed mulattoes as the source of social problems or as prime candidates for assimilation, they could not purge themselves of the idea that there was something—to put it in one of its crudest forms—"in the white blood" that differentiated mulattoes from their black brethren. If there was something in the white blood, it certainly was not socially significant for large numbers of Afro-Americans with white blood who were relegated to the same status as their black brethren. In any event, the "mulatto hypothesis" was diminishing in popularity in the social sciences in the 1920s.

The Thompson questionnaire asked psychologists, sociologists, and anthropologists: "Does experimental evidence support or refute the hypothesis that Negroes of more white blood, are, by virtue of that fact, inherently mentally superior to Negroes of less white blood?" Of the psychologists—many of whom represented the progressive younger generation in that discipline—68 percent thought that the data was inconclusive; 9 percent claimed that the data refuted the hypothesis; and 23 percent believed that the data supported the hypothesis. Of the sociologists and anthropologists who responded to the question, 70 percent felt that the data was inconclusive; 15 percent claimed that the data refuted the hypothesis; and 15 percent thought that the data supported the hypothesis.[52] Despite the presence of reactionaries in the social sciences, it is clear that most competent scholars felt that they did not have sufficient data to make a decision on the issue of whether mulattoes were mentally superior to pure blacks. Concerned with the problem of making their disciplines scientifically respectable and conscious of the biases of earlier scholarship, they assumed a relatively safe position. A more definitive statement, which even today has yet to be reached, could not be made. And perhaps that is fortunate.

THE COLLAPSE OF THE DOCTRINE OF INSTINCTIVE PREJUDICE

Unlike the problem of racial intermixture, which seemed far from being resolved, there was a significant reformulation of ideas among sociologists on the nature of prejudice. Racial prejudice had been viewed by most competent sociologists prior to the 1920s as an instinct. The concept of instinct was undermined, however, by the new emphasis on concrete, empirical research. Ellsworth Faris and Luther L. Bernard, both of whom were transplanted Southerners, led the attack on the concept of instincts. As early as 1921, Faris noted in the *American Journal of Sociology* that the instinct concept was inconsistent. "At the present time," he wrote, "there is the widest diversity of opinion as to what an instinct is, there is the utmost confusion as to how many there are." For Faris, who was the chairman of the prestigious department of sociology at the University of Chicago, "human instincts" were "explanatory assumptions, not observable phenomena." And that accounted for the confusion in the use of the term. A great part of the "difficulty in formulating a doctrine of instincts" stemmed from the fact that "habit and social interaction enter so early that it is difficult to disentangle the original from the acquired." Instincts were not observable in their pure form because they were "constantly being modified by habit and social experience."[53]

In his classic study, *Instincts* (1924), Luther L. Bernard demonstrated that the instinct concept used by social scientists was too broad for scientific use. Bernard, who had received his Ph.D. in sociology from the University of Chicago in 1910, surveyed the works of 412 scholars and found 14,046 instincts listed. The concept was misused to such a great extent, Bernard thought, because most social scientists failed to draw a distinction between instincts and habits. He defined instincts as "patterns of action," which are "determined by the inherited organization of structures." Habits, on the other hand, he defined as "action-patterns," which are "determined by acquired organization and functioning of structure." According to Bernard, the most common error committed by social scientists was the failure to distinguish the "origin" of the "automatism"; thus they labelled "any relatively fixed or definite action pattern . . . an instinct whether it is acquired or inherited." Nonetheless, Bernard thought that "little harm" was done by using the term in a broad inclusive sense to denote "that the act is performed without reflection or consciousness of the purpose of previous plan." Most scholars, however, tended to use the term in its loose sense, "to emphasize the automatic character of the act," and then at another point "fall back upon the recognized or approved meaning of the term, implying that the automatism is an inherited action-pattern."[54]

Bernard was a proponent of behaviorism, perhaps the most influential psychological theory to emerge in the 1920s. According to Edward A. Purcell, Jr., Bernard believed that the instinct theory was an obstacle to the establishment of an objective and quantitative social psychology, not only because the instinct concept lacked scientific precision, but also because the difficulties involved in measuring instincts (if they existed) were insurmountable. It was possible, however, to measure and correlate diverse environmental factors. Thus Bernard attributed the central influence in molding human behavior to the external environment rather than to instincts.[55]

The idea that instincts were "inborn action-patterns" had direct implications for the discussion of racial prejudice. Once again it was a black sociologist who first provided the most trenchant criticism of the proponents of the argument that racial prejudice was instinctive. In 1927, Kelly Miller published an article entitled "Is Race Prejudice Innate or Acquired?" in the *Journal of Applied Sociology*. Miller, who was chairman of the Department of Sociology at Howard University, argued that when two races were involved in a superordinate—subordinate relationship, as was the case with whites and blacks, "race prejudice is mainly a one-sided passion and does not work with equal intensity in both directions." He did not believe that blacks embraced prejudicial attitudes. "This obvious lack of double-acting, reciprocal quality of prejudice," Miller argued, "indicates strongly that it is of the nature of other acquired prejudices and is not a natural antipathy." Furthermore, it was apparent to him that racial prejudice was not manifested by the infant, but appeared "only after it has been stimulated by adult instruction." In the South, white parents felt it was their "social duty to the white child to foster the feeling and belief that he is different from, better than, and superior to the black child with whom he is thrown into contact." The instruction of the white parents, which emphasized the physical, historical, and social differences between blacks and whites, was "calculated to give the acquired prejudice the stubbornness and strength of instinct." The theory of instinctive prejudice, however, could not account for the fact that racial prejudice was "modifiable by time, place, and circumstances." Miller contended that prejudice against blacks was more pervasive in South Carolina than in California while prejudice against the Japanese was more pervasive in California than in South Carolina. Then, too, it was evident that racial prejudice was "exhibited in varying degrees by the different sections of the white race," for racial prejudice seemed "to be stronger in the Nordic than in the Southern European." Furthermore, there was no evidence to suggest that blacks and whites opposed "the closest personal contact and personal association." What was opposed was "social familiarity and the assumption of equality." For Miller, perhaps the most conclusive evidence that undermined the theory of instinctive prejudice was the occurrence of interracial interbreeding and the desire on the part of members of diverse races for intermarriage. He pointed out that in instances where even the most diverse races were brought into contact, those races interbred. The existence of two million mulattoes in the United States was proof of that point. In regard to "cross-marriages," Miller thought they were "so likely that the community with fixed social policies and prejudices, dares not leave the matter to individual preference and predilection." Miller was certain that "unnumbered individuals in both races would prefer to marry across the race line, if they were not forbidden to do so by the ban of public opinion and the restraint of law."[56]

Miller's emphases on the systematic attempts of whites to teach their children racist views, the variability of racial prejudice, the obvious existence of miscegenation, and the social and legal sanctions placed on black and white individuals who might desire to intermarry were intended to demonstrate how ludicrous the idea of inborn prejudice was. Not only would Miller's arguments permeate the writings of many future sociologists, but they would also eventually influence indirectly the thinking of many black and white Americans and provide them with a defense for their liberal views.

One of the more definitive statements on the nature of prejudice, representing the new point of view adopted by sociologists consequent to the decline in appeal of the instinct concept, was offered by Ellsworth Faris in 1929. In an article entitled "Racial Attitudes and Sentiments," Faris began by repudiating the findings of what he called "the mythologic school of sociologists." These sociologists attempted to support the argument that racial prejudice was an organic attitude by relying on data derived from the study of the "olfactory apparatus" and the "gustatory function." Faris pointed out that these sociologists often contradicted themselves. At one point they would suggest "that the strange or unfamiliar is a native stimulus to fear," and at another point they would claim that the strange evoked "curiosity." Furthermore, the theory that racial prejudice was an organic attitude "could not account for the fact that the first Chinese were welcomed and approved" in the United States, nor for the appeal of the first Japanese, nor for the attention given to Mexicans in artistic colonies. A far more convincing theory, Faris argued, gave group consciousness a central role in the formation of racial prejudice.

The assumption is made that the consciousness of one's own group and the consciousness of another group, which require specific and definable conditions for their creation, are held to be necessary for the existence of race prejudice. The group to which I belong is the in-group, but I can belong to an in-group only if there is also present the conception of one or more out-groups. The reaction in race prejudice is never to an individual but always to some person or persons as representing, belonging to, included in, an out-group over against which my own in-group is contrasted.[57]

Faris felt it necessary to stress that "prejudice is a social phenomenon [for] which nothing in the organic or innate constitution of man . . . offers any explanation." Racial prejudice was "rather due to a complex situation in which two or more contrasting or conflicting groups came into contact in such a way that one is set over against the other, with certain emotional aspects to the conflict such as hostility, antipathy and the like."[58]

As was the case with most issues concerning race and race relations, Robert E. Park held a unique point of view. As late as 1919, Park had held that prejudice was instinctive. But he attributed to the environment or culture a strong impact that would significantly modify the potency of instincts in determining human behavior. Park developed the theory of the interaction between heredity and environment in an article, "The Bases of Race Prejudice," which appeared in the *Annals* in 1928. He believed that prejudice had "its source and origin in the very nature of men and their relation to one another. It gets itself fixed and sublimated in the habits of individuals, and enters into the very structure of society." Although he thought that prejudice originated in the "nature of men," his thinking had undergone a transformation, for he no longer believed that prejudice was an instinct. Prejudice for Park was "an attitude, a social attitude."[59] Furthermore, Park incorporated the idea of black progress into his analyses of racial prejudice and racial conflict. He wrote:

every change in status, whether of an individual or of a group, involves a change in social organization. Prejudice—that is caste, class and race prejudice—in its more naive and innocent manifestations, is merely the resistance of the social order to change. Every effort of the Negro—to take the most striking example—to move, to rise and improve his status, rather than his condition, has invariably met with opposition, aroused prejudice and stimulated racial animosities. Race prejudice, so conceived is merely an elementary expression of conservatism.[60]

Park then proceeded to argue that "there is probably less racial prejudice in America than elsewhere, but there is more racial conflict and more racial antagonism. There is more conflict because there is more change, more progress. The Negro is rising in America and the measure of the antagonism he encounters is, in some real sense, the measure of his progress."[61]

As was normally the case, Park's arguments raised several important questions. Did racial prejudice eventuate in racial discrimination? And if so, did not racial prejudice contradict the country's democratic principles? From the perspective of most Afro-Americans, could prejudice be rationalized in such euphemistic terms? Surely most Afro-Americans with the requisite skills and abilities who were attempting to improve their socioeconomic status could not take comfort in being victimized by mere "elementary" expressions "of conservatism." Clearly, Park did not realize how insidious antiblack prejudice was. Finally, although Park was correct in assuming that black progress exacerbated racial conflict, it is doubtful that there was "less racial prejudice in America" than "elsewhere." Certainly, black servicemen who fought in France during World War I would have taken issue with that assertion.

Nevertheless, it is fortunate that the idea that racial prejudice was acquired rather than innate triumphed. It had far-reaching implications, for it opened up the possibility that questions could be raised in regard to the elimination of prejudice. Sociologists in the 1920s had come close to extirpating the biological determinants from their thought.

THE STUBBORNNESS OF THE TEMPERAMENT CONCEPT

But the extirpation, it should be stressed, was not complete, for some distinguished sociologists still thought that the concept of the racial temperament deserved further investigation. Ellsworth Faris, writing in 1921, felt that the temperament was of greater significance to the social psychologist than the concept of instincts: "Instincts tend to describe us *en masse*; the temperament emphasizes the differences." For social psychologists who were confronted with the issue of accounting for differences in personality, the concept of temperament was significant. Faris went so far as to suggest that the study of temperaments would perhaps provide intelligence testers with valuable information. "If temperaments could be adequately classified and a method of determining them could be devised, there would be made available an invaluable supplement to intelligence tests."[62]

As late as 1926, Edward B. Reuter thought there were some valid grounds for the belief that temperaments were racial qualities. "It is possible, and some students consider it probable," Reuter surmised, "that as a result of variations, selection, and adaptation to a peculiar social environment and natural habitat, the Negro people may possess, as a racial heritage, certain characteristic temperamental qualities." In popular terms, blacks were characterized "as sunny, good natured, lively, excitable, kindly, home-loving, convivial, improvident and the like." Surprisingly, Reuter, who believed in the approximate intellectual equality of blacks and whites as early as 1917, argued: "So far as such terms are really descriptive of the people, and so far as the characteristics themselves are not a mere temporary expression of their recent historic status, they lend support to the belief in a racial individuality in temperament." Subscribing to the point of view circulated by sociologists such as Dowd, Faris, and Park, Reuter held that the racial temperament accounted for variations in culture. Blacks, he believed, "showed a tendency to select certain values and reject others." Although the values of blacks had been "selected for them" during slavery, since emancipation, Reuter observed, there had been "significant changes in the behavior of the group." Occupations which blacks had formerly monopolized were now controlled by other groups. Furthermore, blacks showed a tendency to enter "into occupations from which they were previously barred." Reuter admitted that the period of freedom had "been short and their choice of values is still narrowly limited"; yet he still felt that there was a discernable tendency among blacks to "select from the complex American culture the artistic rather than the utilitarian values." Since blacks selected these values that appealed to them, and since their values tended to be different from those selected by whites, Reuter commented that there was a "tendency toward cultural differentiation on the basis of differences in racial temperament." Despite his belief in the existence of distinctive racial temperaments, Reuter felt it necessary to "re-emphasize" that the racial temperament had "not been made the subject of any adequate scientific research."[63] In essence, regardless of how much prominent sociologists such as Reuter, Faris, and Park might emphasize the cultural bases of human behavior, they believed that all cultures had fundamental racial bases.

RACE RELATIONS THEORY

Despite the lingering concern with the concept of racial temperaments in the 1920s, the revolution in sociological thought on the issues of the capabilities of blacks and the nature of white prejudice, which was facilitated by the tendency of sociologists to perceive a steady stream of black progress, undermined the sociological theories which suggested that blacks were unassimilable. That revolution paved the way for the acceptance of a theory of race relations suggesting that the assimilation of blacks was not only inevitable, but also desirable.

During the 1920s, Robert E. Park was the most influential figure in developing the theory that assimilation was a natural and inevitable process in the evolution of society. In 1921 he presented in *The Science of Sociology* a general conceptual system that he had developed which could be applied to the study of race relations in the modern world. For Park, race relations proceeded through four distinct and sequential stages: contact, competition, accommodation, and assimilation. In the first stage, contact occurred when two races met on a "racial frontier" and began to interact. Contact ensued as the races competed for valuable resources. Competition eventuated in conflict. Conflict, which was "conscious competition," was ended by an accommodation in which a stable but unequal social order, such as a caste system, arose. Accommodation was followed by assimilation, when two races merged culturally and, ultimately, physically.[64] In 1926, after surveying Asian–white relations on the Pacific coast, Park presented his classic statement on the race relations cycle when he wrote:

the forces which have brought about the existing interpenetration of peoples are so vast and irresistible that the resultant changes assume the character of a cosmic process. . . . The race relations cycle which takes the form . . . of contact, competition, accommodation and eventual assimilation is apparently progressive and irreversible. Customs, regulations, immigration restrictions, and racial barriers may slacken the tempo of the movement; may perhaps halt it altogether for a time; but cannot change its direction.[65]

It is apparent nonetheless that as late as 1928 Park thought black--white relations had proceeded only to the accommodation stage. Although assimilation logically and inevitably followed accommodation in his cycle, his writings between 1913 and 1928 point to four obstacles—the black's skin color, the black's temperament, an instinctive white racial prejudice, and the failure of the races to maintain primary contacts—that had halted the movement toward assimilation.[66] Park argued in 1928 that there existed a biracial organization in society in which the racial distinctions were preserved, but were different in their content. Although the social distances separating blacks and whites were "maintained," the races exhibited attitudes different from those formerly held. Race relations in the South had changed from a situation in which all whites held a socioeconomic status superior to all blacks, schematically represented as:

$$\frac{All\ White}{All\ Colored}$$

Park conceptualized the change since emancipation—in which there was both social and occupational differentiation despite the persistence of a caste line that "maintained" social distances between the races—in the following manner:

White	**Colored**
Professional occupation	Professional occupation
Business occupation	Business occupation
Labor	Labor

"The races," Park concluded, "no longer look up and down: they look across."[67]

In regard to Park's theory of black–white relations until 1930, E. Franklin Frazier wrote in 1947: It was "a static theory of race relations. His theory not only contained the fatalism inherent in Sumner's concept of mores. His theory was originally based upon the assumption that the races could not mix and mingle freely. This is apparent even in his concept of biracial organization."[68] Until Park altered his belief in the four obstacles to assimilation which infused his theory and focused on the changing currents in the lives of blacks, his theory of race relations would remain static.

Perhaps the most dynamic theory of race relations presented during the 1920s was published by the black scholar Monroe N. Work in the *Publications of the American Sociological Society* in 1924. Work, who was the Director of the Department of Records and Research at Tuskegee Institute, presented statistics demonstrating that blacks had made tremendous economic, educational, health, and political progress since 1912. He concluded that since 1912 there was, first, a tendency of "race friction" to shift from rural to urban areas with the increasing migration. Anticipating Park's argument that black progress exacerbated racial conflict, Work pointed out that "race friction" was a direct product of greater contact between "progressive" blacks and whites. "The agitation and friction," Work argued cogently, "now going on as to where Negroes shall live in cities centers about the efforts of progressive intelligent members of the group to secure better places to live." Second, he argued that there was a "notable growth of race consciousness," which was a direct product of the "rapid economic and educational progress" of blacks, the conditions of World War I, and the contacts that blacks "throughout the world have established in recent years with each other." Finally, he argued that there was an increase in mutual cooperation by blacks and whites, especially in the South. Presenting a theme that had appeared in the writings of Booker T. Washington and that later resurfaced in the writings of Robert E. Park, and even later in the writings of Howard W. Odum and T. J. Woofter, Jr. in the 1930s, Work concluded:

There is a growing tendency, particularly in the South, to endeavor to handle the problems of race relations by whites and Negroes coming together on the basis of co-operation and working together for the best interests of both races. The general advantage of this method is that representatives of both groups may meet face to face and outline policies which are of mutual benefit to each of the groups and to the whole community.[69]

Work's emphases on the changing nature of race relations (especially in the major Northern urban-industrial areas), the increase in black racial consciousness, and the increase of black and white cooperation in the South were all themes that were developed by most prominent social psychologists (both black and white) during the 1930s and 1940s. Indeed, race relations were changing, but there certainly were castelike structures in both the North and South that remained intact. During the 1930s and 1940s these remnants would be the subject of study for W. Lloyd Warner's "caste and class" school of race relations, which confronted directly the proponents of black progress.

Nevertheless, substantial progress towards changing the attitudes of sociologists had reached fruition during the 1920s. These changes on the issues of race and race relations had taken place in sociology because external forces, such as significant economic, educational, and political progress, and internal forces, such as the drive for professionalization and the movement to adopt an empirical worldview, compelled sociologists to reassess the idea that blacks were inherently inferior and therefore unassimilable.

NOTES

1. John Hope Franklin, *From Slavery to Freedom*, 3d ed. (New York: Alfred A. Knopf, 1967), 492.
2. Park, "Negro Race Consciousness as Reflected in Race Literature," in *Race and Culture*, 294–97.
3. Stocking, *Race, Culture, and Evolution*, 300–301.
4. Carl C. Brigham, *The Study of American Intelligence* (Princeton: Princeton University Press, 1923), 182.
5. Ibid., 190–92.
6. Ibid., 194.
7. Ibid.
8. Dale Yoder, "Present Status of the Question of Racial Difference," *JEP* 19 (October 1928) 463–70; Thomas Garth, *Race Psychology* (New York: McGraw-Hill, 1931), 233–46.
9. John Higham, *Strangers in the Land* (Baltimore: Johns Hopkins Press, 1966), 277–86.
10. Franz Boas, "The Problem of the American Negro," *The Yale Quarterly Review* 10 (January 1921): 386–87.
11. Ibid., 386–87.
12. Ibid., 388–89.
13. Ibid., 390.
14. Franz Boas, "What Is Race?" *The Nation* 28 January 1925, 90–91.
15. Boas, "What is Race?" 91.
16. Melville J. Herskovits, "On the Relation Between Negro–White Mixture and Standing in Intelligence Tests," *PS* 33 (March 1926): 41–42.
17. Margaret Mead, "The Methodology of Racial Testing: Its Significance for Sociology," *AJS* 31 (March 1926): 657–67.
18. Carl C. Brigham, "Intelligence Tests of Immigrant Groups," *PR* 37 (March 1930): 158–65.
19. Charles H. Thompson, "The Conclusions of Scientists Relative to Racial Differences, " *JNE* 3 (July 1934): 495–506.
20. Grove S. Dow, *Society and Its Problems* (New York: Thomas Y. Crowell, 1922), 393–95.
21. Jerome Dowd, *The Negro in American Life* (New York: Century, 1926), 393–95.

22. Ibid., 396.

23. Ibid., 369.

24. Hankins, *Racial Basis of Civilization*, 301–2.

25. Ibid., 295–96.

26. Ibid., 297.

27. Ibid., 302.

28. Ibid., 306–7.

29. Ibid., 318–19.

30. Ibid., 323.

31. Ibid., 323–24.

32. Kuhn, *Structure of Scientific Revolutions*, 156–57.

33. Thompson, "Conclusions of Scientists," 499.

34. Ulysses G. Weatherly, *Social Progress* (Philadelphia: J. B. Lippincott, 1926), 35.

35. James M. Reinhardt, "The Negro: Is He a Biological Inferior?" *AJS* 33 (September 1927): 249–55.

36. Ibid., 256–57.

37. Ibid., 257.

38. Ibid., 258–60.

39. Ibid., 258–61.

40. Dow, *Society and Its Problems*, 181–82.

41. L. C. Dunn, "A Biological View of Race Mixture," *PASS* 19 (29–31 December 1924): 55.

42. Ralph Linton, "An Anthropological View of Race Mixture," *PASS* 19 (29–31 December 1924): 69–70.

43. Ibid., 71–72.

44. Ibid., 72–73.

45. Ibid., 73–76.

46. Edward B. Reuter, "The Hybrid as a Sociological Type," *PASS* 19 (29–31 December 1924): 66.

47. Ibid., 68.

48. Kimball Young, "Discussion," *PASS* 19 (29–31 December 1924), 77–78.

49. Ibid., 78–79.

50. Weatherly, *Social Progress*, 39–40.

51. Hankins, *Racial Basis of Civilization*, 347–48.

52. Thompson, "Conclusions of Scientists," 506.

53. Ellsworth Faris, "Are Instincts Data or Hypotheses?" *AJS* 27 (September 1921): 185–89.

54. Luther L. Bernard, *Instincts* (New York: Henry Holt and Company, 1924): 172–220.

55. Purcell, *The Crisis of Democratic Theory*, 37.

56. Kelly Miller, "Is Race Prejudice Innate or Acquired?" *JAS* 11 (July–August, 1927): 520–24.

57. Ellsworth Faris, "Racial Attitudes and Sentiments," in *The Nature of Human Nature* (New York: McGraw-Hill, 1937), 317–19.

58. Ibid., 319–20.

59. Robert E. Park, "The Bases of Race Prejudice," *Annals* 140 (November 1928): 12.

60. Ibid., 13.

61. Ibid.

62. Faris, "Are Instincts Data or Hypotheses?" 196.

63. Edward B. Reuter, *The American Race Problem* (New York: Thomas Y. Crowell, 1926), 82–84.

64. Robert E. Park and Ernest W. Burgess, *Introduction to the Science of Sociology* (Chicago: University of Chicago Press, 1921), 280–783.

65. Robert E. Park, "Our Racial Frontier on the Pacific," *SG* 9 (May 1926): 196.

66. For an illuminating study of the doctrine of obstacles in Park's writings, see Stanford M. Lyman, *The Black American in Sociological Thought: A Failure of Perspective* (New York: Capricorn Books, 1973), 27–70.

67. Park, "Bases of Race Prejudice," 20.

68. Frazier, "Sociological Theory and Race Relations," 270.

69. Monroe N. Work, "Aspects and Tendencies of the Race Problem," *PASS* 19 (29–31 December 1924): 191–96.

6

The Triumph of Assimilationist Theory, 1930–1945

The Great Depression of the 1930s slowed the mass migration of blacks from the South to the North. Americans in general suffered during the Depression; blacks in particular had a hard lot because most of them were in low-paying occupations or on the dole. By the mid–1930s, the great mass of blacks were receiving some form of public assistance. Furthermore, many blacks—especially in some Southern states—were confronted with discrimination when they applied for public assistance. In some sections of the country there were significant differences in the amount of assistance received by blacks and that received by whites. Yet on the whole, the New Deal marked a change in white attitudes toward blacks, for as part of a broader humanitarian interest in the plight of the poor, some politicians expressed their concern with the conditions of blacks. Of far greater significance, however, was the fact that black voting strength in the North had reached a point where the improvement of the socioeconomic status of blacks could not be easily overlooked.

During the World War that followed the Great Depression, most Americans, including blacks, enjoyed prosperity. Once again, Southern blacks migrated North and West by the millions, seeking employment in the war industries. When blacks confronted discrimination in the war industries, a mass march on Washington in 1943 was only averted by President Roosevelt's issuance of an executive order barring discrimination against blacks in industries with government contracts. Thus, during the war years and immediately after, the United States, despite its adherence to white supremacy, became increasingly concerned about its image abroad. As George M. Fredrickson has put it: "As the United States attempted to guarantee its social equilibrium and embarked on efforts to influence the non-Western world in behalf of its interests and ideology, overt and virulent intellectual racism came to be recognized as a dangerous liability."[1]

During the Great Depression and World War II, sociologists began to shift the focus of their attention from the discussion of racial differences to the discussion of cultural differences between the races and the nature of race relations. When the rise of totalitarianism in Europe during the 1930s forced American intellectuals to question the political implications of relativism, the idea of the inequality of cultures was injected into the discussion of the race problem by E. Franklin Frazier and W.E.B. DuBois. They argued that since the culture of most blacks did not provide them with the set of values and behavior required for success in American society, it was, in a pragmatic sense, lower than conventional middle-class culture. The assertion, however, was not an indictment of blacks as persons, but rather an indictment of the total conditions under which they lived, for their culture was a product of these conditions. Thus, despite the fact that these sociologists rejected the idea of cultural relativism, they still viewed the external environment as the central influence in molding human behavior patterns.

The debate that flared up in the discussion of the nature of race relations centered on whether blacks were a caste or a minority group. Robert E. Park's sociological theory of race relations dealt primarily with the social psychological aspects of race relations. As Frazier pointed out: "It was concerned primarily with providing an explanation of behavior in terms of attitudes."[2] Cognizant of the fact that the social psychological approach which characterized the work of Park and his followers ignored the structural aspects of the problem—particularly the unique position of blacks in the stratification system—a school of social anthropologists and sociologists under the leadership of W. Lloyd Warner began in 1936 to advance a social structural approach. By 1939, a debate arose, precipitated by Park's assertion that blacks were a minority group, between the followers of Warner and the followers of Park. From 1939 to 1945, Warner's group suggested persistently that caste was a more precise designation of the status of blacks than minority group since it took into account the permanent disabilities of blacks, while the Park group insisted that the concept of caste was static and hence ignored the dynamic aspects—the changing attitudes and behavior of blacks and whites—of race relations. By 1945, the Park group had forced an important concession from Warner when he agreed that the status of blacks was being redefined. The Park group, however, was forced to contemplate whether the minority status of blacks would accelerate or retard the movement towards assimilation when Louis

Wirth in 1945 suggested that the goals of the minority group directly affected the *modus vivendi* that developed between minority and dominant groups.

E. Franklin Frazier attempted to resolve the issue in 1949. On the basis of his research in history and sociology, Frazier argued that blacks were an assimilationist minority. Sociologists assumed that forces such as urbanization, industrialization, the rising educational levels of blacks and whites, and the position of the United States as the leader of the democratic world were undermining racism and that blacks desired assimilation. They argued that race relations were changing, and that the change would result in the assimilation of blacks into the American mainstream.

THE PERSISTENT ATTACK ON RACISM

Although beliefs in the innate racial inferiority of the full-blooded black and the mulatto had been abandoned by most of the leading authorities on racial issues by 1929, some sociologists writing between 1931 and 1945 felt that it was necessary to convince their remaining incredulous colleagues, popular intellectual racists, the American public, and racists abroad that racist beliefs could not be substantiated by social scientific investigation. On no other sociologist was the impact of the new assumptions on race more evident than on Howard W. Odum. By 1939, Odum, who was then teaching at the University of North Carolina, in a reference to the racist literature published at the beginning of the century to which he had contributed, wrote: "It seems quite likely that a major key to race conflict and exploitation, to misunderstandings and maladjustments is found in the earlier assumptions of superior and inferior races, based upon the premise that races are inherently and innately different." In the past, social scientists had made arguments in support of this assumption, but more recently their point of view had undergone a considerable alteration. The conclusion of the leading social scientists on the question of racial differences, Odum thought, was "stated best negatively" in the following terms: "There does not appear to be adequate data from any sources of historical study, psychological tests, cultural comparison, or biological heritage to justify the conclusion that there are permanent organic differences between the races." Stating his own position lucidly in *American Social Problems*, he wrote: "it is the assumption of this volume that there is a great and cumulative mass of racial differentials due to explainable causes and often so numerous and powerful as to appear in reality to be fundamental differences." For Odum, the problem of primary concern was the elimination of differentials.[3] Clearly Odum, like the new group of Southern professional sociologists who contributed to his journal, *Social Forces*, had accepted during this period the Boasian skeptical position on the capabilities of blacks. Southern sociology was no longer tainted by the provincialism that had characterized its origins.

Transitional figures, such as Park, often intermixed biology and sociology. As late as 1931, Park was still attempting to provide a definitive statement on the issue of whether the superior achievements of mulattoes were due to their biological or to their cultural inheritance. "If the mulatto displays intellectual characteristics and personality traits superior to and different from those of the black man," he wrote in the *American Journal of Sociology*, "it is not because of his biological inheritance merely, but rather more, I am inclined to believe, because of his more intimate association with the superior cultural group." It is clear that although Park placed more emphasis on cultural factors, he did not entirely neglect the purported biological factors; he only relegated them to a position of secondary significance. Biologically speaking, Park believed that the mulatto and the pure black differed in temperament. The differences in temperament were supposedly manifest in the differences in the behavior of the two groups. Park described the mulattoes as "more enterprising than the Negroes, more restless, aggressive, and ambitious." Furthermore, he accepted uncritically Alfred Holt Stone's description of the pure black as "docile, tractable, and unambitious." But Park was unwilling to place too much emphasis on the temperamental differences between the mulatto and the pure black, remarking: "Temperament in the case of the mulatto, has, however, been reinforced by tradition that goes back to the days of slavery and life on the plantation." Like Reuter, Park believed that the mulatto enjoyed superior opportunities during slavery. In addition, the mulatto's conception of himself had also been molded by his consciousness "of his kinship with the dominant white race." The mulatto believed that "whatever justification there was holding the black man in a position of permanent insubordination, it did not apply to the same extent to the brown." Park concluded that the "stimulating influences of his unique environment" were still at work, thereby contributing to the mulatto's superiority.[4] Despite his emphasis on the potency of the environment in determining the status of mulattoes, Park had clearly capitulated to the folklore of the superiority of "white blood" that had characterized Southern sociology before the 1920s. Park's position, perhaps because of his reputation and his role in training most of the prominent students of race relations, was not attacked directly.

Perhaps the most influential scholar to persistently challenge racism during the period was E. Franklin Frazier. Born in Baltimore in 1894, Frazier graduated in 1916 from Howard University, where he took the classical curriculum of courses in language, literature, natural sciences, and some social sciences. From 1916 to 1919 Frazier taught at Tuskegee, Saint Paul's Normal and Industrial School, and Baltimore High School. In 1919, he entered graduate school in sociology at Clark University and came under the influence of Frank H. Hankins, one of the more sophisticated demographers and racists of the period. Although he was influenced by Hankins's statistical approach to sociological analysis, Frazier did not share his mentor's beliefs on black inferiority and social problems. After receiving his M.A. from Clark in 1920, Frazier spent the next year as a research fellow at the New York School of Social Work, where he began a study of black longshoremen in New York City. The study was completed in 1924 and published in the *Howard Review* under the title "A Negro Industrial Group." This was Frazier's first empirical study.

In 1923, Frazier was chosen as a fellow of the American Scandinavian Foundation and spent a year studying Denmark's folk high schools. On returning to the United States, he was appointed professor of sociology at Morehouse College. While at Morehouse, Frazier set up the Atlanta School of Social Work and served as its director. He remained in Atlanta until 1927, when he published an article in *Forum* entitled "The Pathology of Prejudice." The article inflamed the whites of Atlanta, and Frazier's life was threatened, forcing him to leave the city.

Frazier returned to graduate school, attending the University of Chicago, where he received his Ph.D. in 1931 after working under Robert E. Park and Ernest W. Burgess. From 1929 to 1934, Frazier was a professor of sociology at Fisk University. In 1934 he became chairman of the Department of Sociology at Howard University, where he remained until his death in 1962. In recognition of his important contributions to the study of race relations and the family, Frazier was elected president of the American Sociological Society in 1946.

Frazier was one of Park's students who attempted to undermine one corollary of the polygenist argument. He was especially critical of a work published by Corrado Gini, a leading Italian sociologist who taught at the University of Rome. Gini had revived the polygenist argument when he asserted that the "nuptial fecundity" of the mulatto was low. Skeptical of that argument, Frazier examined the 1910 and 1920 census data on pure-blood black and mulatto families in three cities and three rural counties in the South. He found that mulattoes had "a smaller proportion of families without children" and that there was "on the average a larger number of children in the mulatto families." In accounting for the fact that the survival rate of mulattoes was higher than that of pure blacks, he offered an environmentalist argument: "At least two socio-economic differences indicate the cultural rather than the biological factors are responsible for the higher survival rate of mulatto children. Both in respect to literacy and home ownership, which may be taken as an index of more stable family life, the advantage was found on the side of the mulatto."[5]

Frazier's penchant for viewing cultural and social determinants as the central influences in the molding of human conduct was evident in 1940 in his discussion of personality formation. Frazier noted that Park, in the discussion of the racial temperament, had viewed biological traits as "the determining factors in personality formation." Although Frazier did not "deny that intelligence, temperament and physical heredity play a role in the formation of personality," he did suggest that these biological factors were not fixed quantities that determined the individual's "responses to culture," because the organization of the individual's personality occurred in "social interaction." Because social scientists during his day did not have an adequate technique for disentangling the "biological from the social determinants" in the formation of personality, Frazier felt that it was necessary to assume that social determinants, because of their central role in organizing and directing emotions and impulses toward goals, were of greater potency than biological factors.[6]

In his writings on the black family, Frazier employed the environmentalist argument to account not only for the deviation of the great majority of black families from the normative type of family behavior, but also to account for the conformity of a small number of black families to the normative behavior.[7] He called attention to three experiences—slavery, emancipation, and urbanization—that had had a major impact upon black family behavior. By focusing on the experiences of blacks in the United States, Frazier made a significant departure from older studies of the black family. The authors of these older works had insisted that racial and/or cultural traits were acquired in Africa. Such ideas, Frazier commented in 1932, "are based largely upon a conception of primitive peoples that once completed the current evolutionary picture of mankind." After surveying recent anthropological examinations of the sexual behavior of primitive peoples by Bronislaw Malinowski (1927) and Robert Briffault (1927) and an older study by Mary H. Kingsley (1897), Frazier insisted that there was no scientific basis for the belief that blacks and other primitive peoples had strong sexual impulses, or for the belief that the sexual behavior of the primitive was not subject to social control through customs and tradition.

The argument that the deviant sexual morals of blacks were a product of their African heritage also rested on the assumption that African customs and traditions were brought by the slaves to the United States and were perpetuated over time. Drawing on an argument developed by Park in 1918, Frazier stated that while it was possible "that in a few sporadic instances small groups of slaves with a common cultural background might have attempted to perpetuate their customary practices," in most instances, slaves with different traditions and languages were lumped together and consequently they "soon lost the memories of their homeland."[8]

For Frazier, any explanation of the current family behavior of blacks in the United States necessarily began with a discussion of the impact of slavery upon black life. In the earlier scholarship dealing with the black family two diametrically opposed points of view had emerged in regard to the influence of slavery upon the family morals of blacks. One point of view, which had been articulated by Willis D. Weatherford as late as 1924, suggested that slavery had elevated the family morals of blacks. The other point of view, expressed by W.E.B. DuBois in 1908, suggested that the current low moral standards of the black family were a result of slavery. Frazier argued that both of these points of view implied that slavery was a monolithic institution, and hence ignored the different types of treatment accorded to blacks under the varying conditions of the slavery regime. Frazier conceded that the numerous cases of the separation of black families and concubinage supported DuBois's position. He pointed out, however, that these practices, for the most part, were confined to a particular group of whites, and that they occurred in a peculiar environment. "To the slave trader and capitalist the slave might be a utility without a personality involving familial and other social relations. On the frontier of advancing slave power, beyond the reach of a humanizing public opinion, the slave was subject to the arbitrary power of crude adventurers." In other words, in those areas in which slavery was an industrial institution, slaveowners tended to ignore the slave's family ties and the slave's sexual behavior was not subject to control. In areas where slavery was a social as well as an industrial institution, however, slaveowners tended to encourage their slaves to conform to conventional standards of family behavior. As a result of this, the patriarchal family organization emerged within the slave regime among a small number of blacks, mainly composed of house servants and town slaves.[9]

Despite the attention he gave to the varying treatment accorded to slave families, Frazier concluded that, in general, the slave family was in a precarious position because even the family life of the town slaves and house servants "could not avert the changing fortunes of masters and the steady under current of powerful economic forces that tore asunder the strongest family ties."[10] Furthermore, the economic forces inherent in the institution of slavery, Frazier argued in 1939, most frequently undermined the ties between the father and his family. The ties between the mother and her children, however, were not as vulnerable: "Generally speaking, the mother remained throughout slavery the dominant and important figure in the slave family."[11] Frazier identified two types of family patterns that had emerged within the slave regime. The family pattern that developed among the great majority of slaves in response to the unstable conditions inherent within the institution of slavery was matriarchal in organization. The family pattern that developed among the small group of slaves who lived under more favorable conditions was patriarchal.

In 1937, Frazier also gave attention to two family patterns that had developed among two groups of blacks outside the institution of slavery. Of the persons who composed the free black group, many had inherited wealth from their white ancestors, many had social contacts with whites, and many had succeeded in gaining an education. In general, he argued, their families tended to be stable and "assumed an institutional character." Their family pattern was "patriarchal in organization with the female members playing roles similar to those of the slaveholding class in the antebellum South." Another type of family pattern developed among a group of blacks of white and Indian ancestry who lived in communities that were isolated from the currents affecting the lives of the great majority of blacks; their families were "sternly patriarchal."[12]

After emancipation the two types of black families that had emerged under the slave regime exhibited two distinct tendencies. In those few families in which the patriarchal tradition was established, the transition from slavery to freedom, Frazier argued in 1939, was "made . . . without much disturbance to the routine of living." The fathers in these families provided the bulk, if not all, of the family's income and often obtained their own land. Thus, they succeeded in consolidating "the common interests of the family." On the other hand, in those families in which the father's position was marginal during slavery, as was the case in the vast majority of black families, the ties between men and women "broke easily."[13] Thus, by the end of Reconstruction, the maternal family structure was the dominant family pattern for the great mass of blacks who were sharecroppers and tenants on the plantations of the South. On these relatively isolated plantations a black folk culture emerged which had "its peculiar social organization and social evaluation." Despite the fact the illegitimacy was widespread among those blacks in which the family organization was matriarchal, Frazier felt it was "generally a harmless affair, since it [did] not disrupt the family organization and involve[d] no violation of the mores."[14]

When a large proportion of the black population began to migrate to the urban areas after 1900, Frazier noted in 1937 and 1939, the kinds of accommodations they made to their new environment were determined largely by their cultures, of which their family behavior was a product. The vast majority of migrants were poor persons from the rural Southern plantations. On the basis of statistical data obtained from the census, social service agencies, the police and courts, and case histories from social workers, Frazier argued that the majority of those black families that were held together solely by the ties of sympathy and habit between mother and child, and those in which the father's interest was based only upon affectional ties, became disorganized in the urban environment. Furthermore, children from these families often became delinquents, and illegitimacy, which had been a "harmless" affair in the rural areas, in the city became a serious economic and social problem.[15] Frazier thought that the patterns of behavior molded by rural folk culture were not adequate to sustain blacks when they moved to the severely competitive urban areas. On the other hand, these three small groups of blacks whose family patterns approximated those of the white middle class generally succeeded in resisting the destructive forces of urban life. Their families tended to remain stable and some of their children entered the middle class. In view of these developments, Frazier was committed to the view that middle-class culture was a more valuable resource in the urban environment than—to use his value laden terminology—"the simple folk culture."[16]

In 1939, W.E.B. DuBois echoed in the *Journal of Negro Education* the theme of Frazier's position:

Negro self-criticism recognizes that most Negroes in the United States today occupy a low cultural status; both low in itself and low as compared with the national average in the land. There are cultured individuals and groups among them. All Negroes do not fall culturally below all whites. But if one selects any one of the obviously low-cultured groups in the United States, the proportion of Negroes who belong to it will be larger than the Negro proportion in the total population. Nor is there anything singular about it, the real miracle would be if this were not so. Former slavery, present poverty and ignorance with the inevitable sickness and crime, are adequate social explanation.[17]

In recent years, Frazier's and DuBois's position that the culture of most blacks was inferior to that of most whites has come under

criticism. The anthropologist Charles A. Valentine, who views
Frazier as the founder of the "pejorative tradition" of the culture of
poverty debate, has argued that Frazier makes "a direct logical leap
from social statistics, which are deviant in terms of middle-class
norms, to a model of disorder and instability." In assuming that
middle-class culture was an evaluative standard for judging the culture of the black poor, Frazier failed to view the life of the poor from
within and in terms of its own internal logic.[18] Although Valentine's
criticism of Frazier is valid from the cultural relativistic standpoint,
it should be noted that Frazier was concerned with how the black
poor could best escape poverty. Although he was perhaps naive in
believing that escape from poverty was only possible through the
establishment of strong patriarchal families, his belief should not
detract from the fact that he was writing during a period in which
intellectuals were desperate for a solution to the economic plight
crippling the nation. Like many black intellectuals of the period,
Frazier placed the onus of the responsibility of bringing about concrete change on blacks themselves.

Yet even in his own day, Frazier did not escape the criticism of one
student of the social sciences: William T. Fontaine. Fontaine, who
was the head of the Department of Social Science at Southern University of Louisiana, drew on the arguments of Karl Mannheim to
attack the position of black scholars, in general, and Frazier, in
particular. In an article, "Social Determination in the Writings of
Negro Scholars," that appeared in the *American Journal of Sociology* in 1944, Fontaine argued that "there was a correspondence
between the social position of a group and the method employed in
its supporting a body of knowledge." He believed that Afro-American
scholars were environmentalist rather than proponents of geneti-
cism because "the former ascribes the shortcomings of Negroes to a
nonracial factor and, simultaneously, implies demand for social reform." Fontaine argued that each group looks at the "data from his
own position and selects from them the type affording an explanation consistent with his interpretation."[19]

On a more specific level, Fontaine was critical of Frazier's application of the concentric zone theory to blacks in *The Negro Family in
Chicago* (1931). Fontaine was certain that "the absence of thorough
explanation of the numerous mulattoes in the more advanced
'zones' as well as their prominence as leaders in the lesser 'zones'
leaves openings for objections by the Nordicists." For the Nordicists,
Frazier's emphasis on "varying 'zones' of social disorganization"
among blacks would indicate that mulattoes lived in the more advanced zones because of the infusion of white blood. In essence,
Fontaine thought Frazier's emphasis on the environment did not

adequately explain why the mulatto was more "ambitious and energetic" than the pure-blooded Negro. Furthermore, Fontaine felt that Frazier had failed to explain "the correlation between racial characteristics and the degrees of social disorganization," and had not examined the relationship of "environment to ambition, industry, etc." Concluding his polemical analysis of black scholars in general, Fontaine wrote:

Born and confined to a milieu within which struggle against out-group and counterrace status has been waged for generations, his [the black scholar's] action and thought have become interwoven with "defense mechanisms." The defense has become a fixed response. As a result, though his analyses propose to observe scientific method and fact, still they too readily oppose before they have understood, or they halt the analytical attack consciously or unconsciously at those points most convenient for recombination of the data in accordance with group interest.[20]

Frazier's long rejoinder to Fontaine's article was a strong and often disputatious defense of his position. He began by presuming correctly that since Fontaine was "a Negro, he, too, is subject to 'social determinism.'" Frazier emphasized the fact that most psychologists and social scientists were environmentalists. And although he did not mention any names, he noted that some black social scientists were biological determinists. Furthermore, Frazier, who had received his graduate training during the height of scientific naturalism, pointed out that he had followed strict scientific procedures when he applied the concentric zone theory to his study of the black family in Chicago:

I separated the data on Negro homeownership from similar data for whites according to zones of urban expansion in order to find out if the rates for Negroes showed a gradient as did the figures for the total population. Thus I discovered the zones in the Negro community which became a frame of reference for my other data on the family. Somewhere in my unconscious I may have been trying to break up a "morphological category," but as far as my conscious self was concerned, I was engaged in what Lin Yutang has called "playful curiosity."[21]

Frazier was definitely a proponent of scientific naturalism, the major myth in the social sciences during the period. He sincerely believed that his works were not tainted by the value-laden parochialism that characterized the works of lesser scholars. He took pride in the fact that some blacks had criticized him for not representing "Negro women as martyrs in the relations with southern white men," and that he had been criticized "by some whites for being too damned objective." Like a true Kroeberian, Frazier insisted that he did not study the influence of genetic or biological factors on blacks because only the factor of color was "relevant in a sociological and cultural analysis." Frazier concluded that it was "misleading to lump together . . . objective studies which simply reveal variations in the intellectual and cultural development of Negroes and those which are obviously defensive and chauvinistic and emphasize achievements that have no meaning except within the black ghetto."[22]

Unlike Frazier, Edward B. Reuter realized the limitations of objectivity in the social sciences. In his rejoinder to Fontaine's article Reuter presented a balanced assessment. He admitted that it was "exceptional rather than usual for students of social reality to rise to a truly objective analysis. But the proposition assimilates the Negro scholar to, rather than differentiates him from, the current level of scholarly procedure." Accusing Fontaine of implicitly advocating a double standard for black scholars, Reuter commented that: "In the absence of conclusive evidence, we may not assume that white scholars reach a position on the basis of evidence and that Negro scholars reach the same position because of their social bias." And Reuter concluded on a note that is still relevant today: "This is not to deny that there are many Negro students who are unable to recognize and discount their biases, but the Negro group has no monopoly on undisciplined and incompetent scholars."[23]

The Fontaine article raised many significant issues. Like many racial determinists, Fontaine was critical of black scholars because they discounted the relevance of biological factors in their studies of race. By advocating a holistic approach to the problem of race, however, Fontaine was unwittingly falling into the trap of both black and white racists. Despite his trenchant criticism of obvious weaknesses in Frazier's studies—especially on the issue of mulattoes—Fontaine did not fully comprehend (or ignored) Alfred Kroeber's argument that the social sciences had to negate the relevance of biological factors as determinative factors in social and cultural behavior. On the other hand, Frazier recognized the implications of Kroeber's position, but was nonetheless under the illusion that he wrote "objective" sociology. In recent years, social theorists have pointed out correctly that value judgments impinge on the most dispassionate sociological discourse. Much to Frazier's credit, however, he avoided the pitfalls of the slipshod sociological writings published before 1910.[24]

RACE RELATIONS THEORY

Of far more significance than the old nature versus nurture debate during the period 1930–1945 was the debate that developed on the nature of race relations. Robert E. Park, whose theories were being subject to empirical verification by his former students, made an important and somewhat dramatic change in his position. Park's introduction to Bertram Doyle's *The Etiquette of Race Relations in the South* (1937) dealt with the evolution of black–white relations from emancipation to the present. According to Park, the social order that emerged after the abolition of slavery "was a system of caste—caste based on race and color." Park utilized Sumner's concept of "the mores" to explain why caste had survived up until the 1930s. "So firmly," he argued unequivocally, "was the system of caste fixed in the habits and custom—what Sumner called the mores—of both races in the South that all the social organizations incident to the Civil War and Reconstruction were not sufficiently wholly or suddenly to destroy it." Park, in essence, shared Sumner's belief that it was "impossible to reform the mores by law."[25]

Although Park agreed with Sumner's position in regard to the futility of employing legislation to alter the natural laws governing the relations between the races, he did not adopt a fatalistic attitude concerning the future of race relations, for he believed that the progress of blacks was affecting existing relations between blacks and whites. He wrote:

Although caste still persists and serves in a way to regulate race relations, many things—education, the rise within the Negro community of a professional class (teachers, ministers, and physicians) and of an intelligentsia, seeking to organize and direct the Negro's rising race consciousness—have conspired not merely to undermine the traditional caste system but to render it obsolete.

Meanwhile, the slow but steady advance of the Negro, as a result of competition within and without the group, and the gradual rise of a Negro society within the limits of the white man's world have changed the whole structure of race relations in the United States, both in the North and in the South. The restrictions on intermarriage still persist and continue to make of the Negro an endogamous social group, in much the same sense that the Jews, the Mennonites, and any of the more primitive religious sects are endogamous. On the other hand, in view of the fact that he has developed a society in which all the professions and many, if not most, occupations are represented the Negro has an opportunity now, which he did not have earlier, to rise within the limits of the Negro world. Under those circumstances the Negro group has gradually ceased to exhibit the characteristics of a caste and has assumed the character of a racial or national minority.[26]

Park did not explore the implications of blacks' acquisition of minority group status; yet he did suggest in 1939 that the undermining of the caste order, which was a result of the rising standard of education and the dispersion of the black population, tended "to diminish the distances between the races at the different class levels."[27] In the light of his *Applied Sociology* in 1924, it can be inferred that Park thought that the diminution of social distance between the races in the various classes would eventually lead to establishment of intimate understanding between black and white individuals in the same classes. Park wrote in 1924: "We know . . . that under certain circumstances reserves may be 'broken down' and that with this break-down social distances dissolve and the most intimate understandings are frequently established."[28] It followed that the establishment of intimate understanding between the races would inevitably initiate the transition from the accommodation stage to the assimilation stage. "Inter-racial friendships," Park had written in *Survey Graphic* in 1926, "cut across and eventually undermine all the barriers of racial segregation and caste by which races seek to maintain their integrity."[29] Because of the changes that were taking place in the United States, Park thought in 1939 that the completion of the race relations cycle was imminent and that society would be freed of the racial impediments blocking the class struggle that would inevitably follow. Summarizing his position, Park wrote:

Looking at race relations in long historical perspective, this modern world which seems destined to bring presently all the diverse and distant peoples of the earth together within the limits of a common culture and a common social order, strikes one as something not merely unique but millenial! Nevertheless, the new civilization is the product of essentially the same historical processes as those that preceded it. The same forces which brought about the diversity of races will inevitably bring about, in the long run, a diversity in the peoples in the modern world corresponding to that which we have seen in the old. It is likely, however, that these diversities will be based in the future less on inheritance and race and rather more on culture and occupation. That means that race conflicts in the modern world, which is already or presently will be a single great society, will be more in the future confused with, and eventually superseded by, the conflicts of classes.[30]

Although current sociologists disagree over the issue of whether the significance of race has declined, it seems that Park's predictions contain a bit of truth. The increasing cleavages between the black middle class and the black underclass are all too obvious in the 1980s.[31]

During the same decade in which Park was sharpening his insights, one Southern sociologist had moved to a similar position. Thomas J. Woofter, Jr., who had received his Ph.D. under Franklin

H. Giddings at Columbia University in 1920 and taught at the University of North Carolina, emphasized the progress blacks had made since slavery. Drawing on a mass of statistics, the native Georgian documented black progress in terms of: the rapid improvement of black health; the advance in farm ownership; the advance in the number of business enterprises and finance; the entrance of large numbers of blacks into industry and the advance to some degree into semiskilled and skilled positions; the increase in school attendance and the decrease in illiteracy; a growing black political consciousness; and the development of a growing leadership.[32] Yet despite the mountain of facts demonstrating that blacks were progressing, Woofter was convinced that the race problem would persist for a long time. In his *Races and Ethnic Groups in American Life* (1933), Woofter wrote: " Intermarriage having been shown to be a very slow method of eliminating racial difficulties . . . and cultural assimilation proving also to be a slow process, it appears that the United States will, for many years to come, be confronted with the problems of relating the life of unassimilated minorities to the life of the whole community." Like the earlier sociologists who were influenced by Booker T. Washington, Woofter did not propose a role for government in bringing about social change. Rather, he suggested: "The experience of the past ten years indicates that it is through cooperative activities . . . that the most progress may be made toward the development of the healthy tolerance and the elimination of the undesirable manifestations of prejudice."[33]

The optimistic argument that black progress had transformed blacks from a caste into a racial minority, which was explicit in Park's post–1930 writings and implicit in the writings of Woofter, conflicted with the pessimistic argument put forth by W. Lloyd Warner and his followers during the years 1930 to 1945. Warner, a social anthropologist who had been influenced by Alfred Kroeber at the University of California at Berkeley, came to the University of Chicago from Harvard University in 1936 and immediately published a theoretical article on race relations in the Deep South in the *American Journal of Sociology*. Warner argued that in the Deep South blacks and whites formed separate castes—the whites constituting the upper caste, the blacks the lower. He offered the following definition of caste:

Caste . . . describes a theoretical arrangement of the people of a given group in an order in which privileges, duties, obligations, opportunities are unequally distributed between the groups which are considered to be higher and lower. There are social sanctions which tend to maintain the unequal distribution. Such a definition also describes class. A caste organization . . . can further be defined as one where marriage between two or more groups is not sanctioned and where there is no opportunity for members of the lower groups to rise into the upper groups or of members of the upper to fall into the lower ones.[34]

There was also a class structure. Warner argued that the class system and caste system were "antithetical to each other" for the caste system prohibited "movement between the two groups and intergroup marriage" while the class system sanctioned "intergroup movement and at least certain kinds of marriage between higher and lower classes." Nonetheless, Warner argued that both systems "accommodated themselves to each other in the southern community."[35] Thus the social organization of the Deep South was represented by Warner as shown in the diagram.

During slavery the caste line (A, B), which in Warner's diagram ran diagonally between the class system of blacks and whites, was almost horizontal. Yet as a result of "economic, educational and general social activities" of blacks after emancipation, the caste line had swung upward. Feeling that the process would continue, Warner predicted that the caste line would eventually assume a vertical position (D, E). When and if that occurred, Warner believed, "the class situation in either group would not be fundamentally disturbed, except that the top Negro group would be equivalent with the top white, while the lower classes in each of the parallel groups would also be equivalent."[36] Warner felt that the biracial organization that Odum, Bassett, Park, and Booker T. Washington predicted would

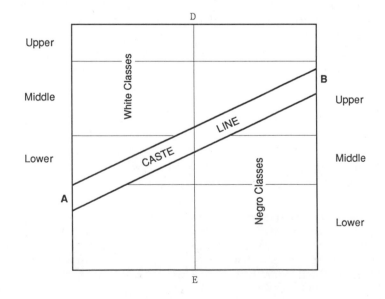

come to pass was a real possibility. In other words, society was not moving towards the assimilation of blacks, but to a true separate but equal society. Finally, Warner argued that upper-class blacks tended to be emotionally unstable because of their "skewed" social position. In regard to the upper-class black's problems, he wrote:

In his own personality he feels the conflict of two opposing structures, and in the thinking and feeling of the members of both groups there is to be found the same conflict about his position. He is known to be superior to the "poor white." (He is a doctor, say, but he is still a "nigger" or "Negro," according to the social context in which the words are used.) Metaphorically speaking, although he is at the top of the Negro class hierarchy, he is constantly butting his head against the caste line.[37]

In 1939, Warner and Allison Davis, a black student of his, coauthored a paper that was intended to demonstrate that the caste interpretation was theoretically adequate. It was Davis who, in a study written in collaboration with Burleigh B. Gardner and Mary R. Gardner, *Deep South*, had provided the empirical evidence supporting the caste and class postulations. Warner and Davis argued that castelike structures existed in Africa, Asia, and even among Indians of the United States. Although they believed castelike structures existed in most of the world, they viewed the East Indian system as the "most ideal form" of caste. Relying on Emile Senart's *Caste in India*, Warner and Davis pointed out that the distinguishing feature of the East Indian system was the tendency of groups "to isolate themselves to prevent intermarriage." Thus hypergamy, when it occurred, was a variation "from the caste ideal." Since intermarriage was prohibited in the South, as in India, Warner and Davis thought they had valid grounds for labeling the structure in the South caste. They stated clearly that although "our caste structure and the Indian caste structure" were not "exactly the same," they were nonetheless "the same kind of social phenomena and therefore" were "forms of behavior which must have the same term applied to them."[38]

In 1941, Warner, Walter A. Adams, and Buford H. Junker went to great lengths to demonstrate that Park, though they did not mention his name, was incorrect in classifying blacks as a minority group. They wrote:

Our social system does not give Negroes the status of a minority group as the term is generally understood in this country, because the members of white minorities may change their culturally inherited attributes for new, typically American ones and live, if they care to, in the larger community according to the general standards they find there. Furthermore, such groups are never subordinated in all their activities to the extent that

Negroes are. On the whole, the social pressure on them is less, and their chance of participation in the larger community is greater. Above all, the dissatisfied member of a white minority in the United States at least has the possibility of escape; he can change his name, his religion, or his cultural behavior, and, if he himself does not succeed entirely in being accepted, there is good reason to hope that his children and grandchildren may. He may marry out of his ethnic group and assimilate to his wife's people. He has some choice in the matter, while the colored person in America has no choice at all.[39]

Warner and his associates perhaps underestimated the strength of anti-Southern and Eastern European prejudice in the United States, yet they were certainly correct in the distinction they drew between the position of blacks and that of white minorities. The term *caste* was to them a more precise designation of the status of blacks than minority group, because it denoted the permanency of that status. To use their words, "the Negro is born into, lives in, and can only die out of the low status to which he is assigned."[40]

The writers went on to suggest that the term caste was not only descriptive of black—white relations in the South, but also in some Northern cities, such as Chicago. They noted that the monographs describing black—white relations in Chicago around 1920 documented the subordination of blacks, the rigid segregation of the races in residences, playgrounds, schools, and available occupations, and the white's primary and secondary beliefs in regard to the characteristics of blacks. After studying black—white relations in Chicago twenty years later, the authors were certain "that, if anything, social relationships had become more clearly defined in the interim and the separation of the races more pronounced." The writers' study of segregation in the city revealed "that the Chicago system of race relations is becoming more like that of the Deep South." Although the writers admitted that there were differences in the position of blacks in different locales in the city, they felt "that if caste . . . is not present [in Chicago] then something very close to it definitely is." Thus they argued that "the situation must be described as at least a castelike system."[41]

THE TRIUMPH OF THE ASSIMILATIONIST PERSPECTIVE

Warner and his associates were indeed correct in pointing to the structural impediments that hampered the socioeconomic mobility of blacks in both the North and South. Nevertheless, liberal and radical sociologists, both black and white, who were aware of the swift changes (and progress) in American race relations tended to argue that Warner's concept of caste was static. It ignored the dynamic forces that were altering traditional patterns of race relations, it mistakenly assumed that blacks approved of the restrictions against intermarriage and segregation, and it ignored the use of violence by whites in their attempt to maintain the status quo.

Elaine Ogden McNeil and Horace R. Cayton pointed out in the *American Journal of Sociology* in 1941 that despite the validity of "the so-called structural approach" in the studies of the Deep South, Northern race relations could not be fully understood by that approach. "In the North," they wrote, "the social structure does not depend on the subordination of the Negro, and rapid changes in his status have occurred within a relatively short period of time. Therefore, in addition to a structural analysis, it is necessary to study the processes which allow the Negro to change his position in the structure."[42]

A more fully developed position on the debate was put forth by Charles S. Johnson, one of the more distinguished sociologists of the period. Johnson was born in Bristol, Virginia, in 1893, the son of a minister who was an emancipated slave. Johnson graduated from Virginia Union in 1917. Though he never received his doctorate, Johnson received valuable training under Park, Thomas, and Faris during his apprenticeship in graduate school at Chicago between 1917 and 1922. During his tenure in graduate school, he was instrumental in the research and writing of *The Negro in Chicago* (1922), a work that identified the underlying causes of the Chicago riot of 1919. In 1923 he moved to New York and served as director of research for the National Urban League and editor of that organization's monthly publication, *Opportunity*. In 1928 he was appointed chairman of the Social Sciences department at Fisk University. Between 1928 and 1947, Johnson published numerous books and articles and established himself as one of the leading students of racial problems. In 1947 he was appointed president of Fisk University, and he remained at the post until his death in 1956.

In addressing himself to the caste interpretation in 1943, Johnson conceded that there were "similarities between Negro–white relations and a caste organization of society." Nevertheless, he felt that "this identification fails to reckon with responsible forces that are actually breaking up such caste organization as exists in the United States as well as other parts of the world where caste has been an accepted and established social order." Johnson argued that since forces such as urbanization, industrialization, the rising standard of black education, the economic progress of blacks, and the social and cultural differentiation within the group were altering the patterns of behavior and modifying the attitudes of both blacks and whites, they were also undermining traditional racial practices.[43]

Johnson argued that of all of the forces affecting changes in interracial behavior, urbanization was the most dominant. In urban areas there was more contact between blacks and whites than in rural areas. "The breadth, strength and variety of these contacts," Johnson commented, "have tended constantly to break down and rearrange the behavior patterns conditioned by custom and tradition in the rural setting." The active participation of blacks in urban life and their mobility directly affected relations between blacks and whites since those activities had "increased the range of communication and helped to develop stronger personal relations across race lines within a class framework."[44]

Another weakness that Johnson identified in the caste interpretation was the assumption that blacks passively accepted the social status that had been assigned to them. He pointed out that as a result of segregation, blacks had developed "a sense of racial solidarity and a consciousness of a struggle for status." Blacks exhibited those characteristics, which Johnson believed "were the essence of minorities, such as Jews, Orientals, and Mexicans, not to mention those transient minorities, the European immigrants."[45]

Writing at the time when the United States was preparing to enter World War II, Johnson was certain that the status of blacks and other minorities would be elevated in the near future. He was convinced that during the war the government would become aware of the fact that the "principle of racialism," which exacerbated the discontent of minority groups, was "dangerous to American Society." He went on to predict that before the war ended the imposition of mandatory controls and regulations "to ensure to all its minorities not only free but equal participation in the economic and political life of the country" would perhaps "become a political necessity."[46] Although Johnson was perhaps too optimistic about immediate reform, he was nonetheless astute in predicting that World War II would precipitate fundamental changes in American society regarding the status of many blacks.

Perhaps the most devastating criticism of the caste interpretation of the "caste and class" school was penned by Oliver C. Cox. Born in Port of Spain, Trinidad, in 1901, Cox migrated to Chicago at the age of eighteen to seek employment and to complete his education. He received his B.S. in law at Northwestern University in 1928. Stricken by poliomyelitis in 1929, he abandoned his legal career for social science, feeling that he could pursue it with less dependence on physical mobility. He entered the University of Chicago, majoring in economics, and received his M.A. in 1932. Yet Cox was not satisfied with economics and changed his major area of specialization to sociology. The reason behind this change he explained as follows: "The Depression caused me to change to sociology. I felt that if economics did not explain what I wanted to know about the Depression, if economics did not help me understand the great economic phenomenon, then I felt I did not need it. Thus, I changed to sociology."[47] Cox pursued his graduate studies in sociology at the University of Chicago, receiving his Ph.D. in 1938.

Unlike the other black sociologists who studied at the University of Chicago, Cox was a Marxist and was critical of Park's approach to race relations. Cox believed racism to be a product of the institutional functioning of a capitalistic society.[48] Although Warner's framework was a viable alternative to Park's and took into account the social structural dimension to race relations, Cox did not think it could be employed to describe black–white relations in the United States. In his discussion of Warner's concept of caste Cox argued that Warner failed to identify the characteristics that distinguished a caste from other social groups. To Cox, it was obvious that a caste was not the only group to prohibit intermarriage. "Endogamy," he wrote, "may be an isolator of social classes, castes, tribes, sects, or any other social group which thinks they have something to protect; hence, the final test of caste is not endogamy but the social values which endogamy secures."[49] Furthermore, Cox thought that Warner's assertion that there were no opportunities for intergroup movement in a caste system needed to be qualified: "To the extent that he [the white male] can have sex relations with Negro women he can 'fall' biologically. The mixed blood children that are born are, in the long run, the most potent equilibrator of the races, and the law makers of the South are by no means unmindful of this fact. The Negro may 'rise' biologically if he is able to pass."[50]

Cox next attacked one of Warner's concealed assumptions. He pointed out that Warner's prediction that the caste line would remain intact even after the races became equal in wealth, education, and political power implied that blacks, even at present, approved of segregation and restrictions against intermarriage. "The caste interpretation of race relations in the South," Cox asserted, "does not see that intermarriage restrictions laws are a social affront to Negroes; it cannot perceive that Negroes are smarting under the Jim Crow laws; it may not recognize the overwhelming aspiration among Negroes for equality of social opportunity." Cox considered it to be obvious that the biracial system in the South remained intact only because whites had "developed the necessary devices for maintaining incontestable control over the shooting iron."[51]

Finally, Cox argued that Warner's assertion that the upper-class black was mentally unstable because he was "constantly butting his head against the caste line," revealed clearly that an analogy could not be drawn between race and caste relations, for the phenomenon that Warner described did not occur in a caste system. Cox believed:

A person belonging to a lower caste is not "constantly butting his head against the caste line." In fact, the absence of such a phenomenon is so vital to the persistence of a caste order that it would hardly be inaccurate to maintain that it is definitely incompatible with a caste system. Caste barriers in the caste system are never challenged. They are sacred to caste and caste alike. The personalities developed in the caste system are normal for that society.[52]

Cox went on to suggest that Warner did not really succeed in establishing that the upper-class black was mentally unstable; the upper-class black's militance and sensitivity to oppression did not necessarily mean he was pathological. In view of the aforementioned weaknesses, Cox concluded that the caste interpretation was purely "fictitious."[53]

In 1945, Warner came close to conceding that blacks were not a caste. He took time to state that he did "not imply that caste is a permanent part of our society," and claimed that his main intention in using the term *caste* was to show "why men capable of reason and endowed with traditions which produced such manifestations of equality and freedom as the Declaration and the Bill of Rights continue to maintain a social world where reason and justice are often conspicuously absent." Thus, despite the incisive criticism of Cox, Warner seemed to be influenced directly by Gunnar Myrdal and the spirit of optimism of post–World War II America. He conceded: "At the present time there are indications throughout the United States and throughout the world that important changes are on their way and that the present system may reform into something quite different which will give Negroes many—if not all—the opportunities now denied them."[54]

Despite the resolution of the conflicts over the caste interpretation, the controversy revealed deep-seated uncertainties about the future of blacks in American society. Although both Warner's caste and class school and the Chicago School social psychologists and radicals believed that blacks had made substantial progress since emancipation, they disagreed over the extent to which blacks would be incorporated into the mainstream of American society. Writing during the 1930s, when many blacks suffered tremendous hardships in both the North and South, the caste and class school believed that blacks in the future would be limited to economic mobility within their caste. The Chicago School liberals and radicals, however, were aware of important changes taking place in the marketplace and within black society, and tended to predict that those changes would stimulate more black progress. When the United States entered World War II, they knew that black participation in the conflict and the desire of the government to cleanse its international image would legitimize greater demands for full inclusion in the American mainstream.

RACE RELATIONS THEORY AFTER 1945

For those sociologists who held that blacks were a racial minority, it was also apparent that they were a political and economic force that had to be reckoned with. Perhaps the most significant theoretical discussion of the political implications of a minority group question was written in 1945 by Louis Wirth, a Jewish scholar who had received his doctorate from the University of Chicago in 1926, a time in which Park, Burgess, and Faris were developing the field of race relations. Wirth, who taught at the University of Chicago and whose "love" was "the field of race relations," wrote "The Problem of Minority Groups" near the close of World War II. It reflected his conviction that a lasting world peace was dependent upon the resolution of the minority group question. "It is becoming clear," Wirth observed, "that unless the problems involved, especially on the continent of Europe, are more adequately solved than they were upon the conclusion of the first World War, the prospects for an enduring peace are slim." In a "shrunken and interdependent world," minority problems represented a threat to world peace, Wirth argued, and "the ideals and ideologies originating in one group are soon shared by others in remote corners of the earth." At that historical juncture Wirth was convinced that the United States had the potential to play an influential role in solving minority problems abroad. He knew that the United States' influence in foreign policy was dependent upon its domestic policy. Thus Wirth suggested that the United States would necessarily have to develop an enlightened program to solve its own problems; it was, he wrote, "unlikely that our leaders in their participation in the making of the peace will be able to advocate a more enlightened course for others than we are able to pursue ourselves."[55]

Wirth's major contribution to the study of minority groups was the development of a typology that delineated the marked differences between minority group movements. After examining the "major goals toward which the ideas, the sentiments and actions of minority groups were directed," Wirth marked off four distinct types of groups: pluralistic, assimilationist, secessionist, and militant. For Wirth, these types represented "successive stages in the life cycle of minorities." He continued:

The initial goal of an emerging minority group, as it becomes aware of its ethnic identity, is to seek toleration for its cultural differences. By virtue of this striving it constitutes a pluralistic minority. If sufficient toleration and autonomy is attained the pluralistic minority advances to the assimilationist stage, characterized by desire for acceptance by incorporation into the dominant group. Frustration of this desire for full participation is likely to produce (1) secessionist tendencies which may take the form either of the complete separation from the dominant group and the establishment of sovereign nationhood, or (2) the drive to become incorporated into another state with which there exists close cultural or historical identification. Progress in either of these directions may in turn lead to the goal of domination over others and the resort to militant methods of achieving that objective.[56]

Wirth believed that the typology had definite policy implications; it could be used by social engineers "to analyze the empirical problems of minority situations and to evaluate the proposed programs for their solutions."[57]

In 1949, E. Franklin Frazier, who always tested theories that were put forth by distinguished scholars at the University of Chicago, drew upon Wirth's typology in order to classify the black minority in the United States. He noted that blacks were unique among minority groups because they were "not distinguished by culture from the dominant group." The language, religion, values, and political ideals of blacks were the same as the dominant group's. And although the rural folk culture of Southern blacks differed from white middle-class culture, Frazier tended to view it as a pathological variant of the general culture. Furthermore, Frazier did not think that blacks themselves considered their culture to be distinct or worth preserving. In view of this, Frazier argued that blacks were neither a pluralistic, nor a secessionist, nor a militant minority. Although the Garvey movement had advocated secession from the United States, Frazier pointed out (erroneously) that the movement had attracted only "a relatively small number of Negroes who recently migrated to the city."[58]

For Frazier, an analysis of the major goals of the black minority indicated clearly that it was an assimilationist minority. He wrote:

The Negro has striven as far as possible to efface or tone down the physical differences between himself and the white majority. He does not take seriously the notion of a separate economy. In his individual behavior as well as his organized social life he attempts to approximate as closely as possible the dominant American pattern. Whenever an opportunity for participation in American culture is afforded, he readily seizes it; that is, so far as his past experience and preparation permit him to take advantage of such opportunities.[59]

By establishing that blacks at that historical juncture were an assimilationist minority, Frazier provided additional support for assimilationist theorists; it could now be argued that the major goals of blacks were not an obstacle to assimilation, once the attitudes of whites evolved.

The ascendancy of the assimilationist perspective in American sociology was undoubtedly related to developments both outside and within the discipline. The origins of an active black protest movement demanding full integration of blacks into the American mainstream, the social, educational, and economic progress of blacks, and the fact that blacks were a political force to be reckoned with in the North convinced many sociologists that there were strong currents that would change the attitudes and behavior of both blacks and whites. Within the discipline of sociology, the emergence of blacks and members of other minority groups, some of whom were activists during their youth, as authorities in race relations no doubt affected the attitudes of the sociological community. The failure of Warner's caste interpretation to gain acceptance in sociology stemmed from the fact that minority group scholars could not concede that blacks, with whose aspirations they were in touch, accepted caste status as part of a natural order. The assimilationist perspective, which had been developed by Park and others at the University of Chicago, prevailed for most scholars despite the challenge it received from Oliver C. Cox in 1948. It was not until sociologists in the late 1960s became aware of the persistence of white racism and the new interest in black nationalism that new questions were raised.

NOTES

1. Frederickson, *Black Image in the White Mind*, 331.
2. Frazier, "Sociological Theory and Race Relations," 270.
3. Howard W. Odum, *American Social Problems* (New York: Henry Holt & Company, 1939), 239–40, 242.
4. Robert E. Park, "Mentality of Racial Hybrids," *AJS* 36 (January 1931): 547–49.
5. E. Franklin Frazier, "Children in Black and Mulatto Families," *AJS* 39 (July 1933): 12–29.

6. E. Franklin Frazier, *Negro Youth at the Crossways* (Washington, D.C.: American Council on Education, 1940), pp. 273–75.

7. For a significant and intellectual biographical profile of Frazier that stresses the attention he gave to "stable and conforming family units," see G. Franklin Edwards, "E. Franklin Frazier," in *Black Sociologists,* ed. James E. Blackwell and Morris Janowitz (Chicago: University of Chicago Press, 1974), 85–117.

8. E. Franklin Frazier, *The Negro Family in Chicago* (Chicago: University of Chicago Press, 1931), 14–24.

9. Ibid., 25–29.

10. Ibid., 29.

11. E. Franklin Frazier, *The Negro Family in the United States* (Chicago: University of Chicago Press, 1939), 41.

12. E. Franklin Frazier, "The Impact of Urban Civilization Upon the Negro Family Life," *ASR* 2 (October 1937): 610–11.

13. Frazier, *Negro Family in the United States,* 61.

14. Ibid., 483.

15. Frazier, "Impact of Urban Civilization," 618; *Negro Family in the United States,* 340–75.

16. Ibid., 618.

17. W.E.B. DuBois, "The Position of the Negro in the American Social Order: Where Do We Go From Here?" *JNE* 8 (July 1939): 352.

18. Charles A. Valentine, *Culture and Poverty* (Chicago: University of Chicago Press, 1968), 20–28.

19. William T. Fontaine, "Social Determinism in the Writings of Negro Scholars," *AJS* 49 (January 1944): 305, 310.

20. Ibid., 312–13.

21. E. Franklin Frazier, "Rejoinder," *AJS* 49 (January 1944): 313–14.

22. Ibid., 314.

23. Edward B. Reuter, "Rejoinder," *AJS* 49 (January 1944): 315.

24. Alvin W. Gouldner, *The Coming Crisis of Western Sociology* (New York: Avon Books, 1970), 20–51.

25. Robert E. Park, Introduction to *The Etiquette of Race Relations in the South,* by Bertram W. Doyle (Chicago: University of Chicago Press, 1937), xvi.

26. Ibid., xxii.

27. Park, "The Nature of Race Relations," in *Race and Culture,* 107.

28. Robert E. Park, "The Concept of Social Distance," *JAS* 8 (1924): 339.

29. Robert E. Park, "Our Racial Frontier on the Pacific," *SG* 9 (May 1926): 196.

30. Park, "Nature of Race Relations," 116.

31. William J. Wilson's *The Declining Significance of Race* (Chicago: University of Chicago Press, 1978), suggests that "race declined in importance in the economic sector" and "the Negro class structure became more differentiated and black life chances became increasingly a consequence of class affiliation" (153). This position has been challenged recently in Alphonso Pinkney's *The Myth of Black Progress* (New York: Cambridge University Press, 1984).

32. Thomas J. Woofter, Jr., *Races and Ethnic Groups in American Life* (New York: McGraw-Hill, 1933), 232.

33. Ibid., 241.

34. W. Lloyd Warner, "American Caste and Class," *AJS* 41 (September 1936): 234.

35. Ibid.

36. Ibid., 235.

37. Ibid., 236.

38. W. Lloyd Warner and Allison Davis, "A Comparative Study of American Caste," in *Race Relations and the Race Problem*, ed. Edgar T. Thompson (New York: Greenwood Press, 1968), 229–34. Warner's theories were subject to empirical verification in a number of impressive monographs. They include: Dollard, *Caste and Class in a Southern Town*; Hortense Powdermaker, *After Freedom* (New York: Viking Press, 1939); Burleigh B. Gardner, Mary R. Gardner, and Allison Davis, *Deep South* (Chicago: University of Chicago Press, 1941).

39. W. Lloyd Warner, Buford H. Junker, and Walter A. Adams, *Color and Human Nature* (Washington, D.C.: American Council on Education, 1941), 10.

40. Ibid., 11.

41. Ibid., 12.

42. Horace R. Cayton and Elaine Ogden McNeil, "Research on the Urban Negro," *AJS* 47 (September 1941): 183.

43. Charles S. Johnson, *Patterns of Negro Segregation* (New York: Harper and Brothers, 1943), 316–20.

44. Ibid., 320.

45. Ibid., 316.

46. Ibid., 324.

47. Quoted in Hubert B. Ross, "In Memoriam Oliver Cromwell Cox (1901–1974)," *Phylon* 36 (Summer 1975): 204.

48. Oliver C. Cox, "The Racial Theories of Robert E. Park and Ruth Benedict," *JNE* 13 (Fall 1944): 453–63. Cox wrote: "Race prejudice . . . constitutes an attitudinal justification necessary for an easy exploitation of some race . . . race prejudice is the socio-attitudinal concomitant of the racio-exploitative practice of a ruling class in a capitalistic society. The substance of race prejudice is the exploitation of a militarily weaker race (460).

49. Oliver C. Cox, "The Modern Class School of Race Relations," *SF* 21 (December 1942), 220.

50. Ibid.

51. Ibid., 221.

52. Ibid., 222.

53. Ibid., 224.

54. W. Lloyd Warner, "A Methodological Note," in *Black Metropolis*, by St. Clair Drake and Horace R. Cayton (New York: Harcourt, Brace and Company, 1945), 774, 782.

55. Louis Wirth, "The Problem of Minority Groups," in *The Science of Man in the World Crisis*, ed. Ralph Linton (New York: Columbia University Press, 1945), 347–48.

56. Ibid., 352–64.

57. Ibid., 364.

58. E. Franklin Frazier, *The Negro in the United States* (New York: Macmillan, 1949), 680.

59. Ibid., 681.

Conclusion

When the distinguished Swedish social economist Gunnar Myrdal published his classic study *An American Dilemma* in 1944, American sociologists had successfully abandoned the last vestiges of nineteenth-century social Darwinist determinism. Such ideas as stages of racial evolution, survival of the fittest, and racial determinism, which had been the cornerstone of the defense of Jim Crow laws, disfranchisement, and extralegalized violence, had been subjected to close scrutiny and found lacking in explanatory power. Without a theory that could rationalize human inequality and suffering as the outcome of the working of natural laws, the proponents of racial determinism were on the defensive. What had happened during the years 1896 to 1930 was a slow transition from a point of view that was conditioned by racial determinism to one based on social or cultural determinism. Such a change in perspective could not have taken place without the transformation in the status of numerous Afro-Americans.[1]

Blacks who left the rural South to migrate to the urban-industrial North had brought the problem of the presence of a large nonwhite minority to the attention of many distinguished scholars who had formerly been able to keep the problem at a distance. Boas and his students anticipated the course that American sociologists would take on the issues of race and race relations. Their position, however, could not have triumphed had it not been for strong forces outside the social science disciplines. It should be remembered that although the Boasian position on blacks had emerged as early as 1894, it only began to gain large numbers of followers in sociology after 1910. Put simply, Boasian theory did not win a wide audience at an earlier period because it emerged during a period in which the

American public was hostile to nonwhites as well as to Southern and Eastern Europeans. Having seen their country succeed in its impe- rialistic ventures in the Spanish-American War, many American in- tellectuals entered the twentieth century determined that its North- ern and Western European heritage would be protected from both the "new immigrants" and nonwhites.

The proponents of racial determinism did not disappear once their arguments came under attack after 1900; rather, their writ- ings became more strident in tone. Furthermore, the timely rein- forcement from psychologists from the 1900s to the 1920s gave them hope that their theories would prevail. But the Boasians were up to the task of refuting the claims and dismantling the methodol- ogy of intelligence testers, and, by the 1930s (with the emergence of a new group of young psychologists), cultural anthropologists re- ceived concessions from psychologists.

For sociologists from 1911 to 1930, the question of whether blacks were innately inferior to whites was quite different from what it had been in the 1900s. Up to 1910, sociologists had been split over the nature versus nurture issue. Southerners, who were usually amateurs, favored the racial determinist theories; Northerners, who were usually concerned with urban-industrial areas, argued, on the basis of Boas's theories or on the basis of the evidence of black progress, for minimizing any purported inherent intellectual differ- ences between blacks and whites. By 1930, the regional and profes- sional boundaries separating Northerners and Southerners had for the most part disappeared. One either had faith in the equality of blacks and whites, or was skeptical of the racists' claims, or accept- ed the shoddy proofs of psychologists who were holdovers from the 1910s.

In the 1930s and 1940s, the ascendancy of the assimilationist perspective in American sociology was undoubtedly related to forces both within and outside the discipline. The gradual emergence of a strong black activist movement demanding the full integration of blacks into the American mainstream, the progress of blacks, the tangible fact that blacks were a political force to be reckoned with in the North, and, perhaps more than anything else, the World War II conditions, convinced sociologists that there were strong currents that would change the attitudes and behavior of both blacks and whites. Within the discipline, the emergence of blacks and other minority group individuals as authorities in race relations influ- enced attitudes in the sociological community.

Forty-five years have passed since the publication of *An American Dilemma,* and the assimilation of most blacks into the American mainstream does not seem imminent. Despite the passage of the

Civil Rights Act of 1964, discrimination in employment and housing still persists and prejudicial attitudes have not disappeared. This leads me to believe, as one of Myrdal's critics has pointed out, that racism is a creed equal in strength to the American Creed—the Christian and democratic value system of Americans.[2] Furthermore, Myrdal did not come to grips with blacks as actors on the stage of history who could play an important role in shaping their destiny.

Recent proponents of black nationalism have asserted that blacks should not assimilate mainstream white ways, but should develop a culture, based on a strong cultural nationalism, that would create a cohesive black community which would bargain effectively for political and economic power and restore the self-respect and dignity of blacks. Nonetheless, as sociologist Howard Brotz has pointed out, Myrdal considered black standards such as family, incomes, nutrition, housing, health, and education to be dependent upon opportunities in employment.[3] For most blacks, the opportunities in employment are severely limited, due primarily to both historical deprivation and present-day discrimination. Given the persistence of racism, despite the voice of social science with which we have been concerned here, it seems as if nothing short of a redistribution of wealth can raise the nonwhite underclasses to the position of social and economic equals in the near future.

NOTES

1. An interesting and important study suggests that British scientists and social scientists were unable to pursue a more enlightened path because they were not compelled by sufficient social structural change in their minority populations. See Nancy Stepan, *The Idea of Race in Science* (Hamden, Conn.: Archon Books, 1982).

2. Nahum Z. Medalia, "Myrdal's Assumptions on Race Relations: A Conceptual Commentary," *SF* 40 (March 1962): 223–27.

3. Brotz, *Black Jews of Harlem*, 118.

Appendix

The Internalist–Externalist Controversy in the History of Racial Thought

In December 1946, E. Franklin Frazier presented a paper to the American Sociological Society entitled "Sociological Theory and Race Relations." After surveying the writings of sociologists published between 1896 and 1945, Frazier, the first Afro-American to serve as president of a national academic association, concluded that most of the sociological theories that appeared during that period "were merely rationalizations of the existing racial situations." Frazier argued that the ascendancy of the assimilationist orientation in post–World War II sociology was due to the emergence of "a sociological theory of race relations . . . formulated independent of existing public opinion and current attitudes." Frazier had completed his graduate training at the famed Department of Sociology at the University of Chicago; thus it is not surprising that he attributed to his former mentor, Robert E. Park, a monumental role in the development of sociological theories free of the idea of black racial inferiority. Such a change in theory, Frazier suggested, could not have occurred without the strong social currents emanating from the migration of blacks to "the metropolitan areas of the North," which "destroyed the accommodation that had been achieved to some extent following the racial conflict during and following Reconstruction." Despite his willingness to concede that social structural changes affected race relations, Frazier insisted that "Park was the chief figure in the formulation of this sociological theory which provided the orientation for empirical studies of race relations."[1]

Frazier's explanation of why most sociologists had by the early 1920s discarded theories that rationalized the castelike social order raises many questions. Most conspicuously absent is the role that anthropology, under the leadership of Franz Boas, played in determining the orientation of many leading professional sociologists. Nevertheless, Frazier's hypothesis of the role of the black migration on theories of race relations is certainly perceptive and his thesis on that issue has been expanded in this book.

Most contemporary scholars who examine the history of the triumph of liberal environmentalism in the American social sciences during the years

1896 to 1945 argue that it was the "internal" developments within the social sciences that generated the movement from racial determinism to cultural determinism. Furthermore, they argue that Franz Boas played the most significant role in the intellectual revolt against racism in the American social sciences.

Typical of the pioneering works that tend to stress the rational aspects of the nature versus nurture debate and to assume that Boas possessed a superior intellect which enabled him to undermine the validity of racist theories is Thomas F. Gossett's *Race: The History of an Idea in America*. Gossett states: "What chiefly happened in the 1920s to set the tide of racism was that one man, Franz Boas, who was an authority in several fields which had been the strongest sources of racism, quietly asked for the proof that race determines mentality and temperament." For Gossett, it is the "illogic of racism" that led to its demise in the American sciences and social sciences. He argues that "racism had developed into such a contradictory mass of the unprovable and the emotional that the serious students eventually recognized that as a source of explanation for mental and temperamental traits of a people it was worthless."[2]

Perhaps the most influential student of Boas's racial thought is George W. Stocking, Jr. Adopting some of Thomas Kuhn's ideas on the emergence of new paradigms in the scientific community—which appeared in his controversial *The Structure of Scientific Revolutions* (1962)—Stocking has argued in his often quoted work, *Race, Culture, and Evolution*, that the "internal . . . development within *each* of the social sciences conditioned the movement toward an explanation of human behavior in purely cultural terms." He proceeds to state that: "In the long run, it was Boasian anthropology—rather than the racialist writers associated with the eugenics movement—which was able to speak to Americans as the voice of science on all matters of race, culture, and evolution."[3]

At the same time as the "internalist" critique was emerging, there was an "external" forces argument emerging in the discussion of racial thought. The proponents of the external forces argument concur in the opinion that internal developments were significant; nevertheless, they argue that those internal developments were a direct product of social structural changes. In response to Gossett, Leonard Lieberman argued in an article that was originally published in *Phylon* in 1968 that: "Gossett's position seems to be that of the historian and humanist: men and ideas make history. The view that must be added concerns the influence of cultural conditions. Boas's ideas could only spread when the social structure was ready. Men make history, but they do not do so immediately."[4]

An important, but overstated, assessment of Boas is the anthropologist Marvin Harris's analysis in *The Rise of Anthropological Theory* (1968). Insisting that the Boas contribution took place in a period of reaction, Harris has written:

The attack on racist theories coincided in the United States with a period of strong democratic countercurrents. Boas was a member of an immigrant minority, who as an individual was obviously unprepared to concede the superiority of the dominant white Anglo-Saxon Protestant intellectual and business elites. Nonetheless, he was no superman; without supporting currents powerfully impelled by the conditions of his adopted social milieu, racism might very well have survived and triumphed in American, as it did in German and Italian, anthropology. But the anti-racist counter-currents in the United States were nourished by the vast influx of Poles, Russians, and Italians, whose Catholicism or Judaism was not easily worked up into a master-race complex. The immigrant groups participated in the political and ideological struggle to break the pattern of unrestricted competition, which marks the beginnings of United States welfare capitalism.[5]

The conflict between those who view the emergence of the culture concept as the product of internal changes in the social science disciplines and those who believe that the social structure determined the emergence of the concept has yet to be resolved. The historian Hamilton Cravens has attempted to reconcile the conflict with his suggestion that Boas and his students were both transforming their discipline "into a respected science and profession in America" and fighting against racist currents in the nation. The position is stated clearly by Cravens when he writes:

The culture idea had obvious implications for the stances men took in the world of politics no less than the world of science. The culture idea was at odds with the notion of "Nordic" superiority, not to mention many other values in WASP culture or the assumptions of "mainstream" middle class progressive ideology. The Boasians were separated from WASP culture; several were immigrants, of Jewish background, or both. If the Boasians had a common political posture, probably it was to the left of mainstream, middle class progressivism; they were not impressed by the progressives' vision of a clean, efficient, and mechanistically democratic society. They believed that ethnic tolerance and pluralism were indispensable prerequisites to American democracy.[6]

Cravens's explanation of the culture idea as a product of "marginal" men and women gives some useful insights into why it emerged during a period of ethnic upheaval in the United States; however, he does not explain adequately why sociologists—most of whom were of British ancestry—eventually accepted the culture idea. It is my argument that for sociologists, imbued as they were with the mainstream progressive ideology, the gradual acceptance of the Boasian position on race relations had more to do with the problems stemming from the migration of blacks into Northern cities than with Boas's stature as an anthropologist. Confronted with the evidence of black progress, the leading sociologists found it exceedingly difficult to reconcile black progress with theories of black inferiority.

NOTES

1. Frazier, "Sociological Theory and Race Relations, 265–71.
2. Gossett, *Race*, 423–30.
3. Stocking, *Race, Culture, and Evolution*, 303, 307.
4. Lieberman, "The Debate Over Race: A Study in the Sociology of Knowledge," in *Race and IQ*, ed. Ashley Montagu (New York: Oxford University Press, 1975), 30.
5. Marvin Harris, *The Rise of Anthropological Theory* (New York: Thomas Y. Crowell, 1968), 297.
6. Cravens, *Triumph of Evolution*, 92.

Bibliography

PRIMARY SOURCES

Books

Baker, Ray Stannard. *Following the Color Line*. New York: Doubleday, 1908.

Bernard, Luther L. *Instincts*. New York: Henry Holt and Company, 1924.

Boas, Franz. *The Mind of Primitive Man*. New York: Macmillan, 1911.

Brigham, Carl C. *The Study of American Intelligence*. Princeton: Princeton University Press, 1923.

Brigham, J. A., ed. *AUP 20*. Atlanta: Atlanta University Press, 1916.

Brinton, Daniel G. *The American Race*. New York: N.D.C. Hodges, 1891.

Cooley, Charles H. *Social Organization*. New York: Charles Scribner's Sons, 1909.

_____. *Social Process*. New York: Charles Scribner's Sons, 1918.

Dollard, John. *Caste and Class in a Southern Town*. New Haven, Conn.: Yale University Press, 1937.

Dow, Grove S. *Society and Its Problems*. New York: Thomas Y. Crowell, 1922.

Dowd, Jerome. *The Negro Races*. 2 vols. New York: Macmillan, 1907–1914.

_____. *The Negro in American Life*. New York: Century, 1926.

Doyle, Bertram W. *The Etiquette of Race Relations in the South*. Chicago: University of Chicago Press, 1937.

DuBois, W.E.B. *The Philadelphia Negro: A Social Study*. 1899. Reprint. Schocken, 1967.

_____. *The Black North in 1901: A Social Study*. A series of articles originally appearing in *The New York Times*, November–December, 1901. New York: Arno Press and The New York Times, 1969.

_____. *The Negro*. New York: Home University Library, 1915.

_____. *Black Reconstruction in America, 1860–1880*. 1935. Reprint. New York: Atheneum, 1969.

———. *Black Folk Then and Now*. New York: Henry Holt and Company, 1939.

———. *The Autobiography of W.E.B. DuBois*. New York: International Publishers, 1968.

Faris, Ellsworth. *The Nature of Human Nature*. New York: McGraw-Hill, 1937.

Franklin, John Hope, ed. *Three Negro Classics*. New York: Avon Books, 1965.

Frazier, E. Franklin. *The Negro Family in Chicago*. Chicago: University of Chicago Press, 1931.

———. *The Negro Family in the United States*. Chicago: University of Chicago Press, 1939.

———. *Negro Youth at the Crossways*. Washington, D.C.: American Council on Education, 1940.

———. *The Negro in the United States*. New York: Macmillan, 1949.

Gardner, Burleigh B., Mary R. Gardner, and Allison Davis. *Deep South*. Chicago: University of Chicago Press, 1941.

Garth, Thomas. *Race Psychology*. New York: McGraw-Hill, 1931.

Giddings, Franklin H. *The Principles of Sociology*. New York: Macmillan, 1896.

Hankins, Frank H. *The Racial Basis of Civilization*. New York: Alfred A. Knopf, 1926.

Isaacs, Harold R. *The New World of Negro Americans*. New York: Viking Press, 1964.

Johnson, Charles S. *Patterns of Negro Segregation*. New York: Harper and Brothers, 1943.

Kelsey, Carl. *The Physical Basis of Society*. New York: D. Appleton and Company, 1916.

Miller, Kelly. *Race Adjustment: Essays on the Negro in America*. New York: Neale Publishing Company, 1908.

Montagu, Ashley, ed. *Race and IQ*. New York: Oxford University Press, 1975.

Odum, Howard W. *Social and Mental Traits of the Negro*. New York: Columbia University Press, 1910.

———. *American Social Problems*. New York: Henry Holt & Company, 1939.

Park, Robert E. *Race and Culture*. New York: The Free Press, 1950.

Park, Robert E., and Ernest W. Burgess. *Introduction to the Science of Sociology*. Chicago: University of Chicago Press, 1921.

Powdermaker, Hortense. *After Freedom*. New York: Viking Press, 1939.

Reuter, Edward B. *The American Race Problem*. New York: Thomas Y. Cowell, 1926.

Ross, Edward A. *Social Control*. New York: Macmillan, 1901.

Sumner, William G. *Folkways*. Boston: Ginn and Company, 1906.

Tillinghast, Joseph A. *The Negro in Africa and America*. New York: Macmillan, 1902.

Thompson, Edgar T., ed. *Race Relations and the Race Problem*. New York: Greenwood Press, 1968.

Ward, Lester F. *Applied Sociology.* Boston: Ginn and Company, 1906.
Warner, W. Lloyd, Buford H. Junker, and Walter A. Adams. *Color and Human Nature.* Washington, D.C.: American Council on Education, 1941.
Weatherly, Ulysses G. *Social Progress.* Philadelphia: J. B. Lippincott, 1926.
Woofter, Thomas G. *Races and Ethnic Groups in American Life.* New York: McGraw-Hill, 1933.

Articles, Discussions, Reviews, Introductions

Bassett, John Spencer. "Discussion," *AJS* 13 (May 1908): 825–28.
Belin, H. "The Civil War as Seen Through Southern Glasses," *AJS* 9 (September 1903): 259–67.
————. "A Southern View of Slavery," *AJS* 13 (January 1908): 513–22.
Boas, Franz. "Human Faculty as Determined by Race," *AAAS* 43 (August 1894): 302–27.
————. "The Mind of Primitive Man," *JAFL* 12 (January–March 1901): 1–11.
————. "What the Negro has Done in Africa," *The Ethical Record* 5 (March 1904): 106–9.
————. "The Negro and the Demands of Modern Life," *Charities* 15 (7 October 1905): 85–88.
————. "The Negro's Past," *AUP* 19 (31 May 1906): 1–15.
————. Review of "The Negro Races," by Jerome Dowd. *PSO* 23 (December 1908): 729–30.
————. "Industries of the African Negroes," *The Southern Workman* 38 (April 1909): 217–29.
————. "Race Problems in America," *Science* 28 (May 1909): 839–49.
————. "The Problem of the American Negro," *The Yale Quarterly Review* 10 (January 1921): 384–95.
————. "What Is Race?" *The Nation* 28 (January 1925): 89–91.
Brigham, Carl C. "Intelligence Tests of Immigrant Groups," *PR* 37 (March 1930): 158–65.
Brinton, Daniel G. "The Aims of Anthropology," *AAAS* 44 (December 1895): 1–17.
Cayton, Horace R., and Elaine Ogden McNeil. "Research on the Urban Negro," *AJS* 47 (September 1941): 176–83.
Cooley, Charles H. "Genius, Fame and the Comparison of Races," *Annals* 9 (May 1897): 317–58.
Cox, Oliver C. "The Modern Class School of Race Relations," *SF* 21 (December 1942): 218–26.
————. "The Racial Theories of Robert E. Park and Ruth Benedict," *JNE* 13 (Fall 1944): 453–63.
Dowd, Jerome. "Discussion," *AJS* 16 (March 1911): 633–34.
————. "Review of *The Negro in the New World* by Sir Harry H. Johnston," *AJS* 19 (March 1913): 343–44.

————. "Race Segregation in a World of Democracy," *PASS* 14 (December 1919): 189–202.

DuBois, W.E.B. "The Conservation of Races," *The American Negro Academy Occasional Papers.* 1897. Reprint. New York: Arno Press, 1969.

————. "Review of *Race Traits and Tendencies of the American Negro* by Frederick L. Hoffman," *Annals* 9 (January 1897): 127–33.

————. "The Study of Negro Problems," *Annals* 11 (January 1898): 1–23.

————. "Review of *The Negro in Africa and America* by Joseph A. Tillinghast," *PSQ* 18 (December 1903): 695–97.

————. "Discussion," *AJS* 13 (May 1908): 834–38.

————. "The Negro in Literature and Art," *Annals* 49 (September 1913): 233–37.

————. "The Position of the Negro in the American Social Order: Where Do We Go From Here?" *JNE* 8 (July 1939): 351–70.

Dunn, L. C. "A Biological View of Race Mixture," *PASS* 19 (29–31 December 1924): 47–56.

Ellwood, Charles A. "The Theory of Imitation in Social Psychology," *AJS* 6 (May 1901): 721–41.

Faris, Ellsworth. "The Mental Capacity of Savages," *AJS* 23 (March 1918): 603–19.

————. "Are Instincts Data or Hypotheses?" *AJS* 27 (September 1921): 184–96.

Ferguson, George O. "The Psychology of the Negro," *AP* 25 (April 1916): 32–126.

Fleming, Walter L. "Reorganization of the Industrial System in Alabama After the Civil War," *AJS* 15 (January 1905): 473–500.

————. "Pap Singleton, The Moses of the Colored Exodus," *AJS* 6 (July 1910): 61–82.

Fontaine, William T. "Social Determinism in the Writings of Negro Scholars," *AJS* 49 (January 1944): 302–15.

Frazier, E. Franklin. "Children in Black and Mulatto Families," *AJS* 39 (July 1930): 12–29.

————. "Impact of Urban Civilization Upon the Negro Family Life," *ASR* 2 (October 1937): 609–18.

————. "Rejoinder," *AJS* 49 (January 1944): 313–15.

Garner, James W. "Discussion," *AJS* 13 (May 1908): 828–31.

Gilman, Charlotte Perkins. "A Suggestion on the Negro Problem," *AJS* 14 (July 1908): 78–85.

Halsey, John J. "Discussion," *AJS* 13 (May 1908): 835.

Haynes, George E. "Conditions Among Negroes in the Cities," *Annals* 49 (September 1913): 105–19.

Herskovits, Melville J. "On the Relation Between Negro-White Mixture and Standing in Intelligence Tests," *PS* 33 (March 1926): 30–42.

Howard, George Elliott. "The Social Cost of Southern Race Prejudice," *AJS* 22 (March 1917): 577–93.

Kelsey, Carl. "The Evolution of Negro Labor," *Annals* 21 (January 1903): 56–75.

————. Discussion of "Social Darwinism," by D. Collin Wells, *AJS* 12 (March 1907): 711.

Kroeber, Alfred L. "Eighteen Professions," *AA* 17(April–June 1915): 283–86.

Lichtenberger, James P. "Negro Illiteracy in the United States," *Annals* 49 (September 1913): 177–85.

Linton, Ralph. "An Anthropological View of Race Mixture," *PASS* 19 (29–31 December 1924): 69–76.

Mead, Margaret. "The Methodology of Racial Testing: Its Significance for Sociology," *AJS* 31 (March 1926): 657–67.

Mecklin, John M. "The Philosophy of the Color Line," *AJS* 19 (November 1913): 343–57.

Miller, Kelly. "Review of Edward B. Reuter's *The Mulatto in the United States*," *AJS* 25 (September 1919): 218–24.

————. "Is Race Prejudice Innate or Acquired?" *JAS* 11 (July–August 1927): 516–24.

Odum, Howard W. "Negro Children in the Public Schools of Philadelphia," *Annals* 49 (September 1913): 186–208.

Park, Robert E. "Negro Home Life and Standards of Living," *Annals* 49 (September 1913): 147–63.

————. "Racial Assimilation in Secondary Groups: With Particular Reference to the Negro," *AJS* 19 (March 1914): 607–23.

————. "Review of *The Psychology of the Negro* by George O. Ferguson," *AJS* 22 (March 1917): 683–85.

————. "Introduction," In *Japanese Invasion* by Jesse F. Steiner. New York: McClurg, 1917.

————. "Education and Its Relation to the Conflict and Fusion of Cultures: With Special Reference to the Problems of the Immigrant, the Negro and Missions," *PASS* 13 (December 1918): 40–60.

————. "The Concept of Social Distance," *JAS* 8 (July–August 1924): 339–44.

————. "Our Racial Frontier on the Pacific," *SG* 9 (May 1926): 192–96.

————. "The Bases of Race Prejudice," *Annals* 140 (November 1928): 11–20.

————. "Mentality of Racial Hybrids," *AJS* 36 (January 1931): 534–51.

————. "The Nature of Race Relations," In *Race and Culture*. New York: The Free Press, 1950.

Reinhardt, James M. "The Negro: Is He a Biological Inferior?" *AJS* 23 (July 1927): 248–61.

Reuter, Edward B. "The Superiority of the Mulatto," *AJS* 23 (July 1917): 83–106.

————. "The Hybrid as a Sociological Type," *PASS* 19 (29–31 December 1924): 62–68.

————. "Rejoinder," *AJS* 49 (January 1944): 315.

"Review of *The Philadelphia Negro* by W.E.B. DuBois," *AHR* 6 (October 1900): 164–65.

Ross, Edward A. "The Causes of Race Superiority," *Annals* 18 (July 1901): 67–89.

———. "Discussion," *AJS* 12 (March 1907): 715–16.

Simons, Sarah. "Social Assimilation, Part I," *AJS* 6 (May 1901): 790–822.

———. "Social Assimilation, Part II," *AJS* 7 (January 1902): 539–56.

Stone, Alfred Holt. "Is Race Friction Between Blacks and Whites in the United States Growing and Inevitable?" *AJS* 13 (March 1908): 676–97.

Thomas, William I. "The Scope and Method of Folk-Psychology," *AJS* 1 (January 1896): 434–63.

———. "On a Difference in the Metabolism of the Sexes," *AJS* 3 (July 1897): 31–63.

———. "The Psychology of Race Prejudice," *AJS* 9 (March 1904): 593–611.

———. "The Province of Social Psychology," *AJS* 10 (January 1905): 445–55.

———. "The Mind of Woman and the Lower Races," *AJS* 12 (January 1907): 435–69.

———. "The Significance of the Orient for the Occident," *AJS* 13 (May 1908): 729–55.

———. "Standpoint for the Interpretation of Savage Society," *AJS* 15 (September 1909): 145–63.

———. "Race Psychology: Standpoint and Questionnaire with Particular Reference to the Immigrant and the Negro," *AJS* 17 (May 1912): 725–75.

Ward, Lester F. "Evolution of Social Structures," *AJS* 10 (March 1905): 589–605.

———. Discussion of "Social Darwinism," by D. Collin Wells, *AJS* 12 (March 1907): 710–11.

Warner, W. Lloyd. "American Caste and Class," *AJS* 41 (September 1936): 234–37.

———. "A Methodological Note," In *Black Metropolis* by St. Clair Drake and Horace R. Cayton. New York: Harcourt, Brace and Company, 1945.

Warner, W. Lloyd, and Allison Davis. "A Comparative Study of American Caste," In *Race Relations and the Race Problem,* edited by Edgar T. Thompson. New York: Greenwood Press, 1968.

Weatherly, Ulysses G. "Discussion," *AJS* 13 (May 1908): 813–25.

———. "Race and Marriage," *AJS* 15 (January 1910): 433–53.

———. "The Racial Element in Social Assimilation," *AJS* 16 (March 1911): 593–612.

Wells, D. Collin. "Social Darwinism," *AJS* 12 (March 1907): 695–716.

Willcox, Walter F. "Preface," In *The Negro in Africa and America* by Joseph A. Tillinghast. New York: Macmillan, 1902.

———. "Discussion," *AJS* 13 (May 1908): 820–23.

Wirth, Louis. "The Problem of Minority Groups," In *The Science of Man in the World Crisis,* edited by Ralph Linton. New York: Columbia University Press, 1945.

Work, Monroe N. "Crime among the Negroes of Chicago," *AJS* 6 (September 1900): 204–23.

———. "Aspects and Tendencies of the Race Problem," *PASS* 19 (29–31 December 1924): 191–96.

Wright, R. R., Jr. "The Negro in Unskilled Labor," *Annals* 49 (September 1913): 19–27.
Young, Kimball. "Discussion," *PASS* 19 (29–31 December 1924): 77–79.

SECONDARY SOURCES

Books

Blackwell, James E., and Morris Janowitz, eds. *Black Sociologists: Historical and Contemporary Perspectives*. Chicago: University of Chicago Press, 1974.
Blumer, Martin. *The Chicago School of Sociology: Institutionalization, Diversity, and the Rise of Sociological Research*. Chicago: University of Chicago Press, 1984.
Broderick, Francis L. *W.E.B. DuBois: Negro Leader in a Time of Crisis*. Stanford, Calif.: Stanford University Press, 1959.
Brotz, Howard M., ed. *Negro Social and Political Thought, 1850–1920*. New York: Basic Books, 1966.
――――. *The Black Jews of Harlem: Negro Nationalism and the Dilemmas of Negro Leadership*. New York: Schocken, 1970.
Cravens, Hamilton. *The Triumph of Evolution: American Scientists and the Heredity-Environment Controversy, 1900–1941*. Philadelphia: University of Pennsylvania Press, 1978.
Crunden, Robert M. *Ministers of Reform: The Progressives' Achievement in American Civilization, 1889–1920*. Urbana: University of Illinois Press, 1984.
Dinnerstein, Leonard. *Ethnic Americans: A History of Immigration and Assimilation*. New York: Harper and Row, 1982.
Faris, Robert E. L. *Chicago Sociology, 1920–1932*. Chicago: University of Chicago Press, 1967.
Fine, William F. *Progressive Evolutionism and American Sociology, 1890–1920*. Ann Arbor, Mich.: UMI Research Press, 1979.
Franklin, John Hope. *From Slavery to Freedom*. 3d ed. New York: Alfred A. Knopf, 1967.
Frederickson, George M. *The Black Image in the White Mind: The Debate on Afro-American Character and Destiny, 1817–1914*. New York: Harper and Row, 1971.
Fullinwider, S. P. *The Mind and Mood of Black America*. Homewood, Ill.: The Dorsey Press, 1969.
Genovese, Eugene D. *The Political Economy of Slavery*. New York: Pantheon Books, 1965.
Gossett, Thomas F. *Race: The History of an Idea in America*. Dallas: Southern Methodist University Press, 1963.
Gouldner, Alvin W. *The Coming Crisis of Western Sociology*. New York: Avon Books, 1970.
Haller, John S., Jr. *Outcasts from Evolution: Scientific Attitudes of Racial Inferiority, 1859–1900*. Urbana: University of Illinois Press, 1971.

Haller, Mark H. *Eugenics: Hereditarian Attitudes in American Thought.* New Brunswick, N.J.: Rutgers University Press, 1963.

Harlan, Louis R. *Booker T. Washington: The Making of a Black Leader, 1856–1901.* London: Oxford University Press, 1972.

———. *Booker T. Washington: The Wizard of Tuskegee, 1901–1915.* New York: Oxford University Press, 1983.

Harris, Marvin. *The Rise of Anthropological Theory.* New York: Thomas Y. Crowell, 1968.

Harris, William H. *The Harder We Run: Black Workers Since the Civil War.* New York: Oxford University Press, 1982.

Herbst, Jurgen. *The German Historical School in American Scholarship: A Study in the Transfer of Culture.* Ithaca, N.Y.: Cornell University Press, 1965.

Herskovits, Melville J. *Franz Boas: The Science of Man in the Making.* New York: Charles Scribner's Sons, 1953.

Higham, John. *Strangers in the Land: Patterns of American Nativism, 1860–1925.* New Brunswick, N.J.: Rutgers University Press, 1966.

———. *Send These to Me. Immigrants in Urban America.* Baltimore: Johns Hopkins University Press, 1984.

Hinkle, Roscoe E., Jr., and Gisela J. Hinkle. *The Development of Modern Sociology: Its Nature and Growth in the United States.* New York: Random House, 1963.

Hofstadter, Richard. *Social Darwinism in American Thought.* Rev. ed. Boston: Beacon Press, 1955.

Kuhn, Thomas S. *The Structure of Scientific Revolutions.* Chicago: University of Chicago Press, 1970.

Logan, Rayford W. *The Negro in American Life and Thought.* New York: The Dial Press, 1954.

———. *The Betrayal of the Negro.* New York: Collier Books, 1965.

Lyman, Stanford M. *The Black American in Sociological Thought: A Failure of Perspective.* New York: Capricorn Books, 1973.

Lyman, Stanford M., and Arthur J. Vidich. *American Sociology: Worldly Rejections of Religion and Their Directions.* New Haven, Conn.: Yale University Press, 1985.

Matthews, Fred H. *Quest for an American Sociology: Robert E. Park and the Chicago School.* Montreal: McGill-Queen's University Press, 1977.

Meier, August. *Negro Thought in America, 1880–1915: Racial Ideologies in the Age of Booker T. Washington.* Ann Arbor: University of Michigan Press, 1963.

Meier, August, and Elliott Rudwick. *From Plantation to Ghetto.* New York: Hill and Wang, 1970.

Moses, Wilson J. *The Golden Age of Black Nationalism, 1850–1925.* Hamden, Conn.: Archon Books, 1978.

Myrdal, Gunnar. *An American Dilemma.* 2 vols. New York: Harper and Row, 1944.

Newby, Idus A. *Jim Crow's Defense: Anti-Negro Thought in America, 1909–1930.* Baton Rouge: Louisiana State University Press, 1965.

Odum, Howard W. *American Sociology: The Story of Sociology in the United States Through 1950.* New York: Greenwood Press, 1951.

Osofsky, Gilbert. *Harlem: The Making of a Ghetto. Negro New York, 1890–1930.* 2d ed. New York: Harper and Row, 1971.

Pinkney, Alphonso. *The Myth of Black Progress.* New York: Cambridge University Press, 1984.

Purcell, Edward A., Jr. *The Crisis of Democratic Theory: Scientific Naturalism and the Problem of Value.* Lexington: University of Kentucky Press, 1973.

Redding, Saunders. *They Came in Chains.* Philadelphia: Lippincott, 1950.

Rex, John. *Race Relations in Sociological Theory.* London: Routledge and Kegan Paul, 1983.

Spear, Allan H. *Black Chicago: The Making of a Ghetto, 1890–1920.* Chicago: University of Chicago Press, 1967.

Spencer, Samuel R., Jr. *Booker T. Washington and the Negro's Place in American Life.* Boston: Little, Brown, 1955.

Spero, Sterling D., and Abram L. Harris. *The Black Worker.* New York: Columbia University Press, 1931.

Stanton, William R. *The Leopard's Spots: Scientific Attitudes Toward Race in America, 1815–1859.* Chicago: University of Chicago Press, 1960.

Stepan, Nancy. *The Idea of Race in Science.* Hamden, Conn.: Archon Books, 1982.

Stocking, George W., Jr. *Race, Culture, and Evolution: Essays in the History of Anthropology.* New York: The Free Press, 1968.

————, ed. *A Franz Boas Reader: The Shaping of American Anthropology, 1883–1911.* Chicago: University of Chicago Press, 1974.

Thorpe, Earl E. *Negro Historians in the United States.* Baton Rouge, La.: Fraternal Press, 1958.

Valentine, Charles A. *Culture and Poverty.* Chicago: University of Chicago Press, 1968.

van den Berghe, Pierre, L. *Race and Racism.* New York: John Wiley and Sons, 1967.

Weinberg, Julius. *Edward Alsworth Ross and the Sociology of Progressivism.* Madison: State Historical Society of Wisconsin, 1972.

Wilson, William J. *The Declining Significance of Race.* Chicago: University of Chicago Press, 1978.

Woodward, C. Vann. *Origins of the New South, 1877–1913.* Baton Rouge: Louisiana State University Press, 1951.

Articles

Baker, Paul J., ed. "The Life Histories of W. I. Thomas and Robert E. Park," *AJS* 79 (September 1973): 243–60.

Diner, Steven J. "Department and Discipline: The Department of Sociology at the University of Chicago, 1892–1920," *Minerva* 13 (Winter 1975): 514–53.

Frazier, E. Franklin. "Sociological Theory and Race Relations," *ARS* 12 (June 1947): 265–71.

Hayes, James R. "Sociology and Racism: An Analysis of the First Era of America Sociology," *Phylon* 34 (December 1973): 330–41.

Jones, Rhett S. "Proving Blacks Inferior: The Sociology of Knowledge," In *The Death of White Sociology,* edited by Joyce A. Ladner. New York: Random House, 1973.

Kroeber, Alfred L. "Franz Boas: The Man 1858–1942," *Mem.* No. 61, *AA* 45 No. 3, Part 2 (July–September 1943).

Lieberman, Leonard. "The Debate Over Race: A Study in the Sociology of Knowledge," *Phylon* 29 (Summer 1968): 127–41.

Medalia, Nahum A. "Myrdal's Assumptions on Race Relations: A Conceptual Commentary," *SF* 40 (March 1962): 223–27.

Murphree, Idus L. "The Evolutionary Anthropologists. The Progress of Mankind. The Concepts of Progress and Culture in the Thought of John Lubbock, Edward B. Tylor, and Lewis H. Morgan," *APS* 105, No. 3 (June 1961): 265–300.

Ross, Hubert B. "In Memorium Oliver Cromwell Cox (1901–1974)." *Phylon* 36 (Summer 1975): 204–7.

Thompson, Charles H. "The Conclusions of Scientists Relative to Racial Differences," *JNE* 3 (July 1934): 494–512.

Yoder, Dale, "Present Status of the Question of Racial Difference," *JEP* 19 (October 1928): 463–70.

Index

Abolitionist movement, 75
Accommodation, 143–44
Adams, Walter A., 165
African inferiority, theory of, 2, 36–37
Afro-Americans; anthropometry of, 119; assimilation of, into American mainstream, 1, 4; character and capabilities of, 59–62, 86–87, 114, 118; stereotypes of, 68. *See also* Blacks
Akron, Ohio, race relations in, 6
Alcoholism, as direct result of prejudice and discrimination, 6
Alpha tests, 82, 114, 115, 116, 119, 120, 131
Amalgamation, 103
American Journal of Sociology, writings published in, 3, 11, 18–19, 20, 39, 46, 56, 70–71, 85, 87, 89, 104, 119, 137, 163
Angell, J. R., 90
Anthropology: American school of, 63; on capabilities of blacks, 81–84, 114; progressive, 114–18
Anthropometry, 2; of Afro-Americans, 119; influence on sociology, 2
Anti-amalgamation argument, 129; proponents of, 135–36

Anti-Semitism, 61, 114, 125
Army Alpha and Beta tests, 82, 114, 115, 116, 119, 120, 128, 131
Art, blacks progressive in, 93
Aryanism, 124
Assimilation: and intermarriage, 74, 77; and slavery, 104–5, 143–44
Assimilationist theory, ascendancy of, 1, 10–12, 15–16, 149–73, 178, 181
Atlanta: growth of, 33; race riots in, 33
Atlanta School of Social Work, 153

Baker, Ray Stannard, 6
Baldwin, James Mark, 71
Baltimore, blacks in, 95
Banneker, Benjamin, 53
Barringer, Paul B., 21
Bassett, John Spencer, 53–54, 55, 164–65
Bastian, Adolf, 60
Bean, Robert B., 125
Behaviorism, 138
Belin, H. E., 35, 39–40, 68
Benington, R. Crewdon, 125
Bernard, Luther L., 137–38

Beta tests, 82, 114, 115, 116, 119, 120, 131
Binet aptitude test, 96
Biological difference argument, 2
Biracial organization, 144
Birmingham, growth of, 33
Black migration, 5–6, 52, 92, 110, 113, 114, 157, 177–78, 181; impact of Great Depression on, 149
Black nationalism, 173; proponents of, 179
Blacks: acceptance of inferior status by, 49–50; achievements of, 19–20; acquisition of minority group status, 161–62; contributions of, to Southern society, 8; "cranial cavities" of, 63–64, 67; and crime, 6, 21, 51, 53; disenfranchisement of, 53–54; effect of "contact with whites," 8–9; hereditary differences between whites and, 130; ideas concerning innate inferiority, 2; illiteracy among, 94; improved home life and standard of living among, 94–95; inherent traits of, 43–44; intellectual inferiority of, 116; as "plastic," 9, 22; psychology and anthropology on the capabilities of, 81–84; rationalization of exclusion from American society, 2–3; role in Southern achievements, 8; as scapegoats, 7; social assimilation of, 10–12
Boas, Franz, 9, 13, 23, 35, 54, 83–84, 85, 90, 91, 95, 97, 116–18, 122, 129, 131, 177–78, 181, 182; influence of, 59–77; progressivism of, 73–74
Boasian anthropology, 84–98; idea of cultural determinism, 1; triumph of, 118–21
Briffault, Robert, 154
Brigham, Carl C., 114–16, 118, 120, 128
Brinton, Daniel Garrison, 59, 65
Broca, Paul, 63, 74
Brotz, Howard, 77, 179

Brown v. Board of Education (1954), 4
Brownsville, Texas, race riots in, 33
Burgess, Ernest W., 85, 153, 171

Calhoun, John C., 53
Caste, 166; definition of, 163–66
Caste-feeling, 47
Caste system, 161; color as basis of Southern, 51; impact on race relations, 107; inferiority of, 16; and innate differences between blacks and whites, 16–17, 18; and position of half-caste, 75; and slavery, 164; Southern whites attempt to consolidate over blacks, 7, 34
Cattell, James M., 82
Cattell and Farrand Cancellation Test, scores of blacks on, 82
Cayton, Horace R., 167
Chamberlain, Alexander, 45
Charleston, blacks in, 95
Chavis, John, 53
Chicago: black-white relations in, 166; race problems in, 5–6; race riots in, 109
Chicago School, 170–71
Civil Rights Act (1964), 179
Civil Rights movement, success of, 4
Columbia Maze Test, scores of blacks on, 82
Concentric zone theory, 158; application to blacks, 158–59
Congo Reform Association, 103
Consciousness of kind, 2
Cooley, Charles H., 16–17, 43, 70, 89–90, 100–101, 108
Cox, Oliver C., 85, 168–70, 173
Craven, Hamilton, 183
Crime: black, 21, 51, 53; as direct result of prejudice and discrimination, 6
Cultural determinism, 62, 66, 177, 182
Cultural differences, between the races, 150

Cultural relativism, 108, 150
Cultural solidarity, 76
Culture concept, 13, 84, 183

Darwin, Charles, 59
Davis, Allison, 165
Degeneracy thesis, 21
Dewey, John, 90
Discrimination, 149, 178–79; as direct cause of black social problems, 6
Disenfranchisement, 7, 33, 53–54
Dow, Grove S., 121–22, 123, 126–27, 130, 136
Dowd, Jerome, 14, 34, 35, 38–39, 68, 69, 98–100, 104–5, 109, 121, 122, 126–27
Doyle, Bertram, 85, 161
DuBois, W.E.B., 6, 9, 21, 41, 50, 54–55, 56, 86–87, 91, 92, 93, 102, 150, 155, 157; and scientism, 26–29
Du Chaillu, Paul, 36
Dunn, L. C., 130–31, 133
Dunning, William A., 41

Ebbinghaus aptitude test, 96
Ebbinghaus Completion Test, scores of blacks on, 82
Education: as lever for black progress, 37; and scores on intelligence tests, 115–16; segregated, rationale for, 86
Ellis, A. B., 36
Ellwood, Charles A., 68, 71
Emancipation, 34; as crisis, 97; impact of, on family, 154, 156
Endogamy, 169
Ethnic-instinct, 75
Ethnocentrism, 2, 25
Evans, Henry, 53
Evolutionists: Boas's criticisms of, 62–63; progressive, 16, 21, 26, 29, 69–70

Faris, Ellsworth, 85, 90–91, 96, 137, 140, 142, 167, 171

Ferguson, George O., 81–83, 85, 86, 115, 118, 119, 135
Fifteenth Amendment, 53–54
Fleming, Walter, 35, 40–41, 56, 68
Fontaine, William T., 158, 159, 160
Ford, Henry, 116
Franklin, John Hope, 113
Frazier, E. Franklin, 85, 108, 110, 144, 150, 151, 153, 155–56, 157–58, 158, 159–60, 160, 172–73, 181
Fredrickson, George M., 10, 25, 149
Frobenius, Leo, 68, 69, 91

Galton, Sir Francis, 16, 63, 70
Gardner, Burleigh B., 165
Gardner, Mary R., 165
Garner, James W., 52–53, 56
Garvey, Marcus, 113
Garvey Movement, 92
Genovese, Eugene D., 34
Giddings, Franklin H., 5, 8–10, 15, 16, 22–23, 24, 25, 43, 45, 74, 93, 122, 123, 162–63
Gillman, Charlotte Perkins, 19–20, 21
Gini, Corrado, 153
Gliddon, George R., 63
Gossett, Thomas F., 182
Gould, B. A., 102
Grant, Madison, 114, 115, 117
Great Depression, impact on black migration, 149
Greensburg, Indiana, race relations in, 6
Gumplowicz, Ludwig, 11

Hagiography, 13
Haines, T. H., 82
Hall, G. Stanley, 45
Halsey, John J., 6
Hankins, Frank H., 67, 123–27, 134, 136, 153
Harlan, Louis R., 7
Harlem Renaissance, 113–14
Harper, William Rainey, 17

Harris, Marvin, 69, 182–83
Hart, Albert Bushnell, 26
Hawkins, Walter Everette, 113
Haynes, George E., 92
Henderson, Charles, 18, 46
Heredity, impact on character and
    capability, 36
Herskovits, Melville J., 35, 118,
    119, 120
Hinkle, Gisela J., 18
Hinkle, Roscoe C. Jr., 18
Hoffman, Frederick L., 20, 21, 75,
    102
Howard, George E., 90, 93, 95–96,
    101–2, 108, 109, 129
Hunt, S. B., 102, 125
Hurston, Zora Neale, 113
Hybrid, achievements of, 133–34
Hypergamy, 165

Instinct concept, 137–38, 140
Instinctive prejudice, 2, 48, 109;
    collapse of doctrine of, 137–41
Instinct theory, 138–39
Intellectual differences, issue of ra-
    cial, 23, 24–25
Intelligence, existence of racial dif-
    ferences in, 131–32
Intelligence tests, scores of blacks
    on, 82–83, 114, 115, 128, 131
Intermarriage, 74–79, 102–3, 118,
    120, 139; and assimilation, 74,
    77; prohibition in South, 165
Internalist critique, 182
Internalist-Externalist controversy,
    in history of racial thought, 181–
    83
Inter-racial friendships, 162

Jackson, Andrew, 53
Jamaica, race relations in, 99
James, William, 71
Jim Crow laws, 8; proliferation of,
    7; defense of, by Southern sociol-
    ogy, 14, 33–57, 98, 177; nation-
    al legitimization of, 33
Johnson, Charles S., 85, 108,
    167–68

Johnston, Sir Harry J., 98
Jones, Rhett S., 83
Jordan, David Starr, 15
Jordan, H. E., 82
Junker, Buford H., 165

Keller, A. G., 13
Kelsey, Carl, 41–42, 68, 73, 102,
    103, 108, 129
Kidd, Benjamin, 23
Kingsley, Mary, 36, 154
Kroeber, Alfred, 83, 84, 86, 109,
    122, 126, 160, 163
Kuhn, Thomas, 2, 127, 182
Ku Klux Klan, 116

Lamarckian doctrine of the inheri-
    tance of acquired characteristics,
    19, 22, 36, 73, 96–97, 123, 130
Lane, Ralph, 53
Liberal assimilationists, theories
    of, 15
Liberal environmentalism, 181–82;
    triumph of, 113–46
Liberal humanitarians, 27, 61–62
Lichtenberger, James P., 92, 93,
    94, 108
Lieberman, Leonard, 182
Linton, Ralph, 131–33
Literature: black progress in, 93;
    rise of black consciousness in,
    113–14
Lubbock, John, 59
Lynching, 7, 113

McGee, W. J., 59
McKay, Claude, 113
McNeil, Elaine Ogden, 167
Malinowski, Bronislaw, 154
Mall, Franklin, 129
Mannheim, Karl, 158
Marginal men, 183
Matthews, Fred H., 87
Mayo, Marion J., 82
Mead, Margaret, 118, 119–20
Mecklin, John M., 99
Meier, August, 7, 33

"Men of high genius" hypothesis, 70, 116

Miller, Kelly, 20–21, 89, 92, 102, 133, 134, 138–39

Minority groups, types of, 171–72

Mississippi, disfranchisement in, 7, 33

Montagu, Ashley, 83

Mores, concept of, 13, 15, 25, 144, 161

Morgan, Lewis Henry, 59

Morse, Josiah, 82

Morton, Samuel George, 63

Moses, Wilson J., 28

Moton, R. R., 102

Mulattoes, 74–77; achievements of, 133–37, 152; advantages over full-blooded blacks, 134; culture of, 107–8; families of, 153–54; fascination of social scientists with, 88–89, 129–30; heredity of, 130; intelligence test scores of, 88–89, 134–35; survival rate of, 154

Murphree, Idus L., 59

Myrdal, Gunnar, 13, 14–15, 27, 76, 104, 170, 177, 179

National Negro Business League, 93

Nativism, 114

National Urban League, 92

Naturalism, adoption as a worldview, 1, 4, 81

Natural selection process, interference of socialism and trade unionism with, 23

Nature versus nurture debate, 36, 160–61, 178, 182

Negro, use of, as term, 9

"Negro problem," 3, 5–29, 34–35; nationalization of, 92

New Deal, and change in white attitudes toward blacks, 149

New Orleans: blacks in, 95; race riots in, 33

New York City: blacks in, 95; race problems in, 5–6

Nonwhites: problem of capabilities of, 22–25; sociologists on the capabilities of, 69–73

Nordicists, 158

North, race problems in, 5–6

Northern sociologists: and the Negro problem, 5–29; on race relations, 98–110

Nott, Josiah, 63, 74

Odum, Howard W., 12–13, 17, 43–45, 76, 77, 91, 96–97, 108, 145, 151–52, 164–65

Park, Robert E., 39, 40, 44, 85, 92, 93, 94–95, 103–7, 104, 105, 109, 113–14, 140–41, 143–45, 150, 152, 153, 155, 161–62, 164–65, 167, 171, 172, 173, 181; theory of black-white relations, 144–45

Pauperism, as direct result of prejudice and discrimination, 6

Peterson, Joseph, 126, 134

Philadelphia: blacks in, 95; race problems in, 5–6, 28

Phillips, Ulrich B., 34, 35

Phillips, Wendell, 75

Plessy v. Ferguson (1896), 8, 33

Polygenist argument, 74, 76–77, 102, 129, 130, 133

Polynesians, 132

Powell, John Wesley, 59

Prejudice, 25–26; as defense of laissez-faire, 46–47; as direct cause of black social problems, 6; distinction between caste-feeling and, 46–47; instinctive, 2, 48, 109, 137–41; and intermarriage, 77; North-South consensus on, 45–57; as physiological expression, 73–74; as radical response, 107–8; and rationalization of black exclusion, 2–3, 25–26, 28; as result of white supremacy, 101–2; as social phenomenon, 140–41

Pressey, S. L., 82

Progressive anthropology, 114–18
Progressive evolution, 16, 21, 26, 29, 69–70
Progressivism, in sociology, 121–29
Proslavery argument, development of, 38–39
Psychological testing, and racial differences, 2, 4, 82–83
Psychology: on capabilities of blacks, 81–84, 114; reactionary, 114–18
Purcell, Edward A., Jr., 81, 138
Putnam, Frederic Ward, 65

Race, definition of, 28
Race mixture: anthropological view of, 131; sociology and, 129–37
Race relations: "caste and class" school of, 28; changes in, 13–14; competitive, 7; economic and political factors as causes of, 52–53; founding fathers on, 7–21; Northern and Southern theorists of, 98–110; and prejudice, 2–3, 25–26
Race relations theory, 143–46, 160–66; in 1945, 171–73
Race riots, 109, 113
Racial antipathy, 48, 52, 55
Racial determinism, 62, 65, 71, 86, 177, 182; proponents of, 178
Racial equality, theory of, 122
Racial evolution, 177
Racial intermixture, 133; problem of, 73–77, 130, 137
Racial solidarity, 76
Racial temperamental differences, theory of, 2
Racial thought, Internalist-Externalist controversy in history of, 181–83
Racism: definition of, 3; persistent attack on, 151–60
Racist orthodoxy, Boas's attack on the, 61
Ratzenhofer, Gustav, 11
Reactionary psychology, 114–18

Reactionism, in sociology, 121–29
Reconstruction: role of blacks during, 8, 40–41; treatment of blacks during, 51–52
Reinhardt, James M., 127–29
Reuter, Edward B., 87–89, 107–8, 129, 133, 134, 135, 142–43, 152, 160
Roosevelt, Franklin D., 149
Roosevelt, Theodore, 55
Ross, Edward A., 5, 15–16, 23, 24, 50
"Ruling ideas," 3–4
Russell, Ira, 125

Schmoller, Gustav von, 26
Scientific determinism, 123
Scientific naturalism, 159–60
Scientism, and DuBois, W.E.B., 26–29
Segregation: causes of, 38; defense of, 86
Senart, Emile, 165
Simmel, Georg, 103
Simons, Sarah, 19, 21, 74, 102
Singleton, Pap, 56
Slavery: and assimilation, 104–5; Boas on, 69; caste line during, 164; family patterns in, 156–57; impact upon black family behavior, 154, 155–56; rationalization of, as solution to race problem, 34, 38–40, 41, 42, 49; Southern defense of, 39–40
Small, Albion W., 5, 17–19, 46, 70
Social Darwinism, 12
Social Darwinist determinism, 1, 177
Socialism, interference of, with natural selection process, 23
Sociology: ascendancy of assimilationist theory in, 1, 10–12, 15–16, 149–73, 178, 181; Boasian critique in, 84–98; defense of Jim Crow by southern, 33–57; and the dynamics of change, 81–110; emergence of, as academic discipline, 5; evolution of black

progress in, 1; mythologic school of, 140; Northern, and the Negro problem, 5–29; reluctance of some to accept new theory, 2; post–World War II, 1, 181; professionalization of, 17; and race mixture, 129–37; reactionism and progressivism in, 121–29; and status quo of black inequality, 3, 8–9
South Carolina, disfranchisement in, 7, 33
Southern sociologists: defense of Jim Crow by, 33–57; on race relations, 98–110
Spencer, Herbert, 64
Springfield, Illinois, race relations in, 6
Stampp, Kenneth, 35
Stanford, Mrs. Leland, 15
Statesboro, Georgia, race riots in, 33
Stocking, George W., Jr., 114, 182
Stone, Alfred Holt, 47–50, 54–56, 152
Suffrage, black, 53–54
Sumner, William G., 5, 12, 23, 24, 25, 144, 161
Superordinate-subordinate relationship of whites and blacks, 14
Survival of the fittest, 37, 177

Tarde, Gabriel, 71
Tempermental differences, theory of, 2
Temperament concept, stubbornness of, 142–43
Terman, Lewis M., 134
Thomas, William I., 18, 45–47, 70–71, 72–73, 85, 90, 96, 97, 104, 106, 127, 167
Thompson, Charles H., 120, 127
Thompson questionnaire, 136
Thorndike, Edward L., 82
Thorndike aptitude test, 96
Tillinghast, Joseph A., 14, 34, 35, 36–38, 39, 42, 68, 69, 121
Todd, Wingate, 125

Topinard, Paul, 37, 63, 64
Totalitarianism, rise of, 150
Trabue, M. R., 116
Trade unionism, interference of, with natural selection process, 23
Tribalism, net effect of, 114
Trinity College, 38
Tylor, Edward B., 37, 59, 64

Universal Negro Improvement Association, 113
University of Chicago, development of sociology department at, 17–18, 46, 85, 137
Urbanization, impact upon black family behavior, 154, 157

Valentine, Charles A., 158
van den Berghe, Pierre L., 3
Vardaman, James K., 53
Vincent, George, 18, 46
Virchow, Rudolf, 60, 63
Vogt, Karl, 74

Ward, Lester F., 5, 10–12, 13, 15, 16, 20, 23–24, 43
Warner, W. Lloyd, 145–46, 150, 163–67, 169–70
Washington, Booker T., 7, 8, 9, 16, 17, 39, 41, 45, 54, 55, 83, 97, 102, 103, 145, 163, 164–65; Atlanta Exposition Address, 7–9; biases of, 14
Washington, D.C., blacks in, 95
Weatherford, Willis D., 155
Weatherly, Ulysses G., 51–52, 72, 74–76, 77, 127, 135–36
Wells, D. Collin, 23
White, Andrew D., 51
Whites, hereditary differences between, and blacks, 130
Whitney, William C., 12
Wilcox, Walter F., 21, 35, 36, 50–51
Wilson, Woodrow, 10
Wirth, Louis, 150–51, 171

Woodworth and Wells Mixed Relations Tests, scores of blacks on, 82

Woofter, Thomas J., Jr., 145, 162–63

Work, Monroe N., 20–21, 92, 96, 129, 145–46

Wright, R. R., Jr., 92, 93

Yerkes, Robert M., 114

Young, Kimball, 134, 136

Znaniecki, Florian, 46

Zueblin, Charles, 18

ABOUT THE AUTHOR

VERNON J. WILLIAMS, JR., is Professor of History and African/
Afro-American Studies at Rhode Island College.